JOSHUA TREE

JOSHUA TREE

ROCK CLIMBING GUIDE

RANDY VOGEL

CHOCKSTONE PRESS

DENVER, COLORADO
1986

Published by
Chockstone Press, Inc.
526 Franklin Street
Denver, Colorado 80218

Printed in the United States of America

ISBN 0-9609452-9-6

PREFACE

Writing a guidebook is a no-win situation. Some climbers are bound to be offended by your guide, and end up disliking you. Because climbers frequently and violently disagree about the rating of routes, a guidebook editor who gives a fixed rating for a particular climb takes his life in his hands. Even the inclusion of a controversial route in a guide book may give rise to complaint. If the climb was put up in unacceptable style, reporting it in print might be construed as condoning poor ethics or bad style.

Probably the most difficult problem a guide book writer encounters is getting climbers to submit route information. Rest assured, however, that these very same uncooperative persons will be the first to level criticism that the guide is incomplete.

With this last bit of complaining, I submit the guide to your criticism and comments. I hope that it serves as a useful aid in the enjoyment of the many climbing delights that Joshua Tree offers.

I strongly suggest that all visiting climbers (and locals alike!) read the section dealing with local practices and ethics. This will save many an hour of futile effort, endless ego-involved debates and claims of ignorance.

The NCCS (a la Joshua Tree) rating system has been abandoned in this guide in favor of the more widely used YDS decimal rating. Very few people ever really used the NCCS, and it remained a constant source of confusion to most. If there is ever going to be a universal rating system it should be the evolutionary end-product of thoughtful reflection, not an artificially imposed system which does little more than arbitrarily renumber.

A comparison chart of some of the rating systems used elsewhere in the world is included in this guide. This chart was designed to serve two purposes. The influx of foreign climbers, unfamiliar with the delights of the YDS, can get a better feel for the difficulty of the climbs before tying on to the sharp end of the rope. Additionally, this chart is an attempt to familiarize American climbers with the other major rating systems. This comparison chart was developed from discussions with many foreign climbers who gladly, and often relentlessly, offered to explain the subtleties of their own systems. The result is hopefully the most accurate rating comparison chart yet devised (but no claims are made of perfection!).

The popular, and sometimes controversial, Star Rating System is again employed in this guide. Reaction to this "Quality" rating has, in general (if not always specifically), been very favorable. To those unfamiliar with its use, the RATINGS section of this guide will provide further explanation.

The information regarding early first ascents of routes, as listed in this guide (as well as previous editions), is only as accurate as known records permit. This information for the period from the early 1950's to the early 1960's has many glaring gaps and inaccuracies. Although many leading climbers of this period climbed many of the obvious lines in Hidden Valley Campground, few took Joshua Tree seriously enough to bother to keep records.

A picture is really worth a thousand words and with this in mind, and the realization that many foreign climbers' English skills may be limited to belay commands, climbing lingo and slang, this guide relies heavily on photographs, maps and topo route descriptions.

These new approaches to the design of the guide have been necessitated by the exponential growth in the number of climbs in the Monument and in order to keep this guide from a similar growth pattern. If past guides serve as exemplars of wasted space and irrelevancy, it is hoped that this guide promotes sensible restraint and intelligent economy.

Joshua Tree is a beautiful and wild place. It provides refuge for several endangered species. For these reasons I ask that climbers treat the Monument with respect and care. If we are careful, no number of climbers can ruin this natural treasure.

Many people contributed to this guide. As with any guide book, it is all the climbers who contribute information and their ideas that make it all possible. I would like to thank all the people who contributed any information and more specifically: John Bachar, Alan Bartlett, Charles Cole, Dave Evans, Craig Fry, Tom Higgins, Dave Houser, Randy Leavitt, Mike Lechlinski, Jack Marshall, Rob Mulligan, Darryl Nakahira, Alan Nelson, Kevin Powell, Rob Raker, Alan Roberts, Todd Swain, Jonny Woodward and Tony Yaniro. I also would like to thank Christine Jenkewitz-Meytras, Charlie Jenkewitz and Hidetaka Suzuki for their translations found in the introduction.

Most of all, climbing is fun. It is in the spirit of fun that this guide is written. Have fun, and foremost, respect the rock.

Randy Vogel, 1985

TABLE OF CONTENTS

INTRODUCTION

Joshua Tree is a wondrous and delightful place to climb. Although there has been a tremendous influx of climbers in the last few years (no doubt due to the guide book), it retains a charm and appeal. One can hike a short distance into the maze of domes known as the Wonderland of Rocks and escape any signs of fellow climbers. This characteristic makes it possible to enjoy both camp scene and wilderness climbing.

The rock formations tend to be dome-like and are usually surrounded by flat sandy washes and open plains. Some of the rock formations appear to be no more than huge piles of stacked boulders. Most formations sport a number of boulders around their base. These rocks offer numerous, excellent problems of the most severe level. While there are many established bouldering spots and problems, there remains a tremendous untapped potential for boulder problems.

Joshua Tree rock is granitic in origin, of a type called Quartz Monzonite. I am certainly no geologist, but here are a few geological highlights. The rock in the Monument is part of a huge underground sea of granite, a batholith that has pushed its way to the surface throughout Southern California.

Due to the particular way that the rock cooled and was subsequently weathered, the rock is generally quite rough in texture. This means there is a high friction coefficient and a need to use care to avoid cuts and scrapes. Fortunately for climbers, this translates into a rock surface that is highly climbable. Sections of formations that look unclimbable or hideously hard often turn out to be only moderately difficult.

The cracks at Joshua Tree are often shallow and tend to flare. There are notable exceptions to this, however. Friends are very helpful in the cracks that are flared and provide good protection in the horizontal cracks that are commonly seen in the Monument.

Generally, the western faces of the rock formations tend to be lower angled and rougher in texture. The eastern faces are much steeper, often overhanging, and this rock is usually much smoother, even polished. This is a result of the way the rock has faulted and weathered.

Crystaline and other intrusion dikes criss-cross many of the formations. It is possible to trace a single intrusion dike as it crosses various different formations. These dikes have provided several traversing and vertical face climbs. *Sidewinder* near Hidden Valley Campground and *I Can't Believe It's A Girdle* are only two examples of the routes that have utilized these dike systems.

HISTORY

Joshua Tree's early climbing days are shrouded in some mystery. Little is known about the period from 1950 to the early 1960's, when Josh's climbing was in its infancy. What is known is that local hardmen such as Royal Robbins, TM Herbert, Mark Powell, Eric Beck, Tom Frost and others frequented the Monument during this time. Various other climbers also found respite in the Monument's temperate winter clime.

For the most part activity was limited to times when poor weather kept the more alpine areas (Tahquitz and Yosemite) closed. In simple words, climbers bided their time at Joshua Tree until some "real" climbing was in condition. It was commonly felt that Joshua Tree was merely a practice area, and for the most part this feeling remained throughout the entire 60's and early 70's.

Unfortunately, no one took the climbing seriously enough to record route names or first ascent parties. It is known, however, that many of the obvious cracks in the Hidden Valley Campground area were free climbed in the late 1950's and early 60's. Nevertheless, in an era when El Cap and Half Dome were the big prizes, it would take more than fun in the winter sun to get Joshua Tree taken seriously.

From the mid 1960's to the beginning of the 70's several new groups of climbers "discovered" Joshua Tree. The predominant group, "The Desert Rats," included Woody Stark, Dick Webster, John Wolfe, Bill Briggs, Dick James, Al Ruiz, Howard Weamer and others. These climbers were generally unaware of their predecessors'—and contemporaries'—accomplishments.

There is a rather exhaustive treatment of this era in the 1979 Wolfe/Dominick guide book. Basically, this group climbed most of the major lines in Hidden Valley Campground, many of which were first aided, then later free climbed. Ironically, some of the "first" aid ascents were made subsequent to the real first free ascent.

Generally, free climbing standards were years (if not decades) behind what was being done at areas like Yosemite, Tahquitz and the Shawangunks. With little exchange with other climbers from other areas, the standards remained low. A few notable exceptions to this rule exist. The most interesting effort was the 1967 first free ascent of the *Left Ski Track* (5.11a), by Tom Higgins.

In 1970 the first guide book was published. There were no routes listed more difficult than 5.9; most routes were 5.7 or under, and aid was in common use. This was soon to change as the guide focused attention on the Monument. About the same period of time, climbing was beginning to experience a boom. As this new generation of young climbers were coming to the forefront, they brought with them the modern free climbing revolution.

The first indications of a change were felt in 1972. In the campground many aid routes were being free climbed, at surprisingly moderate standards. *Half Track* and *North Chimney* both went free at 5.9, and the *Right Ski Track* was freed at 5.10b.

Later that year *Jumping Jack Crack* (5.11a) was discovered and led by John Long. *Comic Book* (5.9) was also first climbed in 1972 by Richard Harrison, Long, Don Watson and Rick Accomazzo. This fun, two pitch crack is tantalizingly obvious from the campground, and this ascent marked the increasingly cloistered environment of Hidden Valley Campground.

The "Stonemasters," a group of talented climbers who turned the climbing world on ear, were instrumental in spurring the rapid development of the Monument's free climbing potential. Tobin Sorenson, John Long, Rick Accomazzo, Jim Wilson, Richard Harrison and John Bachar were some of the hot shots who literally turned the climbing scene at Joshua Tree in a new direction.

Development began to intensify outside the campground, and areas like Saddle Rocks, Hall of Horrors and Rusty Wall saw most of the classic lines completed. The more routes that were put up only revealed more potential yet untapped. Despite the vast potential, development was far from feverish and exploration mainly occurred in group excursions to a few specific areas.

Classics of the early 1970's include *Illusion Dweller* (5.10a, 1973), by Matt Cox, Spencer Lennard and Gary Ayres. Cox was a very motivated and talented young climber who, along with several others were the upcoming "second string" of Joshua Tree climbing. Others in this group include Dave Evans, a climber with a remarkably long and prolific career at J.T., Spencer Lennard, Jim Angione and Randy Vogel.

In 1974 and 1975, Tobin Sorenson spearheaded the ascents of a variety of difficult and excellent routes which include *Harlequin* (5.10d), on Saddle Rocks, with Jim Wilson; *Exorcist* (5.10a), with Dick Shockley, Wilson and Dean Fidelman; *Hyperian Arch* (FFA, at 5.11a), with Long, Kevin Worrall and Accomazzo; *O'Kelley's Crack* (FFA, at 5.10c), with Wilson, Fidelman and Gary Ayres; and *Wangerbanger* (5.11c).

In 1976 exploration began in earnest. Former East Coast climber Herb Laeger moved to Los Angeles with Eve Uiga. Herb wasted no time in exploiting Joshua Tree's potential and together with Jim Wilson completed the unfinished *My Laundry* (5.9), and together with Ed Ehrenfeld and Eve established *Strike It Rich* (5.10b), both on the South Astro Dome.

These latter developments opened many peoples' eyes anew and routes were soon established all over the Astro Domes. *Solid Gold* (5.10a), by Laeger, Jon Lonne, Wilson and Mike Jaffe; *Such a Savage* (5.11a), by Lennard and Craig Fry; and *Figures on a Landscape* (5.10b), by Vogel and Evans are the best of those routes.

For the most part the majority of climbs established in the Monument from the late 1970's to early 80's were accomplished by only a few groups of individuals and a handful of climbers. Several of these climbers have each established over 100 routes in Joshua Tree. These individuals include Dave Evans, Randy Vogel, Charles Cole, Herb Laeger, Craig Fry, Kevin Powell, Gib Lewis, John Bachar, Tony Yaniro and Mike Lechlinski. More recently, Randy Leavitt, Vaino Kodas and Alan Nelson have been extremely active at Joshua Tree.

In the last few years, not only have previously remote areas been extensively developed, but the Wonderland of Rocks has been extensively explored. It can be safely said that although much potential remains in the Wonderland, most of the classic lines have been bagged. The user of this guide will find an immense amount of route information on the Wonderland of Rocks.

Routes will no doubt pour out of Joshua Tree for many years to come, and plans to supplement the material contained herein are already underway. For the guide book editor Joshua Tree is a full time job.

TIPS FOR A PLEASANT STAY

CLIMBING SEASON The single most important factor for Joshua Tree's popularity with climbers lies in its climbing season. When most other areas are covered in snow or rained out, Joshua Tree is often sunny and warm. The season starts in early to mid October and extends to late April or early May. It would be doubtful that so many people would travel to Joshua Tree if it was a summer climbing area. Yosemite, Tuolumne, Tahquitz and Suicide would provide stiff competition.

The best months for climbing are *usually* late October to early December and March through April. But there is no such thing as a sure bet with the weather and some seasons have incredible Januarys and Februarys, and terrible springs.

Unlike other hot spots of climbing activity, there is NO food or water available in the Monument. The nearest source is in the town of Joshua Tree. However, if you get totally desperate and can't make a trip into town, the large motor homes often and generously share of their large water reserves.

Life is pretty slow and easy in the Monument. The night life consists mainly of campfires, moonlight climbing and bouldering and the usual slander and gossip. There aren't any Mountain Room bars in which to while away the evening hours. Many Brits may find this lifestyle a little spartan for their tastes.

CAMPING Out of the many campgrounds in the Monument, there are five campgrounds at which the climber will be interested in staying. On many weekends all of these are congested. The weekend climber should plan on getting a site early or having a friend reserve one. The good news is that there is no fee for camping in the Monument.

Generally, climbers want to stay in Hidden Valley Campground. Not only is this campground the site of many fine climbs (often right outside one's front door), it is very close to most of the other major climbing areas. Unfortunately, staying for long periods of time in Hidden Valley is not suggested lest you raise the ire of the rangers.

Climbers who plan extended stays in Joshua Tree should know that there is a sometimes enforced (often selectively) 14 day per year camping limit in the Monument. Because of the popularity of Hidden Valley with climbers (and most all other campers) this campground is where most camping limit problems arise. Generally it is the climber who fails to maintain a "low profile" who gets cited. For this reason it is probably best, if planning a long stay, to maintain a low profile and whenever possible stay in some of the other campgrounds. This is especially true on weekends.

Other campgrounds that are acceptable for climbers are: Ryan, Jumbo, Belle, and Indian Cove. However, due to its remote location, Indian Cove is really only a practical alternative for climbers intending to climb exclusively in Indian Cove.

A car is helpful to get around from climbing area to climbing area, and to drive to town (Joshua Tree), 14 miles (22.6 km) from the nearest campground.

EATING AND DINING For the many climbers who cook meals over camp stoves, the nearby town of Yucca Valley has several well stocked, modern supermarkets. Additionally, in recent years Yucca Valley has sprouted a virtual swarm of fast food places and reasonably priced restaurants. Many weekenders and bored danglers have been known to never cook an evening meal.

SHOWERS Although Joshua Tree does not generate the excessive amount of dirt like Yosemite, climbers in the Monument have been known to need occasional showers. This necessitates a trip into town. Motels in the town of Joshua Tree have been known to sell showers to climbers. The Yucca Trailer Park in Yucca Valley is also a favorite spot to get clean. Both charge around $1.

RATINGS

All of the climbs listed in this guide are given a difficulty rating, and where applicable, a quality rating.

The difficulty rating used is the Yosemite Decimal System (YDS; although it was first devised and used at Tahquitz rock and should therefore be called the TDS). This system is the same as is used throughout the United States and most climbers will be familiar with its idiosyncrasies.

Climbing routes are rated on an ascending scale from 5.0 (the easiest climbs requiring ropes and belays) to 5.13 (currently the most difficult climbs yet done). Within the 5.10 and 5.11 catagories the subgrades of a, b, c and d are used to denote finer distinctions in difficulty.

Climbers may find the ratings harder or easier than what they are accustomed. However, the ratings given to routes in the Monument are generally consistent. Some exceptions do exist in the upper end of the rating system.

A major problem has developed in the last year in rating climbs. The newly introduced Firé climbing shoe is especially suited to the coarse Joshua Tree rock, often making certain types of climbs far easier than previously rated. It is still difficult to completely ascertain the extent that established ratings have been affected, so these ratings in most cases have not been altered. However, newer routes may be inconsistant in rating with older climbs, so keep this in mind when looking at a rating.

The "star" or "quality" rating used in the 1982 guide and the Tahquitz and Suicide guide is again used here. This system is designed to key climbers to the better climbs.

Climbs are given no stars if they are considered just average or less in quality, and one through five stars (on an ascending scale) if they are thought to be better routes. As this system is highly subjective, coupled with the fact that many routes have not been repeated, this system is far more unreliable than a difficulty rating. Consequently, use it as an indication only, and remember that many unstarred routes may in fact be worthy of your attention.

For those climbers who are unfamiliar with the rating standards at Joshua Tree, what follows is a chart of climbs that more or less typlify a given grade. Additionally, these climbs tend to be picked from those thought to be higher in quality and can be used as a recommended route list.

CLIMBS TYPIFYING PARTICULAR RATINGS

	5.0	*Figures on a Landscape*	5.10b
Right Ski Track Upper	5.1	*Quantum Jump*	5.10c
The Eye	5.2	*Crime of the Century*	5.10d
The Bong	5.3	*Such a Savage*	5.11a
Right On	5.4	*Hot Rocks*	5.11b
Mike's Books	5.5	*Wet T-Shirt Night*	5.11c
Double Dip	5.6	*29 Palms*	5.11d
Mental Physics	5.7	*Sole Fusion*	5.12 –
Flue Right; Sail Away	5.8	*Baby Apes*	5.12
Touch and Go	5.9	*Equinox; The Acid Crack*	5.12 +
Illusion Dweller	5.10a	*The Moonbeam Crack*	5.13

The following rating chart was drawn up and derived from many sources. It can be used to give a general indication of the relative difficulties of any given route.

West German	YDS	British		Australian	East German (Dresden)	French	NCCS *
	5.0						
	5.1						F4
	5.2						
	5.3						F5
	5.4						
	5.5						F6
	5.6						
5+	5.7	4b	VS		VIIa	5a	F7
6−	5.8	4c			VIIb	5b	F8
6	5.9	5a	HVS	16 / 17		5c	F9
6+	5.10a			18	VIIc	6a	F10
7−	5.10b	5b	E1	19	VIIIa		
7	5.10c		E2	20	VIIIb	6b	F11
	5.10d	5c		21	VIIIc		
7+	5.11a		E3	22	IXa	6c	F12
8−	5.11b	6a		23	IXb		
8	5.11c			24		7a	F13
8+	5.11d		E4	25	IXc		
9−	5.12−	6b		26	Xa	7b	F14
9	5.12		E5	27	Xb		
9+	5.12+	6c	E6	28 / 29	Xc	7c	F15
10−	5.13	7a					F16
10			E7				

* as per Joshua Tree/Wolfe

EQUIPMENT

Climbing equipment has changed drastically in the last five years. The advent of Friends, R.P.'s, Rocks and Firé rock boots have had a dramatic effect on the feasibility of both new and existing routes. For some newer climbs, a climber might be well advised to carry some or all of these tools.

For the purpose of discussion, a "standard Joshua Tree rack" (if there is such a thing) would consist of: Friends #1 through 3, small to medium Rocks or Stoppers (¼" to ¾"), R.P.s #2 to 5, a few "quick draws," runners, and the usual assortment of carabiners.

Obviously, a bolted face route would require few nuts, more quick draws and carabiners. On a crack that is uniformly sized, multiples of particular sizes of nuts will be needed. This is only common sense. Some climbers will find that they will be able to climb safely with much less gear than others. However, when a particular size of nut or special gear is required for a route it is often *(BUT NOT ALWAYS)* noted in the route description.

Pitons are rarely if ever needed in the Monument. Only a handful of aid climbs have not been free climbed as of this writing. The trend over the last ten years in the Monument has been away from aid climbing and with few exceptions there is little to attract the aid climber. There are so few climbs in the Monument that require pins that do not have them in place that bringing pitons to Joshua Tree is a waste of time. LEAVE YOUR PITONS AT HOME.

While rarely necessary at Joshua Tree, anyone climbing for very long in California would be best advised to buy a 165' rope. Indeed, a climber may find that on some routes a long rope may be essential.

Climbing gear (shoes, chalk, tape, carabiners, Friends, etc.) can be purchased at Mages Sporting Goods, in the town of Yucca Valley. It is located at 57576 29 Palms Hwy., Yucca Valley, CA; it is in the Alpha-Beta Shopping Center, telephone (619) 365-0656.

ETHICS AND LOCAL STANDARDS

This is always the most controversial section of any guide but also the most important. However, I have never been known to shy away from controversy and the points made here should be mandatory reading for anyone who climbs in the Monument. The rock is all we have. Those climbers who are insensitive to the responsibility to preserve this valuable resource should find another activity to occupy themselves. Although climbing styles and ethics vary drastically from one area to another, these unwritten rules have a common basis in rock preservation.

Strictures as to the acceptable manner in which one may climb a rock are the natural result of an increasingly large climbing population, respect for the rock, and the peculiar nature of an area's rock. Whether one agrees with the ethics of a particular area is irrelevant. When climbing in someone else's area, respect for their views should override any personal opinions. Of course one can always climb in better style than the local prevailing ethic, but local standards should be considered the minimum.

It should be carefully noted that there is a big difference between ethics and style. Style is a matter that is of concern merely to the individual climber, or climbing party. Ethics are something that has a more lasting effect and as a result alters the rock in some manner. It is the alteration of the rock itself that gives the climbing community the right to dictate the manner in which we may climb. Bad style, at worse, erodes a climber's personal integrity; Bad ethics brutally violate the rock, and as a result undermine the foundations of climbing.

CHOPPING HOLDS The worst thing a climber can ever do is to chop holds. The climber who feels it necessary to "improve" on nature is arrogant and should not be climbing. Obviously, too, the person who feels it necessary to add a hold to a route must envision himself to be the best climber in the world. After all, if they could not climb the route as it existed, no one else could either.

The shortsightedness of such an approach to climbing is apparent when one takes an historical look at rock climbing. How would today's climbers feel about our predecessors if they had resorted to chopping holds and such on 5.9's or even 5.6's? Certainly, these levels of difficulty, in the not too distant past, were at the extreme of what was thought possible. It is essential for all climbers to understand our position as it relates to history and the future of climbing.

People will climb better and at a higher standard in the years to come. If a particular route or move is beyond your ability, even though it may be a "first ascent," retreat and a recognition of your own limits requires more bravery and maturity as a climber than any "artificial" forcing of a route. Whatever puny accomplishments we as climbers attain must be measured by the yardstick of historical prospective. One's peers rarely have the requisite distance from our actions to be true sounding boards of the propriety of particular acts.

BOLTS It has been often said that the bolt is the great equalizer. On one hand it has the capacity to remove the element of the unknown and adventure in climbing, but it also makes possible routes of uncomparable boldness and beauty. Restraint in the use of the bolt is the fine dividing line between such extremes. Just as the game of climbing itself involves the balance of restraint and resourcefulness, so must we temper our use of bolts.

Placing bolts on rappel should never be considered justified. The entire concept of climbing involves the ascent of the crags from the bottom to the top. By rappelling down a route to preprotect it, we cross that line where caution is outweighed by ethical considerations. At Joshua Tree the climbs are generally short (one or two pitches). If a climber feels that protection placed on the lead is inadequate, then a top rope is almost always a viable alternative. Bolts, if essential, should be placed on the lead, by a climber climbing the route for the first time.

If our motive is safety, and not the pursuit of a name in the guidebook, a top rope should make no difference. Just as with chopping holds, let's not let our personal arrogance and ego get in the way of exercising restraint. Rest assured that what is considered impossible by today's standards will be commonplace in the future.

To rap down and preinspect or rehearse moves before leading a route is dishonest to those who attempt to repeat a route in good style. Without the benefit of familiarity with the moves, a climber may end up hopelessly sandbagged. Advance familiarity with a route certainly takes away any credit for boldness which would ordinarily be due.

If a climb is simply too steep to let go and place a bolt on the lead, one should consider two alternatives. One is to retreat and save the route for another day when you are feeling particularily bold, or to use a hook to provide balance while drilling the bolt. Using hooks should only be considered in the most extreme circumstances, and after much thought and consideration. Ask youself if this route should be left as a top rope problem and what is the real reason for your placing the bolts? Additionally, if hooks are necessary they should never be used in lieu of bold climbing. Remember, "When in doubt, run it out."

Putting up routes is not for everyone. It requires a great deal more boldness, insight and boredom with existing routes than repeating established climbs. As snobbish as it sounds, establishing new routes should be left to those who have a large amount of experience in doing established routes.

Adding bolts to established routes is so seldom justified that it should not even be considered. Times when it is necessary usually arise when: 1) Belay bolts are inadequate or need reinforcing. (I've never seen anyone complain about triple bolt belays!) 2) An existing bolt has come out or is in such poor shape as to justify replacing. In these cases the old bolt should be PULLED directly out, not "chopped." This leaves no scar and the hole can be filled with epoxy and the mouth covered with granite dust.

BOLTS SHOULD NOT BE ADDED TO EXISTING ROUTES. If you are not up to a particular route, don't do it. No one is holding a gun to your head forcing you to climb it. There is no constitutional guarantee to "safe routes." Since at some level we are all "wimps," recognize this fact and climb accordingly. Best of all, to avoid any of these problems, leave your bolt kit in the car if you're doing an established route. Except for some Yosemite Big Walls, there is absolutely no reason to carry a bolt kit on an established route!

CLEAN CLIMBING As is discussed earlier, (under *EQUIPMENT*) there is very little reason to use pitons at Joshua Tree. The iron age ended fifteen years ago, so practice your aid at some more obscure climbing area where no one minds. The routes at Joshua Tree protect very well with the assortment of clean climbing equipment available to the modern climber.

HOW TO USE THIS GUIDE

MAPS There is an extensive use of overview maps to aid the location of the various formations in each area. Immediately following this introductory material is an overview map of the entire Monument which further shows the areas covered by the other overview maps.

Although the formations in Joshua Tree are often very complex and surrounded by talus, these domes have been simplified in the maps to simple closed lines.

ROUTE INFORMATION This guide uses a variety of photographs, verbal descriptions and "topo" drawings to locate and describe routes in the Monument. Since many of the climbs are quite short, if you find the base, and see where the climb goes on a photo, you're in there. If this information is not enough, you have picked the wrong sport.

Distances may often be approximate, but every attempt is made to make these as accurate as possible. Overview maps and area introductions are given to get you to the general area of a formation or climb. After that, photos, topos, and descriptions will tell you where the climb is, where it goes, the rating, and any particular gear that might be needed. Climbing is your responsibility.

For those unfamiliar with the use of topos, what follows is a representation of the various symbols used to describe a climbing route. While topos tend to be more accurate in showing the line of ascent, they often tell less about how to climb the route itself. Of course this is as it should be. The symbols used in this guide are essentially the same as used in the Yosemite, Tuolumne and Tahquitz and Suicide guides.

TOPO SYMBOLS

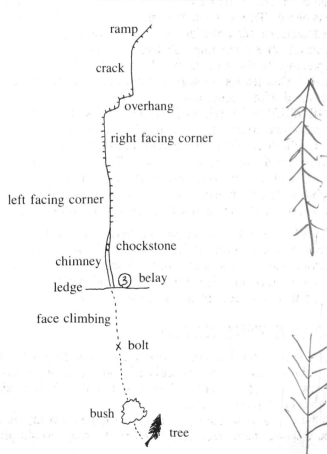

SUMMARY

The following section has been translated into French, Japanese and German in
an attempt to help realize the goal of this guide to present universally understand-
able route information:

This guide book is generally laid out in the order in which one would
encounter the various areas as he/she drove into the Monument from the town
of Joshua Tree. In this regard there is very little difference from previous Joshua
Tree guidebooks.

Directions such as north, south etc. or right and left are often used. I recognize
the fact that climbers at Joshua Tree don't carry compasses. Therefore, north,
south, east and west are often approximates, and should not be taken as
absolutes.

This guide contains several specific sections in the introductory material which
explain many diverse aspects of climbing in Joshua Tree such as Ratings, Ethics,
Equipment, Eating and Dining, The Rock, and Tips for a Pleasant Stay (eg:
avoiding raising the ire of the rangers).

Generally:

(A) There is NO food or water available in the Monument. (The nearest stores
    are in the town of Joshua Tree, 14 miles (22.6 km) from Hidden Valley
    Campground).

(B) There is a sometimes-enforced 14-day camping limit, but the campgrounds
    are free.

(C) The texture of the rock is very rough.

(D) The chopping of holds, adding of bolts, and use of pitons on existing routes
    is not tolerated by locals.

(E) Hang-dogging, pre-inspection, and wild yo-yoing is considered bad style.
    But this is really your own business.

(F) People are generally much friendlier than in Yosemite Valley.

(G) Equipment thieves should stay home.

(H) The climbing here is basically fun.

Remember, a good climbing guide helps you find the climbs, not climb them.
Good judgment and clear thinking are needed for safe climbing. This book is
no substitute for experience and good sense. Climbers are responsible for their
own safety!

SOMMAIRE

Ce guide est généralment présenté dans l'ordre où l'on trouverait les différents emplacements si l'on arrivait dans le "Monument" depuis la ville de Joshua Tree. De ce fait, il y a trés peu de différence avec les guides précédents sur Joshua Tree.

Les directions telles: Nord Sud, etc . . . , ou à droite et à gauche sont souvent utilisées. Je me rends compte du fait que les grimpeurs à Joshua Tree ne transportent pas de boussole. Aussi, Nord, Sud, Est et Ouest sont souvent approximatifs et ne devraient pas être pris dans leur sens absolu.

Ce guide comprend plusieurs parties spécifiques dans la documentation d'introduction qui expliquent les nombreux et divers aspects de l'escalade à Joshua Tree tels que les classifications, les éthiques, l'équipement, la nourriture et les repas, le rocher et les tuyaux pour un séjour agréable. (Eviter de mettre les Rangers en colère.)

En général:

-A- Il n'y a PAS de nourriture ou d'eau dans le "Monument," les magazins les plus proches se trouvent dans la ville de Joshua Tree, à 14 miles, 22.6 km du camping de Hidden Valley.

-B- Il y a, parfois, une limite, mise en vigueur, de 14 jours de camping, mais les camping sont gratuits.

-C- Le grain du rocher est trés rugueux.

-D- Le taillage de prises, l'addition de spits et l'utilisation de pitons sur des voies déjà existantes ne sont tolérés par les gens de la région.

-E- Se pendre sur les protections, inspecter la voie précédemment à l'escalade et le yo-yo sauvage sont considérés mauvais style. Mais, en général, c'est votre propre affaire.

-F- Les gens sont en général plus amicaux dans la vallée de Yosemite.

-G- Les voleurs de matériel devraient rester chez eux.

-H- L'escalade est ici fondamentalement du plaisir.

Souvenez-vous, un bon guide d'escalade vous aide à trouver les voies, mais pas à les grimper. Un bon sens du jugement et penser clairement sont nécessaires pour grimper en sécurité. Ce livre n'est pas un remplacement pour l'expérience et le bon sens. Les grimpeurs sont responsables de leur propre sécurité.

このガイドブックは、大体 彼 あるいは 彼女が ジョシュア・ツリーの町から モニュメントに 入ってくる時、通ってくる地域の順序で書かれています。この点が以前のジョシュア・ツリーのガイドブックと異っています。 方角は、しばしば 北、南、あるいは右、左 というふうに 表現されていますが、 ジョシュア・ツリーのクライマー達がコンパスを持っていないことは、わかっています。ですから北、南、東、西は、おおよそであって絶対的なものと取らないで下さい。このガイドブックは前置きとして、多くの独特な項目がありそれは、グレーディング、クライミングの倫理、道具、食事、岩、そして レインジャーの怒りをかわずに楽しく滞在する秘訣等です。

(概要)

A) モニュメント内では、水、食料は得られません（最も近いストアはヒドン・ヴァレーキャンプ場から、14マイル（22.6km）離れた ジョシュア・ツリーの町にあります）

B) 時々、14日間のキャンプ制限をされることがありますが キャンプ料金は無料です。

C) 岩肌は非常に荒い。

D) 既成のルートで、ホールドを刻んだり、ボルトを打ち加えたり、ピトンを使うことは 認められません。

E) プロテクションにぶら下がって休むこと、事前にラッペルでルートを

下見すること. ひどいヨーヨーイング(何回も墜落を重ねて登ること)は. 悪いスタイルとみなされます. しかし これは実際, あなた自身の問題ですが.

F) ここの人々は. 大体ヨセミテよりも友好的です.

G) 泥棒は家にいるべきです.

H) ここのクライミングは. おおむね良好で楽しいものです.

(次のことを忘れないで下さい)

ガイドブックというものは, あなたが良いルートを見つける為の手助けをするものであって. クライミングそのものを手助けする訳ではありません. この本は経験とグッドセンスの代りには. なりえません. 安全なクライミングは, 良き判断と明確な考えが必要です. クライマー自身の安全は. 自分自身で責任をおうべきです.

ÜBERSICHT

Dieser Führer ist in der gleichen Ordnung angelegt, wie auf die verschiedenen Klettergebiete trifft, wenn man von dem Ort ,,Joshua Tree" aus in das Monument hinein fährt. In diesem Sinne unterscheidet sich dieser Führer von dem vorhergegangenem kaum.

Richtungen wie ,,Nord", ,,Süd" etc. oder links und rechts sind häufig im Gebrauch. Ich bin mir darüber klar dass Kletterer keine Kompasse mit sich herumschleppen, deswegen sind die Richtungsangaben wie ,,West" und ,,Nord" etc. nur als appoximale Angaben anzusehen.

Dieser Führer enthält spezifische Auskünfte über Schwierigkeitsbewertungen, Ethic, Ausrüstung, Felsbeschaffenheit und verschiedene Tips für einen angenehmen Aufenthalt. (z.B. wie man die Rangers nicht verärgert.)

Generell gilt folgendes:

A; Es gibt keine Lebensmittel und kein Wasser im Monument. Die am nächsten gelegenen Geschäfte sind im Ort ,,Joshua Tree" der etwa 22 Km (14 mi.) von dem ,,Hidden Valley Campground" entfernt ist.

B; Es besteht eine 14 – tägige Aufenthaltsbegrenzung. Die Zeltplätze sind aber ohne Gebühr.

C; Die Felsbeschaffenheit ist sehr rauh.

D; Folgendes wird von den Einheimischen auf Keinen Fall toleriert werden: Dass ein meisseln von Griffen! Dass zusätzliche einschlagen von Bohrhaken und der Gebvauch von Haken in schon existievenden Routen.

E; Ausruhen an Zwischensicherungen, Vorinspection von Routen, und wildes Yo-yoing sind stark verpönt und als slechter Kletterstil anzusehen.

F; Die Szene hier ist viel freundlicher als im Yosemite Valley.

G; Ausrüstungs Klauer sollen zu Hause bleiben.

H; Wir klettern hier weils uns Spas macht.

Merke: Ein guter Fhrer hilft dir Routen zu finden, klettern must Du sie selber. Gutes Einschätzungsvermögen des eigenen Könnens und klares Denken sind Voraussetzungen für sicheres Klettern. Dieser Führer ist kein Ersatz für Erfahrung und Vernunft. Alle Kletterer sind verantwortlich für ihre eigene Sicherheit.

NEW ROUTE INFORMATION

Although there has been a concerted effort to gather all the route information possible into this guide, many routes are no doubt missing. Additionally, as many as 150 new routes may be "put up" in one season, so it is nearly impossible for this guide to remain totally current. New route supplements are planned, so if you know of a route not listed in this guide, please send me the information. Even if it is an established route that no First Ascent information is available, this information is very helpful. **ROUTES OF ALL DIFFICULTIES ARE SOLICITED.** Please send your new routes and comments to:

Randy Vogel
P.O. Box 4554
Laguna Beach, CA 92652
Your help is appreciated.

John Bachar on Acid Crack – Arid Piles

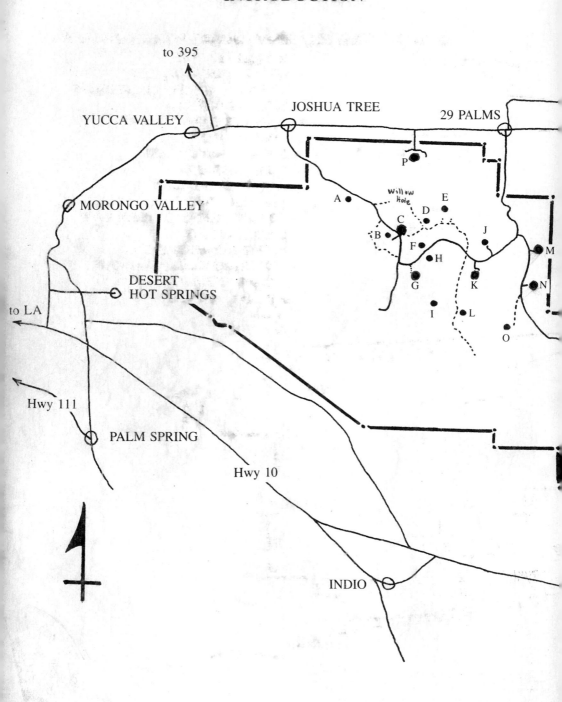

JOSHUA TREE NATIONAL MONUMENT OVERVIEW

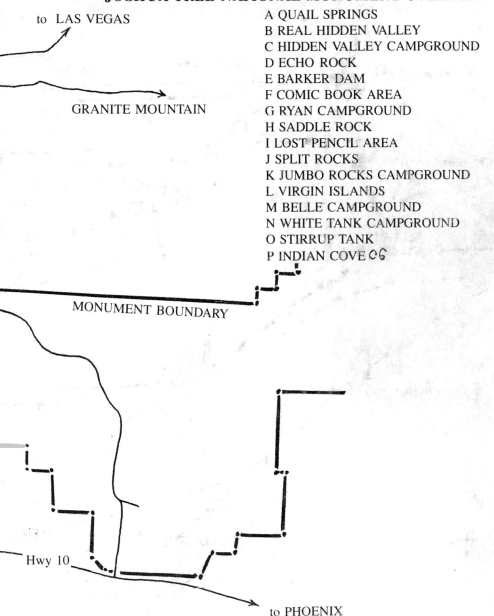

to LAS VEGAS

GRANITE MOUNTAIN

A QUAIL SPRINGS
B REAL HIDDEN VALLEY
C HIDDEN VALLEY CAMPGROUND
D ECHO ROCK
E BARKER DAM
F COMIC BOOK AREA
G RYAN CAMPGROUND
H SADDLE ROCK
I LOST PENCIL AREA
J SPLIT ROCKS
K JUMBO ROCKS CAMPGROUND
L VIRGIN ISLANDS
M BELLE CAMPGROUND
N WHITE TANK CAMPGROUND
O STIRRUP TANK
P INDIAN COVE CG

MONUMENT BOUNDARY

Hwy 10

to PHOENIX

Reproduced from TWENTYNINE PALMS and LOST HORSE

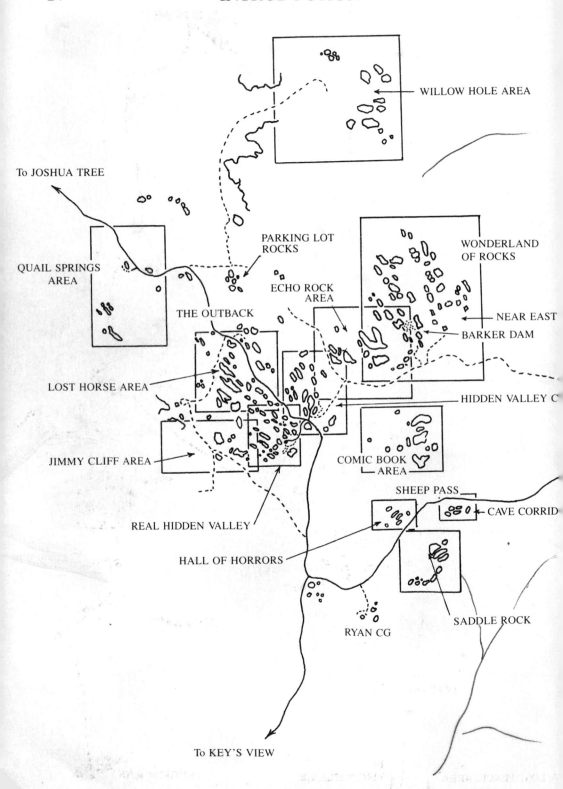

To JOSHUA TREE

WILLOW HOLE AREA

PARKING LOT
ROCKS

WONDERLAND
OF ROCKS

QUAIL SPRINGS
AREA

ECHO ROCK
AREA

THE OUTBACK

NEAR EAST

BARKER DAM

LOST HORSE AREA

HIDDEN VALLEY C

JIMMY CLIFF AREA

COMIC BOOK
AREA

SHEEP PASS

CAVE CORRID

REAL HIDDEN VALLEY

HALL OF HORRORS

SADDLE ROCK

RYAN CG

To KEY'S VIEW

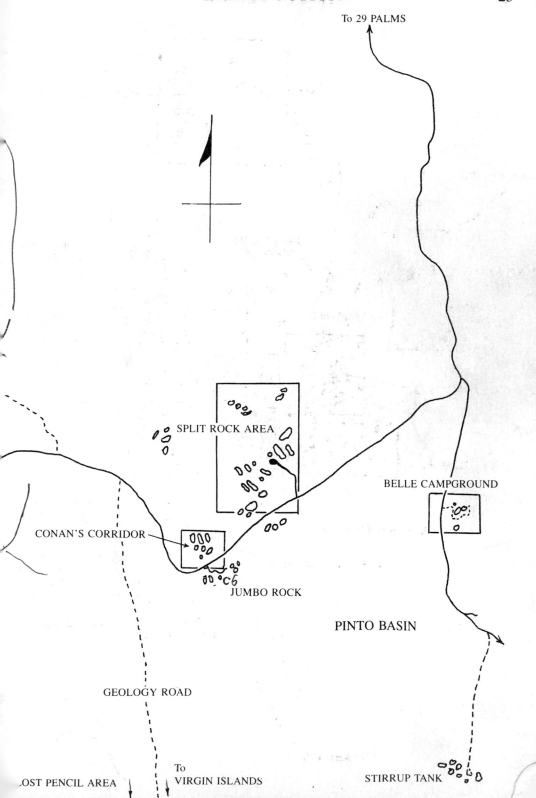

To 29 PALMS

SPLIT ROCK AREA

BELLE CAMPGROUND

CONAN'S CORRIDOR

JUMBO ROCK

PINTO BASIN

GEOLOGY ROAD

OST PENCIL AREA

To VIRGIN ISLANDS

STIRRUP TANK

Randy Leavitt on Ionic Strength　　photo by Karin Bozzo

LIZARD'S LANDING

This somewhat obscure area lies approximately one mile north by northeast of the main road into the Monument (Quail Springs Road). The usual approach is made from the Quail Springs Road at a point about 1.8 miles (2.9 km) towards Hidden Valley Campground, and past the Joshua Tree entrance to the Monument. A small pullout will be found on the left side of the road (as coming into the Monument), just where the road makes a sharp right (southerly) turn. Hike to the north along an obvious wash; the formations will be seen on the right, beyond intervening hills.

Although much recent route exploration has occurred in this area, descriptions for many routes were unavailable for this book. Several formations are located here. The first encountered is the Central Formation, which contains two routes.

CENTRAL FORMATION

1 LAST TICKET TO OBSCURITIVILLE 5.7 ★   On the central rock formation is a giant flake that starts out of an alcove located half way up the south face of the rock. Climb up to the alcove and then up the flake to the summit.   FA: Craig Fry and Marchello, February 1982.

2 ON THE BACK 5.11c (TR)   On the north face of the summit block of the Central Formation is a steep 1¼" crack.   FA: Roy McClanahan, 1982.

EAST FORMATION

3 LIZARD'S LANDING 5.7 ★   This route follows the west buttress of the formation to the east of the Central Formation. Climb ledges and cracks to a chimney which leads to the summit.   FA: Craig Fry and Lynn Hill, November 1979.

4 JET STREAM 5.10b ★★ (TR)   On the right hand arête of the second terrace of the East Formation is this interesting face which has been top-roped.   FA: Craig Fry and Lynn Hill, November 1979.

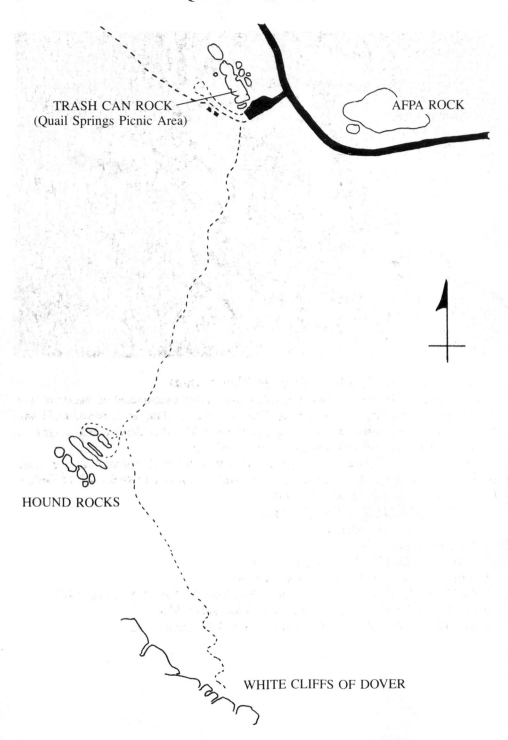

TRASH CAN ROCK
(Quail Springs Picnic Area)

AFPA ROCK

HOUND ROCKS

WHITE CLIFFS OF DOVER

TRASHCAN ROCK (Quail Springs Picnic Area)

Trashcan Rock is the first formation of major importance encountered on the drive into the Monument from the town of Joshua Tree. A paved parking area, picnic table and bathroom are found here, but no camping is allowed. The Park Service has designated this area for day-use only. This is a fine beginners' area.

Trashcan Rock is located on the right (west) side of the road, approximately 6 miles from the Park entrance. This area also provides parking for Hound Rocks and The White Cliffs of Dover, located to the southwest.

TRASHCAN ROCK – EAST FACE

5 FILCH 5.5   FA: unknown
6 RIPPER 5.11a   FA: unknown
7 WALLABY CRACK 5.8   FA: unknown
8 HERMANUTIC 5.10c ★★   FA: unknown
9 BUTTERFLY CRACK 5.11a ★★★   FA: John Bald and John Long, 1973.
10 LEFT SAWDUST CRACK 5.10c   FA: John Long, 1973.
11 RIGHT SAWDUST CRACK 5.8 ★★   FA: John Long, 1973.

TRASHCAN ROCK – WEST FACE

12 EYESORE 5.1   FA: unknown

13 SIMPATICO 5.1   FA: unknown

14 BLACK EYE 5.9   FA: unknown

15 BLOODYMIR 5.9   FA: John Long and John Wolfe, November 1972.

16 CRANNY 5.7 ★   FA: Scott Little, November 1972.

17 ESCHAR 5.4   FA: unknown

18 BIMBO 5.8   FA: unknown

19 TULIP 5.6   FA: John Wolfe and Margie Creed, October 1972.

20 BABY-POINT-FIVE 5.8   FA: unknown

TRASHCAN ROCK – WEST FACE

21 WALKWAY 5.3   FA: unknown

22 B-1 5.1   FA: unknown

23 TIPTOE 5.7 ★★   FA: Dave Stahl and Mona Stahl, October 1972.

24 B-2 5.3   FA: unknown

25 PROFUNDITY 5.10a (or 5.10c)   Going straight up past the bolt is more difficult than going slightly right, then up.   FA: Chris Wegener, February 1973.

26 B-3 5.3   FA: unknown

27 KARPKWITZ 5.4   FA: unknown

28 THE TROUGH 5.0   FA: unknown

HOUND ROCKS

These rocks are located approximately ½ mile (.8 km) southwest of Trashcan Rock. Park at the Trashcan Rock parking area and follow rough trails to this area. Many fine crack routes are found here. Map, page 28.

29 WEATHERING FRIGHTS 5.9 (TR)　FA: Alan Nelson, December 1981.

30 STEMULATION 5.9 (TR)　FA: Alan Nelson and Sally Moser, December 1981.

31 SOUND ASLEEP 5.10b (TR)　FA: Mike Beck and Alan Nelson, September 1982.

32 LEFT BASKERVILLE CRACK 5.10b　FA: John Long and Dan Dingle, May 1977.

33 RIGHT BASKERVILLE CRACK 5.10a ★★★　FA: John Long and Janet Wilts, May 1977.

34 DIRECT WRENCH 5.11a (TR)　FA: unknown

35 CRESCENT WRENCH 5.10c ★　FA: Mike Laughman and Amy Laughman (TR), October 1979. First lead unknown.

36 AN EYE TO THE WEST 5.9 ★　FA: Randy Vogel and Lyman Spitzer, November 1979.

37 TOSSED GREEN 5.10a ★★★　FA: John Long, Randy Vogel, Mike Lechlinski, Craig Fry and Mari Gingery, December 1977.

38 WHITE POWDER 5.7　FA: Janet Wilts and John Long, May 1977.

39 OVER THE HILL 5.9　FA: Alan Bartlett and Don Wilson, April 1981.

40 ANIMALITOS 5.11b ★★ (TR)　FA: John Long and Eric Ericksson, 1980.

41 ANIMALARGOS 5.11c ★★★ (TR)　FA: John Long, Randy Vogel and Lynn Hill, 1980.

BACK OF HOUND ROCKS

On the west face of the formation containing *Tossed Green* are several unnamed cracks that range in difficulty from 5.6 to 5.8.

HOUND ROCK AND WHITE CLIFFS OF DOVER FROM TRASHCAN ROCK

WHITE CLIFFS OF DOVER

This band of cliffs is located approximately ¾ mile (1.2 km) south of Trashcan Rock, and approximately ⅓ mile south-southeast of Hound Rocks. The approach to the White Cliffs of Dover is essentially the same as that for Hound Rocks. Most routes are located near the left end of the outcrop; however, several fine routes have been added further right. Map, page 28.

42 *MAKE OR BREAK FLAKE* 5.10b   This route ascends a flake/crack on a small face furthest left. A bolt protects the entry move.   FA: Craig Fry, Randy Vogel, John Long, Mike Lechlinski and Mari Gingery, December 1977.

43 *QUEST FOR FIRE* 5.11a   Just right of *Make or Break Flake* is this thin crack. #4 Friend is useful.   FA: Tom Gilje.

44 *DIGITAL WATCH* 5.11c ★★   Just left of *Jack of Hearts* is this short but thin finger crack; start out of an ant-covered tree. Poor protection.   FA: Ray Olson (TR), 1985. FA: (lead) Paul Craven and Jim Dunn, 1985.

WHITE CLIFFS OF DOVER FROM HOUND ROCK

45 JACK OF HEARTS 5.9 ★★★   This route follows a hand crack on the left side of the tiered pinnacle left of **Popular Mechanics**.   FA: John Long and Janet Wilts, May 1977.

46 CARD CHIMNEY 5.5 (descent route)   The obvious clean chimney right of **Jack of Hearts**.   FA: John Long and Janet Wilts, May 1977.

47 POPULAR MECHANICS 5.9 ★★★   This ascends the attractive white dihedral to the right of **Jack of Hearts**. Descend to the right.   FA: Mari Gingery, Mike Lechlinski and John Long, November 1977.

48 ACE OF SPADES 5.9 ★★★   Follows the left of two parallel hand cracks which are located on the left wall of the **Popular Mechanics** dihedral.   FA: Mike Lechlinski, John Long and Craig Fry, December 1977.

49 VOICE BUDDY 5.9   This route lies approximately 100 yds to the right of **Popular Mechanics**. Climb a right facing corner system right of a large face with a roof near the bottom.   FA: unknown, 1985.

50 RED SNAPPER 5.11a ★★★   A difficult entry move/ overhanging crack leads to a right facing corner, 40 yards right of **Voice Buddy**.   FA: Kevin Powell, Paul Schweizer, Alan Roberts and Randy Vogel, 1985.

51 SOVIET UNION 5.11c ★★   The crescent crack on the steep face 100ft. right of **Red Snapper**. Protection difficult.   FA: Ray Olson and John Long (TR), 1985. FA: (lead) Paul Craven and Jim Dunn, 1985.

AFPA ROCK

This nondescript formation faces the main road and lies about 200 yards east of and further down the road from Trashcan Rock. Map, page 28.

52 BOULDER CRACK 5.8   The boulder to the left of the main face has a crack on its west side.   FA: unknown

53 UNKNOWN 5.10a   FA: Randy McDonald and Don Wilson.

54 ANDROMEDA STRAIN 5.7   FA: Dave Davis, Don O'Kelley and Bruce Andre, November 1971.

55 RIP OFF 5.6   FA: Rob Stahl, John Wolfe and Dave Stahl, November 1972.

56 WHICH WITCH 5.9   FA: Don O'Kelley and Bill Mikus. FFA: John Wolfe, December 1972.

57 TWO OUR SURPRISE 5.9   FA: Brad Johnson and Mike Orr, February 1984.

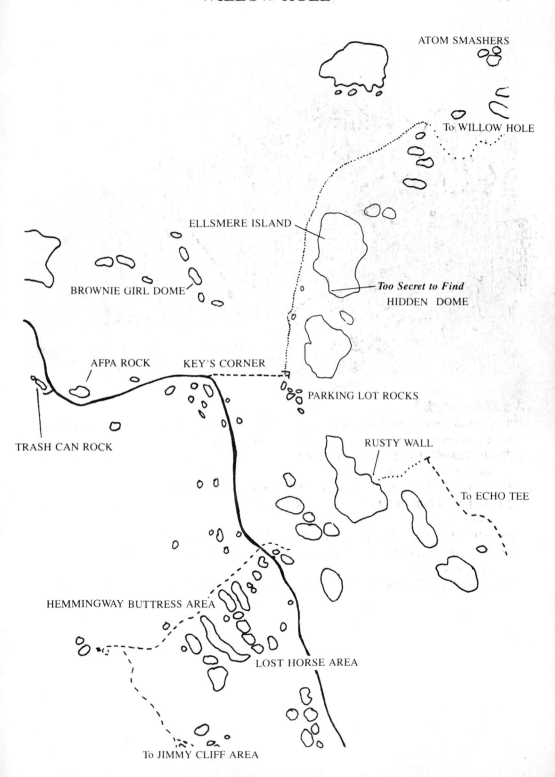

ATOM SMASHERS

To WILLOW HOLE

ELLSMERE ISLAND

BROWNIE GIRL DOME

Too Secret to Find
HIDDEN DOME

AFPA ROCK   KEY'S CORNER

PARKING LOT ROCKS

TRASH CAN ROCK

RUSTY WALL

To ECHO TEE

HEMMINGWAY BUTTRESS AREA

LOST HORSE AREA

To JIMMY CLIFF AREA

WILLOW HOLE AREA

The Wonderland of Rocks constitutes the largest concentration of rock formations in the entire Monument. This area (in excess of 9 square miles) is bounded by Indian Cove to the north, Barker Dam to the south, Key's Ranch to the west, and Queen Mountain to the east.

Due to its vast size, exploration has been made from and around two separate points of entry. At Key's Corner (a sharp right hand turn in the road .7 miles (1.1 km) east of Trashcan Rock), a dirt road continues straight east for about ½ mile (.8 km). At its end is a small parking area. The Wonderland of Rocks is approached via a sandy trail (a closed road) which proceeds to the north.

To the south of the parking area are several formations. Although there has been climbing activity on these formations for several years, only one route has been reported in this guide. No doubt many more routes will be discovered here in the years to come.

PARKING LOT ROCKS

On the west face of a formation about 200 yards south of the parking lot is a fine thin crack/dihedral. Hike south from the parking lot on the left (east) side of the first formation, then cut right (west) between the first formation and the next dome to the south. A short walk south will bring you to the base of the following route.

58 PRIVATE IDAHO 5.11b   FA: Mike Paul and Bob Gaines, 1983.

(routes 60 & 61)

approach

59

WILLOW HOLE PARKING AREA

The approach to Willow Hole and the formations in the surrounding Wonderland of Rocks follows an abandoned dirt road, now a trail. On your right is a series of low hills and formations which extend for approximately 1.1 miles (1.8 km) along the trail. About ½ mile (.8 km) from the parking lot, the trail passes a small rock on the right and jogs to the right. An unused road heads south from here, nearly paralleling the trail. About 150 ft. south is a cliff with a thin crack going over a roof; this is *Breaking Away*.

59 BREAKING AWAY 5.11a (TR)   FA: Bruce Howatt, Alan Roberts and Pete Charkin, 1985.

HIDDEN DOME

Just beyond the pile of rocks that holds **Breaking Away** is an open valley. Further down the trail (.8 mile, 1.25 km) the hill side again lies adjacent to the road. A formation high on the hill side has parallel cracks that face the road. This is Hidden Dome; a ten minute scramble leads to the base. Map, page 37.

60 TOO SECRET TO FIND 5.10d ★★★★ (large rack, ½" to 3")   FA: Pete Charkin, Bruce Howatt and Alan Roberts, spring 1985.

61 CALGARY STAMPEDE 5.9 ★★   FA: Roberts, Charkin and Howatt, spring 1985.

ELLSMERE ISLAND
About a .1 mile down the road, a left-facing red dihedral can be seen low on the hillside. Map, page 37.

62 MADE IN THE SHADE 5.9   FA: Bill Meyers, spring 1985.

63 THE GREAT ESCAPE 5.12a ★★★★ (many RP's, 3 #1 Friends)   FA: Bill Meyers, spring 1985.

64 FOREIGN LEGION 5.10d ★★★★   FA: Pete Charkin, Alan Roberts, Bruce Howatt and Swane Swaine, spring 1985.

65 AFTERMATH 5.10b ★★★★   FA: Charkin, Roberts, and Howatt, spring 1985.

66 BABY ROOF 5.8 ★★★   FA: Roberts, Charkin and Howatt, spring 1985.

67 ROUTE 66 5.4 ★   FA: unknown

68 AS THE WIND BLOWS 5.7   1.2 miles (1.9 km) along the road are cliffs. Walk east along the northern end of these cliffs for ¼ mile (.4 km); this is the highest formation along the hillside, above a long talus gully.   FA: unknown

_____ High and Dry

69

70-72

69 HIGH AND DRY 5.11a   FA: Alan Roberts and Bill Meyers, spring 1985.

To the right of the **High and Dry** formation is a boulder-filled gully which leads up to a hidden, dark face that faces that same rock. Three routes lie on this solution-pocketed wall.

70 WREN'S NEST 5.11a (TR)★★★   FA: Craig Fry and Alan Roberts, April 1985.

71 RED EYE 5.8 (TR) ★★   FA: Craig Fry, April 1985.

72 JAH LOO 5.10c (TR) ★★★   FA: Fry, Roberts, April 1985.

THE BROWNIE GIRL DOME

This obscure formation is about .6 mile directly north of Key's Corner, and about .3 mile directly west of the Willow Hole Parking Trail at a point just past route #59, **Breaking Away.** Map, page 37.

73 BUSTER BROWN 5.9 ★★   This route follows the obvious dike (large at bottom) on the west face. Climb past two horizontal bands and one bolt to the top.   FA: Kevin Powell, Paula Chambers and Darrel Hensel, 1983.

Randy Leavitt on 5 Crying Cowboys   photo by Dan Hershman

THE ATOM SMASHERS
This area lies about 3 miles (4.8 km) from the Willow Hole Parking Area. Hike along the main trail (do not take the trail heading to Indian Cove located about 1.2 mile north of the parking area) to where the trail/road ends in a sandy wash. Straight ahead (east by northeast) a group of angular-shaped boulders and formations can be seen. Although the main wash now heads south, follow a narrow streambed east until an open basin is reached. The main Atom Smashers area lies directly ahead. Map, page 37.

MAIN AREA (aka TIMBUKTU TOWERS)
74 SINE WAVE 5.9   (1 bolt)   FA: Tony Yaniro and Brett Maurer, 1983.

75 GRAVITY WAVES 5.11a ★★★★★   FA: Tony Yaniro, Graham Peace and Bill Leventhal, February 1984.

76 GRAVITY WORKS 5.11c ★★★   FA: Yaniro and Toivo Kodas, 1983.

77 OFFSHOOT 5.10b   This is the obvious wide, offwidth crack in the middle of the face.   FA: Gib Lewis and Charles Cole, 1982.

78 POLYTECHNICS 5.10c ★★   Three bolts on the wall to the left of **Psychokenesis.**   FA: Yaniro, Peace, and Kodas, 1983.

79 PSYCHOKENESIS (aka MISSING IN ACTION) 5.11a ★   Two bolts to the dihedral   FA: A. Bell and Vaino Kodas, April 1983.

80 FAMOUS POTATOES 5.11c ★   This follows 2 bolts on the east face of the Leaning Pillar.

Several face routes have been done by Vaino Kodas on the east face of the Main Area. No information is available to these.

ATOM SMASHER BOULDERS
These boulders lie about 125 yards south southeast from the Main Area, and down the hill. These boulders are generally about 50' high. Many face climbs are found on the sharp arêtes. Map, page 37.

81 NUCLEAR ARMS 5.12a ★★★   Climb west face of Boulder I, starting above the overhanging bottom via either **Atom Ant** or **Gumshoe.**   FA: Tony Yaniro and Randy Leavitt, March 1984.

82 ATOM ANT 5.11b ★★   Start left of the northwest arête of Boulder II and continue up and left past bolts to top.   FA: Yaniro and Leavitt, March 1984.

83 GUMSHOE 5.10c ★★★   Start as **Atom Ant;** from 1st bolt traverse up and right around the arête to summit.   FA: Gib Lewis and Charles Cole, 1982.

84 IONIC STRENGTH 5.12a ★★★   This climbs the steep arête on the southwest corner of Boulder II.   FA: Yaniro and Ron Carson, 1983

85 SHIN BASHERS 5.11c ★   Climb just right of the northeast arête of Boulder III.   FA: Yaniro, Brett Maurer and Carson, 1983.

86 QUANTUM MECHANICS 5.11b ★★   Climbs the center of the north face of Boulder III.   FA: Yaniro and Carson, 1983.

87 ISOTOPE 5.8 ★★   Climbs the northwest arête of Boulder III.   FA: Yaniro and Carson, 1983.

LEANING PILLAR

79

ATOM SMASHER BOULDERS

74
75
76
77

TIMBUKTU TOWERS

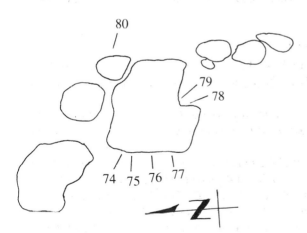

80

79
78

74 75 76 77

TIMBUKTU TOWERS

81

Boulder I

85

Boulder III

82

83

84 87

86

Boulder II

THE ATOM SMASHERS

JUMBO ROCKS

EAST
VIRGIN
ISLES

VIRGIN
ISLES

LOST PENCIL

ASTRO
DOMES

COMIC
BOOK

SADDLE ROCKS

HALL OF
HORRORS

ECHO ROCK

To PARKING LOT

To ATOM SMASHERS

WILLOW HOLE

WONDERLAND OF ROCKS

photo by Dave Houser

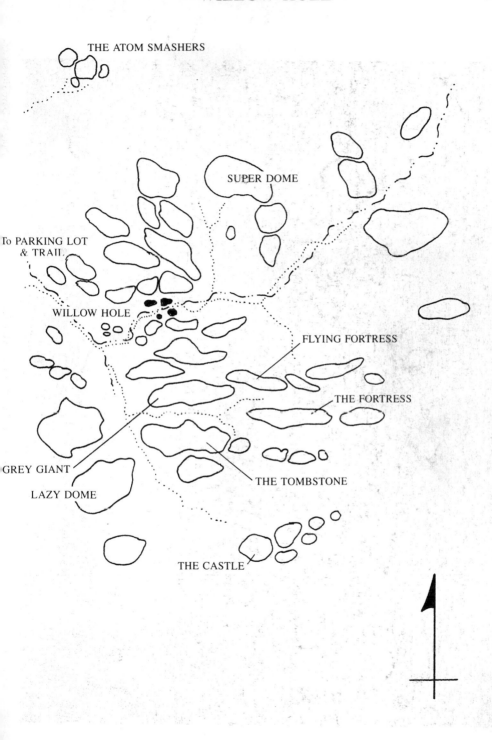

THE ATOM SMASHERS

SUPER DOME

To PARKING LOT
& TRAIL

WILLOW HOLE

FLYING FORTRESS

THE FORTRESS

GREY GIANT

LAZY DOME

THE TOMBSTONE

THE CASTLE

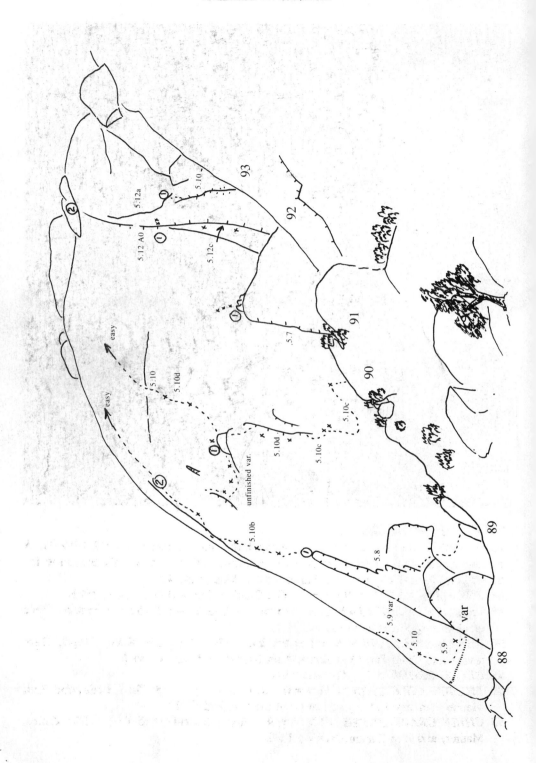

THE SUPER DOME

From Willow Hole proper, walk east along Rattlesnake Canyon about 200 yards. A narrow canyon can be seen from here to the north. Follow talus up this canyon to the base of the obvious and beautiful Super Dome. Map, page 47.

88 THE COLE-LEWIS 5.10a ★★   FA: Charles Cole and Gib Lewis, 1983.

89 THE GREAT UNKNOWN 5.10b ★★★   FA: unknown **5.10a Var.** ★★★   Take crack in left corner up to face.

90 THE LAST UNICORN 5.10d ★★★★★   FA: (1st pitch) Randy Vogel, Dave Evans and Craig Fry. (2nd pitch): Alan Bartlett and Dan Michaels.

91 BLEED PROOF 5.7   FA: unknown

92 THE MOHAWK 5.12b A0 ★★★★   Runout at top.   FA: Tony Yaniro and Brett Maurer, January 1982. (one rest point used on 2nd pitch)

93 CHIEF CRAZY HORSE 5.12a ★★★   First pitch runout (5.10b)   FA: Yaniro, Maurer, and Ron Carson, January 1982.

DISNEYLAND DOME

FREAK BROTHERS DOME

THE INAUGURON

ONE MOVE

POODLE SMASHER

LOST IN THE WONDERLAND

THE FORTRESS

THE TOMBSTONE

FLYING FORTRESS

BACK OF GREY GIANT

RATTLESNAKE CANYON

To WILLOW HOLE PARKING LOT

To SUPER DOME

WILLOW HOLE

WONDERLAND OF ROCKS (Looking southeast from near the Atom Smashers)

photo by Dave House

GREY GIANT, TOMBSTONE, FORTRESS AREAS

From the major wash that leads to Willow Hole, take the second side wash to the right (the Grey Giant can just be seen). Follow this wash in a southeasterly direction until rock scrambling leads to the west end of the Grey Giant. Map, page 47.

On the right a large face can be seen. This is Lazy Dome. To the left, a rock-filled side canyon separates the Grey Giant, on the north side, and the Tombstone, to the south. The Castle is located further southeast down the major wash.

LAZY DOME

This formation lies west of the Grey Giant and Tombstone, just across the canyon. It is to your right as you approach the Grey Giant. Map, page 47.

94 COMMON LAW MARRIAGE 5.10c   FA: Mike Lechlinski and Mari Gingery, 1985

FLYING FORTRESS   THE FORTRESS   BACK OF HYPERION

VIEW FROM SUPER DOME

GREY GIANT – SOUTH FACE

95 ILLUSION 5.7   FA: Dennis Bird and Chris Wegener, January 1971.

96 TRANSFUSION 5.12a ★★   FA: Bob Dominick and Mona Stahl, March 1972. FFA: Tony Yaniro, Mike Lechlinski and Mari Gingery, 1980.

97 LITHOPHILIAC 5.11a ★★★   FA: Don O'Kelley and Dave Davis, December 1970. FFA: Lechlinski, Yaniro and Gingery, 1980.

98 HYPERION 5.11a ★★★★ many nuts 1½-3", & 4"   FA: O'Kelley and Davis, November 1970. FFA: (1st pitch) John Long, Kevin Worrall, Tobin Sorenson and Rick Accomazzo, February 1974. (second pitch) unknown. (3rd pitch) Tony Yaniro.

98a (Var) JANUS 5.10d   FA: John Wolfe and Bill Mikus, December 1970. FFA: unknown, 1979.

98b (Var) VORTEX 5.10a   FA: Long, Sorenson and Jack Roberts, June 1974.

99 THE DMB 5.9 ★★   FA: Randy Vogel and Craig Fry, January 1978.

100 DIMORPHISM 5.7   FA: Ken Stichter and Rob Stahl, January 1971.

101 DAWN YAWN 5.11d ★★★   FA: Tony Yaniro, 1981.

THE TOMBSTONE
102 CINNAMON GIRL 5.10d ★★   FA: Dan Michaels
103 THE TOMBSTONE 5.11c ★★   FA: Tony Yaniro, Randy Leavitt and Dan Michaels
104 THE S CRACKER 5.10c ★★★   FA: Dan Michaels
105 HEAVEN CAN WAIT 5.10c ★★★   FA: Tony Yaniro and Viano Kodas

rope drag

106

photo by Roger Linfield

THE FORTRESS AREA

Continue east in the rock-filled gully between the Grey Giant and Tombstone. Heading straight east to the right hand canyon leads to the back (south) face of the Fortress proper. The *Book of Brilliant Things* and *Rope Drag* are located in this canyon.

If you head slightly left and around the west buttress of the Fortress you will find yourself in a wide flat valley. The north face of the Fortress is located on the south side of this valley. The north side of the valley is bounded by the Flying Fortress. The north side of the Grey Giant is reached easily by walking west from this valley. Map, page 47.

106 ROPE DRAG 5.10b   This route lies on the south side of the right hand canyon.   FA: Dennis Yates and Roger Linfield, april 1985.

107 BOOK OF BRILLIANT THINGS 5.12+★★★★★   This route is located on the south face of the Fortress, on the opposite side of the canyon containing *Rope Drag*. This route is best approached from the north face of the Fortress, near its left (east) end, via a "tunnel" which leads through the formation.   FA: Randy Leavitt, 1985.

Randy Leavitt on Natural Selection   Dan Hershman

THE FORTRESS – NORTH FACE

108 *IT'S EASY TO BE BRAVE FROM A SAFE DISTANCE* 5.12a ★★   FA: Randy Leavitt and Mike Geller, 1984.

109 *IT'S EASY TO BE DISTANT WHEN YOU'RE BRAVE* 5.11c ★★   FA: Leavitt and Geller, 1985.

110 *TOAD WARRIOR* 5.10b (Var) ★   FA: Paul Schweizer and Mike Geller, 1985. (Direct start) Roger Linfield and Dennis Yates

111 *WEEKEND WARRIOR* 5.11a ★   FA: Mike Lechlinski and Tony Yaniro, 1983.

112 *SUBLIMINATION* 5.10a   FA: Linfield and Yates, December 1983.

113 *NATURAL SELECTION* 5.11a ★★★★   FA: Leavitt and Geller, 1984.

114 *GRUNGY* 5.10d   FA: Leavitt and Rob Slater, 1985.

115 *TOWER OF GODLINESS* 5.10a ★   FA: Leavitt and Slater, 1985.

116 *TOWER OF CLEANLINESS* 5.10b ★★★   FA: Leavitt and Slater, 1985.

117 *CATAPULT* 5.11b ★★★★   FA: Tony Yaniro, Brett Maurer and Suzanne Sanbar, 1984.

118 *ARMS CONTROL* 5.12a ★★★   FA: Leavitt and Slater, 1985.

119 *ROARK* 5.10c   FA: Linfield and Yates, May 1985.

120 *THE OLD MAN DOWN THE ROAD* 5.10a   FA: Linfield, April 1985.

121 *JULIUS SEIZURE* 5.10a   FA: unknown FFA: (direct start) Linfield and Yates, April 1985.

THE FORTRESS – NORTH FACE

THE FLYING FORTRESS – SOUTH FACE

122 NO SAN FRANCISCO 5.11a (TR)   FA: Randy Leavitt and Bob Horan, 1984.

123 NO SELF CONTROL 5.12c ★★★★   poor pro.; many RP's, wires   FA: (TR)
Tony Yaniro, 1983. First lead: Randy Leavitt, 1984.

124 NO SELF RESPECT 5.10d ★★★   FA: Leavitt and Glen Svenson, 1984.

125 NO SELF CONFIDENCE 5.10c ★★   FA: Leavitt and Mike Geller, 1984.

126 42N8 5.10a   FA: Dennis Yates, Roger Linfield, 1985.

FLYING FORTRESS – RIGHT SIDE
127 HYPERVENTILATION 5.10d   FA: Linfield and Yates, April 1985.
128 NEW DAY YESTERDAY 5.10a   FA: Yates and Linfield, January 1984.
129 THUMBS UP 5.10a   FA: Yates and Linfield, April 1985.
130 TROGLODYTE CRACK 5.8   FA: Linfield, Yates, January 1984.

GREY GIANT – NORTH FACE
131 THE MALTESE FALCON 5.10b ★   Climb the obvious corner left of *5 Crying Cowboys*.   FA: Mike Geller and Randy Leavitt, 1984.
132 DROP A FROG 5.9 ★   This squeezes up the offwidth chimney that closes to a finger crack on a slab, immediately left of *5 Crying Cowboys*.   FA: Leavitt and Geller, 1984.
133 5 CRYING COWBOYS 5.12b ★★★★   Climb this thin finger crack for 50' to rappel bolts (rock deteriorates above this point).   FA: Leavitt and Geller, 1984.

THE CASTLE
This formation lies to the south of the Grey Giant. Walk about 250 yards south along the main canyon between Lazy Dome and Grey Giant. The Castle lies to the east from here and contains two short routes. A left-facing dihedral is on the left, a widening crack to the right. Map, page 47.
134 WARRIOR EAGLE 5.12b ★★★   This is the left-facing corner.   FA: Tony Yaniro and John Allen, 1981.
135 THE KNIGHT IN SHINING ARMOR 5.11b ★★★★   Finger crack widening to 2".   FA: Yaniro and others, 1981.

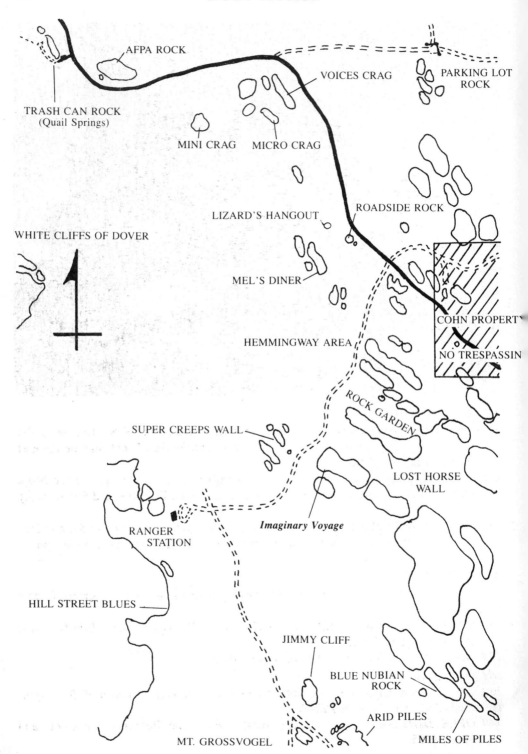

VOICE'S CRAG

This long, low, reddish colored crag lies .2 mile (.3 km) south of Key's Corner on the west side of the road. These two routes lie directly opposite the 25 mph sign on the east side of the road. Map, page 60.

136 WAR CRIMES 5.10a   This follows the slanting crack on the right of the black buttress which angles up and left.   FA: Alan Roberts, Don Reid and Shari, spring 1985.

137 DWINDLING GREENBACKS 5.11a ★★   This route is just right of the previous route and follows a thin RP crack that curves right to left, with poor protection.

MICRO CRAG

This small crag lies about 75 yards off the road, just south and slightly behind Voice's Crag. Map, page 60.

138 WIRED 5.10b ★★★   (RP's and small nuts)   FA: Alan Roberts, Don Reid and Bob Harrington, 1985.

139 O.W. 5.10a   (offwidth)   FA: unknown, 1985

MINI CRAG

Just west of Micro Crag is another little outcrop. On the west face is a 35 foot right-facing dihedral. This is *Opus Dihedral.*

140 OPUS DIHEDRAL 5.9   (medium nuts)   FA: Alan Roberts, Don Reid, and Shari, 1985.

ROADSIDE ROCK

South ¾ mile (1.2km) on the Quail Springs Road from Key's Corner, a rock formation lies just west of the road, at a sharp left hand corner. This is Roadside Rock.

141 JUST ANOTHER ROADSIDE ATTRACTION 5.9 ★   FA: unknown, 1981

LIZARD'S HANGOUT

Approximately 100 yards northwest (to the right) of Roadside Rock and about 50 yards from the road is this small rock. The routes are located on the back, west side of the rock. Map, page 60.

142 ALLIGATOR LIZARD 5.10a   FA: Kevin Powell and Darrell Hensel, May 1983.

143 PROGRESSIVE LIZARD 5.7   FA: Powell and Hensel, May 1983.

144 CHICKEN LIZARD 5.10b (TR)   FA: Powell and Hensel, May 1983.

to #151
on face
around corner
150 yds.

MEL'S DINER Map, page 60.

145 SHAMROCK SHOOTER 5.11c (TR)   FA: Kevin Powell, April 1983.

146 MODERN JAZZ 5.10c (TR)   FA: Alan Nelson and Karl Mueller, December 1981.

147 ROCK & ROLL GIRL 5.9   FA: Alan Nelson, December 1981.

148 KICKIN' BACH 5.10a (TR)   FA: Mueller and Nelson, December 1981.

149 RIGHT MEL CRACK 5.10a ★★   FA: Kevin Powell, Mike Waugh and Darryl Nakahira, April 1983.

150 LEFT MEL CRACK 5.10d ★★   FA: Darryl Nakahira, Alan Roberts, Mike Waugh and Kevin Powell, April 1983.

151 OTHER VOICES 5.7   About 125 yards to the right and west of the main face of Mel's Diner is this separate face.   FA: Powell and Darrell Hensel, April 1983.

photo by Dave Houser

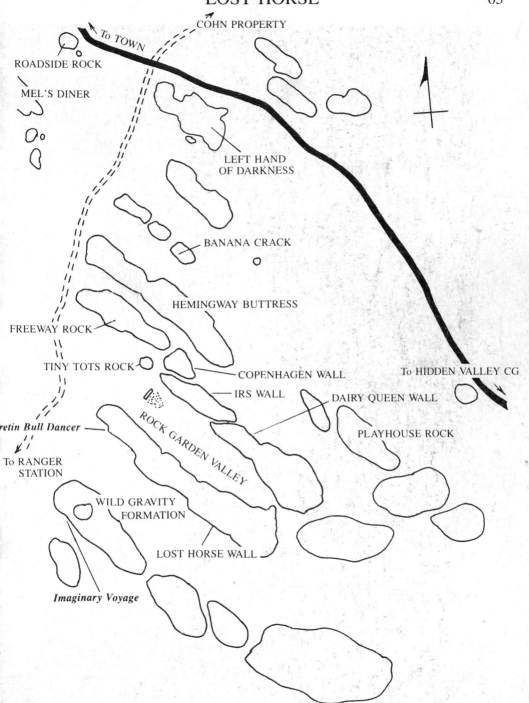

HEMINGWAY BUTTRESS AREA

LEFT HAND OF DARKNESS – EAST FACE

This formation is located at the southwest corner of the junction of Quail Springs Road and the Lost Horse Ranger Station dirt road. Map, page 65.

152 ROUTE 152 5.10a (TR)   FA: unknown, 1984

153 LEFT ROUTE 5.10a (poor protection)   FA: Chick Holtkamp and John Lakey, February 1978.

154 RIGHT   ROUTE 5.10c   FA: Holtkamp   and   Lakey,   1978.
    Variation   5.11c (climbs straight up the crack via TR)   FA: unknown, 1979.

155 UNCLE FESTER 5.10d   FA: Kevin Powell, Randy Vogel, Rob Raker and Darryl Nakahira, May 1983.

156 WHISTLING SPHINCTER 5.11c (TR)   FA: Kevin Powell, May 1983.

157 GRANNY GOOSE 5.7   FA: Fred East and John Edgar, 1973.

LEFT HAND OF DARKNESS – WEST FACE

The west side of the Left Hand of Darkness has a steep orange-colored face about 100 yards south of the Ranger Station Road. A large pillar lies about 5 feet away from the center of the face. Map, page 65.

158 BABY HUEY SMOKES AN ANTI-PIPELOAD 5.11d (TR)   This route lies near the center of the face, just left of the pillar.

159 ANTI-GRAVITY BOOTS 5.11c (TR)   FA: unknown

HEMINGWAY BUTTRESS – EAST FACE

160 MORE FUNKY THAN JUNKY 5.10a (TR, but could be lead)   FA: Roger Whitehead, Mike Ayon, Mike Wolfe and Ed White, March 1985.

161 SMOKE-A-BOWL 5.9   (one bolt)   FA: Ayon and Whitehead, March 1985.

162 FUNKY DUNG 5.8   FA: John Long and Kevin Worrall, December 1974.

163 OVERSEER 5.9 ★★   FA: Dan Ahlborn and Tim Powell, April 1977.

163a DIRECT START 5.10a ★   FA: Jonny Woodward and others, January 1983.

164 DUNG FU 5.7   FA: John Long, Rick Accomazzo and Richard Harrison, February 1973.

165 PIG IN HEAT 5.9   FA: Matt Cox, Randy Vogel and Jim Dutzi, February 1976.

165a DIRECT START 5.10b   FA: unknown

166 WHITE LIGHTNING 5.7 ★★★   FA: Chris Wegener and Roy Naasz, March 1973.

167 POODLES ARE PEOPLE TOO 5.10b ★★★★   FA: Randy Vogel and Charles Cole, February 1980.

168 POODLESBY 5.6   FA: Darryl Nakahira, November 1982.

169 SUCH A POODLE 5.8+   FA: Nakahira and Vogel, November 1982.

170 FELTONEON PHYSICS 5.8   FA: Vogel and Cole, February 1980.

171 PREPACKAGED 5.9 – ★★   FA: John McGowen, Rick Smith and Herb Laeger, February 1977.

HEMINGWAY BUTTRESS – EAST FACE   Map, page 65.

172 THE IMPORTANCE OF BEING ERNEST 5.10c ★★★★   FA: Darryl Nakahira and Randy Vogel, 1982.

173 SCARY POODLES 5.11b ★★★   FA: Nakahira and Vogel, November 1982.

174 POODLE IN SHINING ARMOR 5.8   FA: Vogel, Nakahira and Charles Cole,
November 1982.

175 ON THE NOB 5.10b   FA: Scott Erler, 1981.

HEMINGWAY BUTTRESS – EAST FACE

176 THE OLD MAN AND THE POODLE 5.8   FA: Randy Vogel, Darryl Nakahira and Maria Cranor, November 1982.

177 FOR WHOM THE POODLE TOLLS 5.9   FA: Vogel, Cranor, Nakahira and Marjorie Shovlin, November 1982.

178 A FAREWELL TO POODLES 5.9   FA: Charles Cole, Shovlin and Cranor, November 1982.

179 HEAD OVER HEALS 5.10a ★★★   FA: Herb Laeger and others, 1979.

180 MIND OVER SPLATTER 5.10a   This lies about 40 feet left of #179; climb a thin flake/crack to an obvious clean dihedral which is followed to the top.   FA: Todd Swain, April 1985.

181 FUSION WITHOUT INTEGRITY 5.10b   FA: Todd Gordon and others.

182 ROUTE 182 5.9   FA: unknown

183 EASY AS PI 5.7   This follows the 2" left leaning crack located about 80' right of *Fusion Without Integrity.* A small pine marks the start.   FA: Todd Swain, 1985.

HEMINGWAY BUTTRESS – WEST FACE

Map, page 65.

184 AMERICAN EXPRESS 5.9 ★   FA: John Yablonski and Mike Lechlinski, December 1979.

185 LAYAWAY PLAN 5.11a (TR) ★   FA: John Bachar, Lechlinski and Yablonski, December 1979.

BANANA CRACKS

This formation lies between the Quail Springs Road (near Left Hand of Darkness) and Hemingway Buttress. The Banana Cracks lie on the west side of the summit block. Map, page 65.

186 LEFT BANANA CRACK 5.10b ★   FA: John Lonne, Dave Ohlsen and Martin McBirney, April 1976.

187 RIGHT BANANA CRACK 5.11b ★★   FA: Lonne, Ohlsen and McBirney, 1976.

188 TAILS OF POODLES 5.9 This takes the crack in the corner around to the right of the previous route.   FA: Charles Cole, 1982.

THE IRS WALL – EAST FACE   Map, page 65.

189 SQUATTER'S RIGHT 5.10d   FA: Jon Lonne and Dave Ohlsen, February 1976.

190 NUCLEAR WASTE 5.10b   FA: Mike Lechlinski, Mari Gingery, Randy Vogel and Maria Cranor, 1982.

191 ATOMIC PILE 5.9   FA: Vogel and Cranor, April 1980.

192 TAX FREE 5.10d   FA: Tom Gilje and others, 1982.

193 TAX MAN 5.10a ★★★★   FA: Tim Powell and Dan Ahlborn, April 1976.

194 TAX EVASION (var) 5.10a ★★   FA: Lechlinski and others, 1982.

195 BLOODY TAX BREAK 5.10b ★   FA: Steve Gerberding and Jay Punkman, February 1983.

196 MR. BUNNY vrs. SIX UNKNOWN AGENTS 5.8   FA: unknown

197 MR. BUNNY'S REFUND CHECK 5.10a ★   FA: Vogel and Cranor, April 1980.

descent into corridor

200

198

199

COPENHAGEN WALL

This wall can be reached from the south end of Hemingway Buttress or via the "Pass" just south of the Freeway Formation. Map, page 65.

198 QUANTUM JUMP 5.10c ★★★★   FA: Herb Laeger and others, February 1977.

199 THE SCHRODINGER EQUATION 5.10b (TR) ★★★   FA: Dave Evans, Mike Lechlinski, Craig Fry and John Long, November 1979.

200 HEAVY WATER 5.10a   FA: John Bachar and Lechlinski, spring 1982.

DAIRY QUEEN WALL

This formation lies to the left of the IRS Wall. Its right section is very knobby and has several cracks of varying widths. At the left end of the formation is a severely overhanging right-facing dihedral: the **Pat Adams Dihedral**. Map, page 65.

201 PAT ADAMS DIHEDRAL 5.11b ★★★   FA: Pat Adams, 1979.

202 SCRUMDILLISHUS 5.7 ★★   FA: Tim Powell and Dan Ahlborn, 1976.

203 FROSTY CONE 5.7 ★★   FA: unknown

204 DILLY BAR 5.5   FA: Tim Powell, April 1976.

205 MR. MISTY KISS 5.7   FA: Ahlborn and Powell, April 1976.

206 DOUBLE DECKER 5.6   FA: unknown

D.Q. WALL (Left)

DAIRY QUEEN WALL (Right)

descent

201

202-206

PLAYHOUSE
ROCK

207 208 209 210

PLAYHOUSE ROCK

This nondescript formation lies approximately .6 mile past the Ranger Station Road turnoff, along Quail Springs Road, just past a 50' pillar next to the road. Map, page 65.

207 FINAL ACT 5.4   FA: Dave Davis and Don O'Kelley, March 1976.

208 CURTAIN CALL 5.6   FA: O'Kelley and Davis, March 1976.

209 I'M SO EMBARRASSED FOR YOU 5.7   FA: Randy Vogel and Charles Cole, February 1980.

210 BECK'S BEAR 5.7   FA: Tom Beck, Tim Ramsey and Curt Shanebeck, November 1978.

THE (LOWER) FREEWAY WALL – WEST FACE

This formation lies parallel to Hemingway Buttress, to the west. The upper (right-hand) portion ends just north of Copenhagen Wall, and it is possible to walk through a narrow corridor behind (west) of the Copenhagen Wall to the IRS Wall. Map, page 65.

211 SMOOTH AS SILK 5.7   This is the smooth low angle slab with finger crack that faces the road.   FA: John Bald and John Edgar, 1973.

212 START TRUNDLING 5.10a   FA: Darryl Nakahira, Randy Vogel and Maria Cranor, 1980.

THE (MIDDLE) FREEWAY WALL – WEST FACE

213 FREEWAY 5.7   FA: John Wolfe and Chris Gonzalez, November 1974.
214 TOTALLY NUTS 5.9   FA: Gib Lewis and Charles Cole, 1981.

THE (UPPER) FREEWAY WALL – WEST FACE

215 NOBODY WALKS IN L.A. 5.9 ★★★   FA: Charles Cole, Steven Anderson and Marjorie Shovlin, 1981.

216 PRETTY GRITTY 5.10a   FA: Lewis and Cole, 1981.

217 ANACRAM 5.10c ★★★   FA: Cole, Lewis and R. Smith, 1981.

THE (UPPER) FREEWAY WALL – WEST FACE

218 CAKE WALK 5.9 ★★★   FA: Chick Holtkamp and John Lakey, February 1978.
219 JUNKYARD GOD 5.9   FA: Lewis and Cole, 1981.

TINY TOTS ROCK – EAST FACE

This pillar of rock lies opposite the upper Freeway Wall. Map, page 65.

220 TINKER TOYS 5.10b ★★   FA: unknown, 1977

221 DINKEY DOINKS 5.8 ★★   FA: unknown, 1977

222 COLE-LEWIS 5.9   FA: Charles Cole and Gib Lewis, 1981.

223 FATAL FLAW 5.8   Climbs the crack in the corner, going over a small overhang.   FA: Randy Vogel and Charles Cole, 1982.

ROCK GARDEN VALLEY

224 227 231 234

IMAGINARY VOYA
FORMATION

WILD GRAVITY
Routes 249-250

ROCK GARDEN VALLEY – EAST FACE

The Rock Garden Valley is formed by the back (west) side of the IRS Wall on one (left) side, and the back (east) side of the Lost Horse Wall on the other (right) side. All of the recorded routes lie on the right hand side (East Face of Lost Horse Wall).

224 POP ROCKS 5.10b   Near the upper end of the Rock Garden Valley climb straight up a face (one bolt) to a nice crack, then left; then climb straight up and over a roof to the top.   FA: Mike Hord and Mike McMullen

SHORTER WALL

To the right of route #224 is a short wall with four distinct cracks. A broken area at the base is for reference.

225 SPITWAD 5.10a   Start at the lower left-hand part of the broken area. A crack that goes left and up is followed until you can stem back right into a layback crack near the top.   FA: Keith Cunning and others, 1979.

226 EUTHYPHRO 5.9   This is a hand crack which goes up and left from the top of the broken section.   FA: Cunning and others, 1979.

227 YOUNG LUST 5.9   Ten feet right of the broken area, follow another thin crack to the top.   FA: Cunning and others, 1979.

228 SMITHEREENS 5.9   Follow to the top a thin crack located at the extreme right-hand section of the wall.   FA: Cunning and others, 1979.

229 ROCK-A-LOT 5.7   Climb the somewhat wide crack left of *Rock Candy*.   FA: Cunning and others, 1979.

230 ROCK CANDY 5.9 ★★★   Climb this steep face just left of *Double Dogleg*. Unfortunately, this route is overbolted despite good nut placements; bolts were placed on rappel, ignoring good stances.   FA: Cunning and others.

231 DOUBLE DOGLEG 5.7 ★★★   In the middle of a brown and white pocketed face, this crack heads up, doglegs left, then jogs back right.   FA: Kevin Powell, Dan Ahlborn and Tim Powell, April 1976.

232 SPLIT PERSONALITY 5.9 ★★★   Start up *Double Dogleg* but stem out right to a very thin crack on the right.   FA: unknown

233 BECK'S BET 5.8   This crack lies about 30 feet right of *Double Dogleg* and is fairly obvious.   FA: Tom Beck and others.

ROCK GARDEN VALLEY   Map, page 65.

234 WHAT'S HANNEN 5.10a   Starts in a chimney/alcove. (need #4 Friend)   FA: Jack Roberts, Kevin Powell and Alan Roberts, 1981.

235 SWISS CHEESE 5.6   Climb solution pockets right of route #234.   FA: Tom Beck

236 BOLIVIAN FREEZE JOB 5.9   FA: Kelly Rich and others, January 1980.

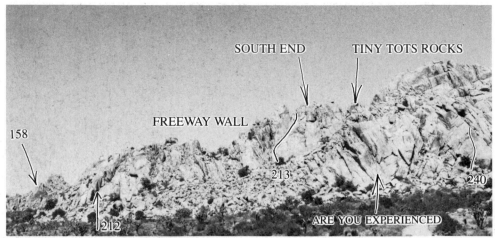

LOOKING EAST FROM SUPER CREEPS WALL

LOST HORSE WALL – NORTH END

About .5 mile southwest along the Ranger Station Road from Quail Springs Road is a valley with a large west-facing formation (the back side of the Rock Garden Valley). The stream bed in the middle of this valley can be followed south to the Real Hidden Valley. Map, page 65.

237 *ENOS MILLS GLACIER* 5.10a ★   FA: unknown

238 *CRETIN BULL DANCER* 5.11a ★   (loose)   FA: Tom Gilje and others, 1981.

239 *ARE YOU EXPERIENCED?* 5.11a ★   FA: John Long, Rick Accomazzo and Richard Harrison, December 1973. FFA: (TR) John Bachar, Mike Lechlinski, John Yablonski, John Long and Lynn Hill, 1979.

240 *JUST ANOTHER CRACK FROM L.A.* 5.9 ★   FA: Dave Evans and Jim Angione, January 1979.

LOST HORSE WALL – SOUTH END

241 WILSON REGULAR ROUTE 5.5   FA: Don Wilson, 1979.

242 THE SWIFT 5.7   This follows upper dihedral on the left side of the face.   FA: Bob Dominick and John Wolfe, April 1976.

243 BIRD ON A WIRE 5.10a ★★★   Climb up and left to a thin crack which leads straight to the top. FA: Dave Evans, Kevin Powell and Dan Ahlborn, 1977.

244 DAPPLED MARE 5.8 ★★   Climb up twin cracks and corner to a small belay stance with a bolt. Traverse along the crack down and left, then up and left to the top.   FA: John Long, Richard Harrison and Rick Accomazzo, January 1973.

245 ROAN WAY 5.8 ★   From belay on route #244, climb straight to the top.   FA: Chris Gonzalez and John Wolfe, May 1975.

246 HAIRLINE FRACTURE 5.9 ★★   Climb thin cracks 15 feet left of *Dappled Mare* up to the traverse.   FA: Charles Cole, Gib Lewis, Jessica and Darryl Nakahira, 1980.

247 MARE'S TAIL 5.9   Climbs straight up crack 40' left of *Dappled Mare,* past wedged block.   FA: Paul Neal and Charlie Saylan, December 1976.

248 LOST IN SPACE 5.8   About halfway up *Mare's Tail* traverse right to another straight-up crack which is followed to the top.   FA: Dave Evans and Jim Angione, March 1977.

WILD GRAVITY FORMATION

This formation lies opposite the south end of the Lost Horse Wall, facing east. The cliff is characterized by numerous vertical crack systems and many large roofs. Several routes have been done on this wall. Map, page 65.

249 TOP FLIGHT 5.10a This route takes the second crack to the left of route #250. FA: John Sherman, Todd Skinner and Kelly Rich, January 1983.

250 WILD GRAVITY 5.9 This takes the crack directly under the left side of the largest, highest roof on the wall. An incipient crack marks the start, which leads to a right-facing corner just below the roof. FA: Rich, Skinner and Sherman, 1983.

Several other cracks and roofs have been climbed further to the right of route #250, and range from 5.9 to 5.10b. These were all first ascended by Ken Black in 1983.

LOOKING SOUTH EAST FROM SUPER CREEPS WALL

IMAGINARY VOYAGE FORMATION

This formation consists of a fifty foot summit block lying atop the Wild Gravity face. A large cave/crack is located on its west side. Map, page 65.

251 ROUTE 251 5.10a (TR) This is the face on the north side of the block. FA: Mike Lechlinski and others.

252 IMAGINARY VOYAGE 5.10d ★★★★ This route starts inside the cave/crack. FA: John Long and Richard Harrison, November 1977.

SUPER CREEPS WALL – EAST WALL

This small formation lies just north of the Ranger Station Road approximately one mile from the junction with the Quail Springs Road. Map, page 60.

253 TALES OF POWDER 5.10b   FA: Randy Leavitt and Tony Yaniro, 1980.
254 SCARY MONSTERS 5.11d ★★★   FA: Yaniro and Leavitt, 1980.
255 YOUNG FRANKENSTEIN 5.11a ★   FA: Leavitt and Yaniro, 1980.
256 WALTZING WORN 5.12a ★★   FA: Yaniro and Leavitt, 1980.

LOOKING SOUTHWEST FROM NEAR SUPER CREEPS WALL

LOST HORSE RANGER STATION WALL

This formation lies behind the Ranger Station located about ¼ mile past the Super Creeps Wall. Map, page 60.

257 BUSHCRACK 5.7 ★   FA: unknown, 1972

258 HERCULES 5.11c ★★★   FA: (TR) John Long, October 1976. First lead: Dale Bard, November 1979.

259 SWAIN IN THE BREEZE 5.6 ★★   Climbs the face above the left side of sunken garden. (Numerous bolts, without hangers, were placed on the second ascent.)   FA: Todd Swain, 1985.

260 OWATAFOOLIAM 5.8   Climb a flake/crack to sunken garden; above, follow left-facing flake to yucca, and follow face above to the top.   FA: Swain, April 1985.

261 WALL OF 10,000 HOLDS 5.4   Friends in pockets are helpful. Approach by scrambling the groove and chimney on the right of the sunken garden to a 20' by 100' ledge; above, the climb follows "swiss cheese" wall above a block, just right of the approach chimney.   FA: Swain, April 1985.

S CRACK FORMATION

This rather small, dark rock is located about 300 yards south of the Ranger Station and about 100 yards west of the dirt road. It sits at the base of the hillside.

262 LEFT S CRACK 5.7   FA: Dave Ohlson and Jon Lonne, April 1976.

263 MIDDLE S CRACK 5.11a   FA: Ohlson and Lonne, April 1976.

264 RIGHT S CRACK 5.8   FA: Ohlson and Lonne, 1976.

265 ANDROID LUST 5.11a (TR) ★   FA: Todd Swain, April 1985.

266 ROBOTICS 5.8   FA: Todd Swain and Kip Knapp, April 1985.

HILL STREET BLUES

This formation lies uphill and left of the S crack Formation. Map, page 60.

267 ONCE IN A BLUE MOON 5.4   Climb the low angle face around and left of route # 268.   FA: Patty Furbush and Todd Swain, April 1985.

268 BLUE NUN 5.8   Climb the zigzag crack 20 feet left of the obvious corner and just left of the offwidth crack.   FA: Swain and Furbush, 1985.

269 BLUE BAYOU 5.4   Climb the right facing exfoliated corner system.   FA: Furbush and Swain, 1985.

270 BLUES BROTHERS 5.10a ★★★   Climb the obvious thin crack that runs up the center of the slab.   FA: Swain and Kip Knapp, April 1985.

271 RHYTHM & BLUES 5.10b ★★   Very short. Uphill and right of route #270, climb a thin crack/flake system to a ledge.   FA: Swain and Furbush, April 1985.

272 BLACK & BLUE 5.6   This starts atop a boulder 100 feet right of route #271, and follows a thin crack that leads to boulders at the top.   FA: Swain and Furbush, April 1985.

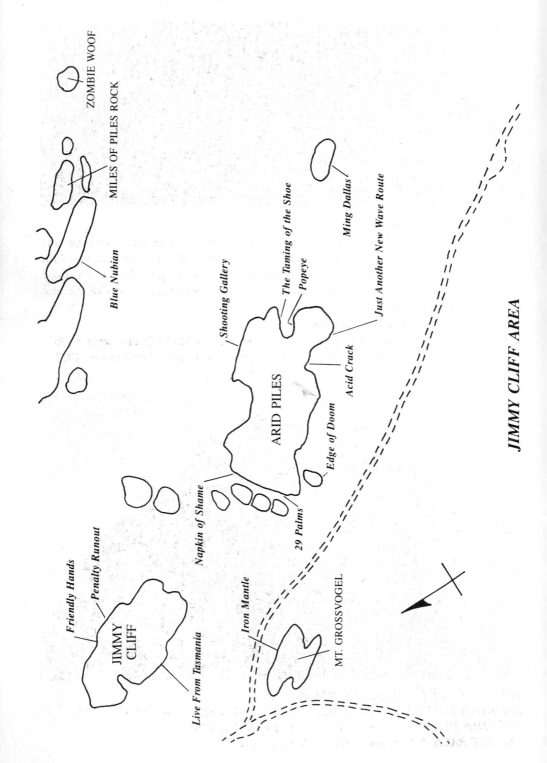

JIMMY CLIFF AREA

JIMMY CLIFF AREA

This area is about ⅔ mile southeast from the Lost Horse Ranger Station. The main dirt road passes just west of the two largest formations (Jimmy Cliff to the north, and Arid Piles to the south) and just east of the smaller Mt. Grossvogel. This area's close proximity to the Real Hidden Valley makes it possible to walk here by way of the trail leading past Houser Buttress.

JIMMY CLIFF – WEST FACE

273 GRAIN OF TRUTH 5.10d ★   FA: Charles Cole and Maria Cranor, spring 1982.
274 LIVE FROM TASMANIA 5.9 ★   FA: Kevin Powell and Alan Roberts, 1981.
275 LURLEEN QUITS 5.8   FA: Darryl Nakahira, 1982.

JIMMY CLIFF – SOUTH FACE

276 DOWNPOUR 5.9   FA: Randy Vogel, Craig Fry and Steve Quinlin, 1975.
277 THIN FLAKES 5.9 ★★ (TR)   FA: Tom Gilje, 1982.
278 RAT RACE 5.10d ★★ (TR)   FA: Gilje, 1982.

JIMMY CLIFF – EAST FACE

279 UNKNOWN 5.10

280 LAST MINUTE ADDITIONS 5.6   FA: Alan Bartlett and Alan Roberts, 1983.

281 PENALTY RUNOUT 5.8 ★★   FA: Randy Vogel, Maria Cranor and Alan Roberts, 1980.

282 SUDDEN DEATH 5.10a ★   FA: Dave Katz, Jack Roberts and Bob Gaines, November 1982.

283 THIRD WORLD 5.9 ★★   FA: Mike Paul and Jeff Elgar, 1980.

JIMMY CLIFF – EAST FACE
284 THE HARDER THEY FALL 5.9 ★★★   FA: Alan Bartlett and Alan Roberts, 1983.

285 THE BRONTO'S OR US 5.11c ★★   Three bolts   FA: Gordon Brysland and Eric Easton.

286 THE DIKE 5.10c ★★   FA: Mike Paul and others, 1980.

287 FRIENDLY HANDS 5.10b ★★★★   FA: Kevin Powell and Alan Roberts, 1981.

288 FIENDISH FISTS 5.9   FA: unknown

ARID PILES – NORTH FACE

This formation lies just south of Jimmy Cliff and consists of a complex series of faces and corridors. Map, page 90.

289 THE OUTSIDERS 5.11a   FA: Russ Raffa, Paul Trapani, Lori Chaiten and Iza Trapani, 1983.

290 QUARTER MOON CRACK 5.10a ★   FA: Alan Bartlett, Alan Roberts and Sally Mosher, 1983.

291 NAPKIN OF SHAME 5.10b ★   FA: Charles Cole, Jim Ducker, Randy Vogel and Maria Cranor, 1982.

ARID PILES – NORTHWEST FACE

These routes lie in a narrow corridor to the right of route #289. Some routes are located on the northern side of the corridor. Map, page 90.

292 29 PALMS 5.11d ★★★★ This route takes the beautiful dihedral on the left side of the coridor, 100 feet right of route #289. FA: Tony Yaniro, Mike Lechlinski, Vaino Kodas and Allen Nelson, 1981.

293 FACE ROUTE 5.10a This route lies on the face of one of the rocks forming the right side of the corridor; bolts for protection. FA: unknown.

294 MR. BUNNY QUITS 5.10a ★ This takes the thin finger crack opposite *29 Palms.* FA: Darryl Nakahira, Rob Raker and Dan Leichtfuss.

295 U.B. KOOL 5.10b Follows an undercling flake start, up and left to overhanging hand crack, then up and left to the top of *29 Palms.* FA: Gordon Brysland and Dan Sullivan, April 1985.

296 EDGE OF DOOM 5.10b ★★★ FA: Charles Cole and Majorie Shovlin, fall 1982.

ARID PILES – SOUTHWEST FACE

297 SWIFT 5.11a ★   FA: John Bachar, 1982.

298 THE ACID CRACK 5.12d ★★★★   FA: Bachar (TR), 1982. First lead: Bachar, 1983.

299 JUST ANOTHER NEW WAVE ROUTE 5.9   FA: unknown, 1982.

300 POPEYE 5.11a ★★   This route climbs the left side of the hourglass formation opposite route #301.   FA: Alan Roberts and Alan Bartlett, 1983.

301 THE TAMING OF THE SHOE 5.11a ★★   (RP's useful)   FA: John Bachar, Mari Gingery and Randy Vogel, 1981.

302 GENERIC ROUTE 5.8   In front of the east face is a smaller wall separated from the main formation by a boulder-filled corridor. This climb is a right-slanting crack which starts wide and peters out into face climbing; it is just right of a chimney system with a tree in it.   FA: Alan Bartlett and Dave Black, January 1983.

descent

29 Palms
corridor

303

290

302

ARID PILES – EAST FACE
303 SHOOTING GALLERY 5.10b ★★ FA: Bartlett and Roberts, 1983.

MT. GROSSVOGEL – EAST FACE

This formation lies just west of the dirt road. A branch in the main road heads to the right (southwest) and behind this rock. Map, page 90.

304 BLIND ME WITH SCIENCE 5.10d   FA: Todd Swain and Kip Knapp, April 1985.

305 RANGER DANGER 5.8   FA: Swain and Knapp, 1985.

306 IRON MANTEL 5.10c   FA: Darryl Nakahira, Charles Cole, Steve Anderson and others, October 1982.

307 ROBAXOL 5.6   FA: Susan Ducker, Jim Ducker and others, 1982.

MT. GROSSVOGEL – WEST FACE

308 KILLER BEES 5.9   FA: Charles Cole, 1983.

309 CHAFFE N' UP 5.8   FA: Steven Anderson and Charles Cole, 1983.

310 CRAZY CLIMBER 5.10d   One bolt and fixed pin.   FA: Dave Wonderly, Charles Cole and Steven Anderson, 1983.

311 BERSERK 5.10a   FA: Charle Cole, 1983.

312 POETRY IN MOTION 5.9   This route lies across the branch in the road on the west side of Mt. Grossvogel, on a small pinnacle. Two bolts, without hangers, protect the west face of the pinnacle, from a start at a left-diagonaling crack.   FA: Todd Swain and Kip Knapp, April 1985.

MT. GROSSVOGEL – WEST FACE

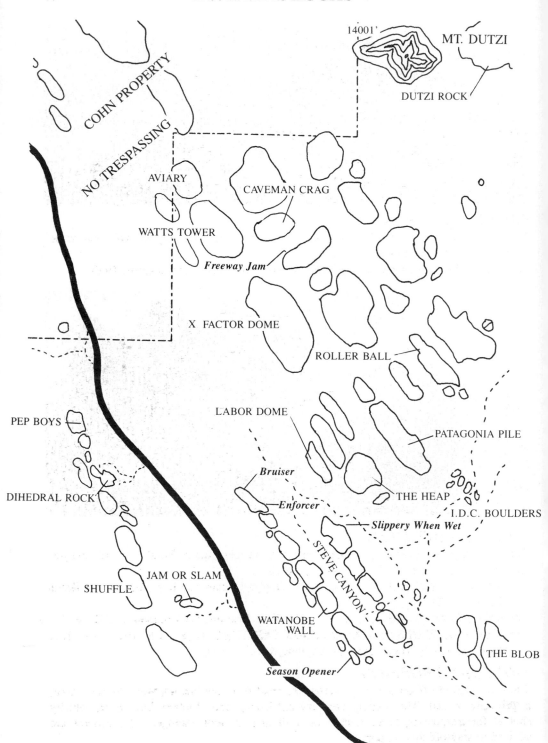

14001'

MT. DUTZI

DUTZI ROCK

COHN PROPERTY

NO TRESPASSING

AVIARY

CAVEMAN CRAG

WATTS TOWER

Freeway Jam

X FACTOR DOME

ROLLER BALL

PEP BOYS

LABOR DOME

PATAGONIA PILE

Bruiser

DIHEDRAL ROCK

Enforcer

THE HEAP

I.D.C. BOULDERS

Slippery When Wet

STEVE CANYON

JAM OR SLAM

SHUFFLE

WATANOBE
WALL

THE BLOB

Season Opener

PRIME TIME CRAG

This small rock lies about 100 yards south of Arid Piles. The only known route is on the west side. Map, page 90.

313 THE MING DALLAS 5.10b   FA: Randy Vogel and Charles Cole, 1983.

THE PEP BOYS CRAG

This formation lies ¾ mile past the Lost Horse Ranger Station Road turn off, and just west of the Quail Springs Road. Map, page 100.

314 YABO PHONE HOME 5.10c   FA: Darryl Nakahira, Mike Waugh and Kevin Powell, 1983.

315 DOS PEROS NEGROS 5.9 ★   FA: Todd Gordon, Pat Brennan, and Dave Evans

316 THE THREE BEST FRIENDS YOUR CAR EVER HAD 5.10c ★★   FA: Todd Gordon, Randy Vogel and Jim Angione, October 1985.

THE COHN PROPERTY

The area marked off on the map, across the road from the Hemingway Buttress Area, is privately owned. The owners are very unfriendly, and climbers have been actually shot at for trespassing here. Unless or until this situation changes, all climbers are advised to stay off this property.

DIHEDRAL ROCK

This formation lies about 100 yards further south of the Pep Boys Crag; the large left-facing dihedral on its left side can be seen easily from the road. Map, page 100.

317 COARSE AND BUGGY 5.11a ★★★★   FA: Bill Mikus and Bob Dominick, December 1970. FFA: Spencer Lennard, February 1978.

318 ROTS O' ROCK A3   FA: Bill Mikus and Steve Godshall, November 1970.

319 TONS OF JUNK A3   FA: unknown, 1982.

320 TOP OF THE ROPE 5.11c (TR) ★   FA: Craig Fry and Mike Lechlinski, April 1984.

321 THIN LINE 5.11c (TR) ★★   This route follows a very thin diagonalling crack which faces the road (west) but lies in the descent gully.   FA: Roy McClanahan and others, 1984.

DIHEDRAL ROCK

THE PEP BOYS

DAIRY QUEEN WALL

IRS WALL

HEMINGWAY BUTTRESS

BANANA CRACK

LEFT HAND OF DARKNESS

PLAYHOUSE ROCK

LOOKING NORTHWEST FROM NEAR LABOR DOME

THE AVIARY

This formation is about 150 yards east of the Quail Springs Road and roughly opposite the Playhouse Rock/Pep Boys Crag areas. The property to the north, as shown on the map, is private. Avoid crossing this private land in approaching the Aviary. Map, page 100.

322 *BIRDMAN FROM ALCATRAZ* 5.9   Climbs finger crack over a small roof.   FA: Mike Law and Bob Gaines, 1983.

323 *STUDEBAKER HAWK* 5.10c ★★   FA: Mike Paul, Banny Root and Bob Gaines, 1983.

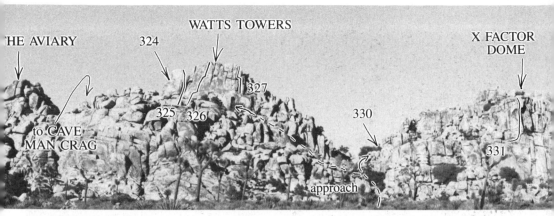

WATTS TOWERS Map, page 100.

324 INFECTIOUS SMILE 5.9 This climbs a narrow, north-facing arête with one bolt near the bottom. FA: Alan Nelson and Ken Black, March 1983.

325 JEMIOMAGINA 5.10b ★★ This is the left-most crack on the west face, and it goes over a roof formed by a huge block. FA: Alan Bartlett and Alan Roberts, 1983.

326 SOLE FOOD 5.10a ★★ Left of the center of the west face is an extremely thin RP crack which disappears after 40', before reappearing higher up, but 10' to the right. FA: Bartlett and Roberts, 1983.

327 ADULT BOOKS 5.11a ★★ On the right end of the west face are disconnected right-facing dihedrals; climb the lower book, then move left and climb the upper (crux) book. FA: Bartlett and Roberts, 1983.

CAVE MAN CRAG

This small cliff is to the east of **Infectious Smile** and faces to the south and east. Many short cracks are located on the south face and are all 5.9 or 5.10. An arching crack on the right end is **Cave Man Crack**, 5.11a.

328 PTERODACTYDL CRACK 5.9 This is just left of **Monster Mash**, on the east face. FA: Ken Black, 19183.

329 MONSTER MASH 5.10a This takes the 80' overhanging crack on the east face. FA: Ken Black and Alan Nelson, 1983.

INTERSTATE CRAG

This short cliff lies 100 yards southeast of Watts Towers and faces north. Several cracks are located on this crag, but all are short.

330 FREEWAY JAM 5.10d ★★ This is the longest crack (apprx. 35') on the right hand side and is about 1-1¼" in width. FA: Alan Bartlett, Alan Roberts and Roy McClanahan, 1983.

X FACTOR DOME

This formation is very complex and has several crack systems that lead through roofs on its upper west face. Several top rope problems have been done on the south end of the rock. Map, page 100.

331 T.K.O. 5.10c FA: Bill Critchlow and Don Reid, March 1985.

LOST IN THE SHUFFLE CRAG

This formation is almost directly across the Quail Springs Road, on its west side, from Watanobe Wall and Steve Canyon. It is about ¼ mile south along the road from Dihedral Rock. The formation to its right has one or two routes, but no information is available. Both recorded routes on Lost in the Shuffle Crag are on the east face. Map, page 100.

333 DADDY LONG LEGS 5.10c ★   FA: Mike Waugh, Darryl Nakahira, Kevin
       Powell and Dan Leichtfuss, 1983.

334 SUGAR DADDY 5.9   FA: unknown

JAM OR SLAM ROCK

This small rock is just west of a small parking lot on the west side of the road, across from Steve Canyon. Map, pages 100, 108.

335 CRANKING SKILLS OR HOSPITAL BILLS 5.10a   FA: unknown, 1984

336 FIRE OR RETIRE 5.10a ★   FA: Randy Vogel and Randy McDonald, 1979.

SLUMP ROCK

This rock lies ¼ mile south from the Jam or Slam parking area, on the west side of the road, just where the road takes a turn to the left. Map, page 108.

337 NIP IN THE AIR 5.10a   On a subsequent ascent an unknown party added several bolts to the lower section of the face, previously protected by nuts.   FA: Charles Cole, Darryl Nakahira and Randy Vogel, 1981.

338 THE PILE 5.7   FA: unknown

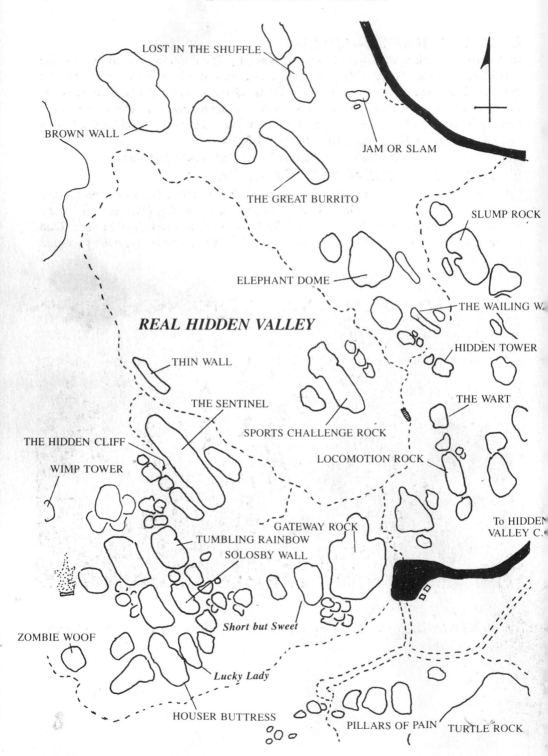

LOST IN THE SHUFFLE

BROWN WALL

JAM OR SLAM

THE GREAT BURRITO

SLUMP ROCK

ELEPHANT DOME

THE WAILING W.

REAL HIDDEN VALLEY

THIN WALL

HIDDEN TOWER

THE SENTINEL

THE WART

SPORTS CHALLENGE ROCK

THE HIDDEN CLIFF

LOCOMOTION ROCK

WIMP TOWER

GATEWAY ROCK

To HIDDEN
VALLEY C.

TUMBLING RAINBOW

SOLOSBY WALL

ZOMBIE WOOF

Short but Sweet

Lucky Lady

HOUSER BUTTRESS

PILLARS OF PAIN

TURTLE ROCK

UP 20 AND JBMF BOULDERS

In the roughly triangular shaped area bordered by Quail Springs Road on the the northeast, the Real Hidden Valley Road on the south and a broken rock formation on the west, is an area of several excellent boulders. Good bouldering is also found below the broken rock formation. This lies just south of Slump Rock. A lieback flake on a boulder is the **Up 20**. Steep face problems lie on the east face of the boulder to its north; this is the **JBMF** (John Bachar Memorial Face).

Several routes have been done on the east face of the broken formation.

THE REAL HIDDEN VALLEY AREA

Just before getting to Hidden Valley Campground (*just* before!), is a road which heads southwest from the Quail Springs Road. This road leads to the Real Hidden Valley. Approximately 1/10 mile southwest from the Real Hidden Valley and Quail Springs Road a blocky crag can be seen on the right (north). This is Three Pile Island. One route has been recorded.

THREE PILE ISLAND

339 THE COLOSSUS OF RHOIDS 5.11a   FA: Perry Beckham and W. Ravitch, January 1984.

At the end of the paved section of the Real Hidden Valley Road is a parking area. The entrance to the Real Hidden Valley is to the north; a sign and trail marker make this obvious. Map, page 108.

GATEWAY ROCK

340 FALSE TUMBLING RAINBOW 5.8   Approach is best made up hidden crevice by *In the Pit*, route #345.   FA: Dave Evans, 1977.

341 HANDS AWAY 5.9   FA: Steven Anderson and others, 1980.

342 LAY BACK AND DO IT 5.11a (TR)   FA: Dale Bard, John Yablonski and others, 1980.

Just as you enter the Real Hidden Valley, two obvious cracks can be seen on the east side of Gateway Rock.

343 SOLO 5.8   FA: Tobin Sorenson, 1976.

344 BROKEN GLASS 5.10a   FA: Charles Cole, Gib Lewis and Randy Vogel, December 1979.

Route #344, *Broken Glass*, lies on the east side of a buttress. To the right of this buttress is a narrow crevice, a gully. Route #345 lies in this crevice system.

345 IN THE PIT 5.10a ★   FA: Dan Michaels and others, 1980.

346 SEMI TOUGH 5.10d ★★   FA: Mike Lechlinski, Mari Gingery, John Yablonski, Charles Cole and Dean Fidelman, October 1979.

347 MARTIN QUITS 5.10c ★   This thin crack lies on a small east-facing rock 50 yards west of route #346.   FA: Jon Lonne and Dave Ohlsen, September 1976.

secret entrance ↗ to crevice

GATEWAY ROCK

TURTLE ROCK

To TUMBLING RAINBOW

347

346

344

343

341

To ROAD

trail loop

REAL HIDDEN VALLEY – Looking south

SADDLE ROCK

HALL OF
HORRORS

CAVE CORRIDOR

WATERGATE ROCK

THE COMIC BOOK AREA

THE WART

352

348

354

355

353

LOCOMOTION ROCK

This small crag lies in the extreme southeast corner of the Real Hidden Valley.   Map, page 108.

348 JUMPING JEHOSAPHAT 5.7 ★   FA: Tim Powell and Dan Ahlborn, April 1977.

349 LEAPING LEANER 5.6 ★★   FA: Powell and Ahlborn, 1977.

350 LUMPING FAT JENNIE 5.7   FA: unknown

351 SNNFCHTT 5.8   (Starts in pit on right)   FA: Randy Vogel, Darryl Nakahira and Charles Cole, 1981.

352 HHECHT 5.6   FA: Cole, Nakahira and Vogel, 1981.

THE WART – WEST FACE

This small formation is just east of the trail, right after it passes over the bridge.   Map, page 108.

353 PREPARATION H 5.11a (TR)   FA: John Bachar and Kevin Powell, December 1979.

354 COMPOUND W 5.11b (TR)   FA: John Bachar, December 1979.

355 THE GOOD, THE BAD AND THE UGLY 5.10a   FA: Chick Holtkamp and John Lakey, February 1978.

SPORTS CHALLENGE ROCK – WEST FACE

This excellent formation lies roughly in the central part of the Real Hidden valley. The west face sports mostly vertical crack routes; the east face is continuously overhanging. Map, page 108.

356 SPHINCTER QUITS 5.9 ★★★   FA: Dave Evans and Randy Vogel, December 1978. *Variation* 5.11a FA: same

357 WHAT'S IT TO YOU 5.10d ★★★   This is a very serious lead.   FA: Maria Cranor and Randy Vogel (TR), November 1979. First lead: Tom Gilje, 1982.

358 RIDE A WILD BAGO 5.10a ★★   FA: Randy Vogel and Dave Evans, December 1978.

359 NONE OF YOUR BUSINESS 5.10b ★★   (a serious lead)   FA: Vogel and Cranor (TR), October 1979. First lead: Gib Lewis and Charles Cole, December 1979.

360 I JUST TOLD YOU 5.10a ★   FA: Lewis and Cole, December 1979.

361 RANGER J.D. 5.6   FA: Vogel and Cranor, October 1979.

362 RANGER J.B. 5.6   FA: unknown

357.5 RAP Bolters Are Weake
FA. Paul Borne

descent route

361

362

To EAST FACE

To WEST FACE

SPORTS CHALLENGE ROCK FROM THE SOUTH

SPORTS CHALLENGE ROCK – EAST FACE

363 CLEAN AND JERK 5.10b ★★★★   FA: Kevin Powell and Dan Ahlborn, April 1977.

364 DICK ENBERG 5.11a ★★ (with tree)   FA: Dan Ahlborn, April 1977. FFA: Jeff Elgar (lead), 1979. *Direct Start (The Lobster)* 5.12a ★★★ (no tree) (TR)   FA: John Bachar and Mike Lechlinski, 1980.

365 LEAVE IT TO BEAVER 5.11d ★★★★★   FA: Dave Evans and Jim Angione, January 1978. FFA: John Bachar (TR), March 1978. First lead: Bachar, 1979.

366 CHAMPIONSHIP WRESTLING 5.10a ★   FA: Ahlborn and Powell, January 1977.

367 COOL BUT CONCERNED 5.11c ★★★ (TR)   FA: Bachar, Lechlinski, Lynn Hill and John Yablonski, 1980.

368 DISCOY DECOY 5.11a ★★ (TR)   FA: Bachar, Lechlinski, Hill and Yablonski, 1980.

369 HANG AND SWING 5.10d ★★   FA: Bachar, Lechlinski, Hill, and Yablonski (TR), 1980. First lead: Charles Cole and Gib Lewis, 1981.

SPORTS CHALLENGE ROCK – EAST FACE

rap off
or down climb

370

HIDDEN TOWER

This small tower is to the east of Sports Challenge Rock and just east of the Nature Trail. The formation can also be easily reached from Quail Springs Road by walking southwest from the vicinity of Slump Rock. Map, page 108.

370 NOT FORGOTTEN 5.10a FA: John Wolfe, 1966. FFA: John Long and others, spring 1979.

371 WILD WIND 5.9 ★★ FA: John Lakey, Chick Holtkamp and Randy Russell, February 1978.

372 SAIL AWAY 5.8 ★★★★ FA: Holtkamp, Russell and Lakey, February 1978.

373 SPLIT 5.6 This route lies in a deep groove 25' left of route #371. FA: John Wolfe, Rich Wolfe and Stu Harris, 1966.

374 SPLOTCH 5.6 This route lies in the chimney system which splits the summit; face moves lead to the crack. This also serves as a down climb route. FA: unknown

HIDDEN TOWER – NORTHEAST FACE

THE WAILING WALL – WEST FACE

Approximately 65 yards north of Hidden Tower is an extremely narrow wall with several large summit blocks. The east face has a ramp system which provides the easiest descent. Map, page 108.

375 DECENT BUCKETS 5.2　This may be used for descent, although a bit loose.　FA: unknown

376 BURN OUT 5.10b ★　FA: Chick Holtkamp and Randy Russell, February 1978.

377 GOOD GRIEF 5.10c (TR)　FA: Karl Mueller and Alan Nelson, December 1981.

378 COMIC RELIEF 5.11a ★　FA: Holtkamp, February 1978.

379 PUSSY GALORE 5.10d ★　FA: Holtkamp and Bob Yoho, February 1978.

380 LEGAL BRIEFS 5.9　FA: Yoho and Holtkamp, 1978.

381 BRIEF CASE 5.10c (TR)　FA: Mike Paul, 1981.

ELEPHANT DOME

THE GREAT BURRITO

BROWN WALL

SPORTS CHALLENGE ROCK

382

REAL HIDDEN VALLEY – LOOKING NORTH

ELEPHANT DOME
North of Sports Challenge Rock 200 yards is a rock with an elephant-shaped flake on the southwest face. This is Elephant Dome. Map, page 108.

382 PACHYDERMS TO PARADISE 5.9   FA: Robert Fainberg and Howard King, 1977. FFA: Randy Vogel and Dave Evans, December 1979.

THE GREAT BURRITO
This light-colored face lies about 200 yards north of Elephant Dome. Although a bit loose, it promises to clean up in time, providing good, moderate routes. Five or six routes rated from 5.6 to 5.10a have been done on this face.

THE BROWN WALL

This formation is approximately 500 yards north of Sports Challenge Rock and just east of the terminus of the Nature Trail Loop. Map, page 108.

383 CAPTAIN KRONOS 5.7 ★   FA: Howard King and Rob Fainberg, 1977.

384 BROWNIAN MOTION 5.10c   FA: Steve Bartlett and Steve Untch, March 1984.

385 JERRY BROWN 5.10a ★★   FA: Randy Vogel, Mari Gingery, Mike Lechlinski and John Yablonski, December 1979.

386 BROWN 25 5.11a ★★★   FA: unknown (TR), December 1979. First lead: Alan Bartlett, 1981.

387 IF IT'S BROWN, FLUSH IT 5.11 (TR) ★   FA: unknown, 1983.

388 SAVWAFARE IST EVERYWHERE 5.8   This route lies about 100 yards left of the Brown Wall on a buttress that falls almost straight into the wash. A Mojave cactus marks the route's start. The route takes a direct line up a discontinuous crack system, on desert varnished rock.   FA: Steve Untch and Steve Bartlett, March 1984.

THE THIN WALL – EAST FACE

This formation lies northwest of Sports Challenge Rock and just east of the Nature Trail. Map, page 108.

389 CHILD'S PLAY 5.10d ★★ (TR)   FA: Mike Tupper and Greg Mayer, December 1982.

390 CONGRATULATIONS 5.11a ★★ (TR)   FA: unknown, 1979.

391 NO CALCULATORS ALLOWED 5.10a ★★   FA: unknown, 1979.

✳ THE THIN WALL – WEST FACE

392 SANDBAG 5.10c (TR)   FA: Mike Beck and others, 1979.

THE WIMP TOWER

This formation is about ¼ mile northwest of the Sentinel and is noted by a thin crack, located on the east face, that leads to a large crystal dike. Map, page 108.

393 MAGNETIC WOOSE 5.10b   This route follows the above crack which diagonals left after passing the dike.   FA: John Long, Lynn Hill and Randy Vogel, January 1980.

THE SENTINEL – EAST FACE

This large formation lies on the west side of the Real Hidden Valley and sports two large faces. The east face is next to the Nature Trail, and the west face lies in a canyon and is approximately 200 feet high at its tallest point. Map, page 108.

394 BALL BEARING 5.10a ★★   FA: Herb Laeger and John McGowen, November 1976.

395 FOTE HOG 5.6 ★★   FA: Bob Dominick and John Wolfe, September 1976.

396 WESTERN SAGA 5.9 ★   FA: Dan Ahlborn and Maria Cranor, December 1976.

THE SENTINEL – WEST FACE

397 FLARED BEAR 5.8   This route takes the right-arching chimney at the extreme left side of the west face. Rappel from a horn, below a cubbyhole.   FA: James Barnett and Ted Doughty Jr., May 1965.

398 WHERE JANITORS DARE 5.7   FA: unknown.

399 WHERE EAGLES DARE 5.11d ★★   FA: Kevin Powell and Dan Ahlborn, January 1976. FFA (1st pitch): John Long, December 1979. FFA (2nd pitch): Jonny Woodward, April 1984.

400 CRYSTAL KEYHOLE 5.9   FA: unknown, December 1981.

401 NOT FOR LOAN 5.10b ★★★   (5.10c if join route #399 to top)   FA: Jeff Morgan and Tony Zeek, 1975. FFA: Gib Lewis and Charles Cole, December 1979.

402 DESERT SONG 5.11b ★★★★   FA: (1st pitch) Roy Naasz and Chris Wegener, February 1970. FFA (1st pitch) and FA (2nd pitch): John Bachar, 1977.

402a SCARED BARE (Variation) 5.10d (loose)   FA: Naasz and Wegener, February 1970. FFA: unknown.

403 NAMELESS A3 (var)   FA: unknown.

404 ILLUSION DWELLER 5.10a ★★★★★   FA: Matt Cox, Spencer Lennard and Gary Ayres, 1973.

405 THE CHAMELEON 5.12b (TR) ★★★   FA: John Bachar and Mike Lechlinski, December 1979.

406 THE RUBBERFAT SYNDROME 5.11a (TR)   FA: John Bachar, Mari Gingery and John Yablonski, December 1979.

TUMBLING RAINBOW
FORMATION

THE SENTINEL – EAST FACE

SOLOSBY FACE

descent

409

411

412

descent

394 395 396

To WEST FACE

To THIN WALL

NATURE TRAIL

THE SENTINEL – WEST FACE

THE SENTINEL – WEST FACE

THE HIDDEN CLIFF

This cliff lies directly opposite *Illusion Dweller – Rubberfat Syndrome* and in the canyon/gully area. It is an outstanding face. Map, page 108.

407 BIKINI WHALE 5.12a (TR) ★★★   Climbs knobs and horizontal bands left of route #408.   FA: by visiting French climbers, 1984.

408 AGAINST THE GRAIN 5.10a (TR)   Climb knobs up to a crack, thin at first, that gradually widens.   FA: Charles Cole, Gib Lewis and Randy Vogel, December 1979.

TUMBLING RAINBOW FORMATION

409 RUN FOR YOUR LIFE 5.10b ★★★★   FA: Charles Cole, Dave Houser and Herb Laeger, 1978.

410 TUMBLING RAINBOW 5.9 ★★   FA: John Long, Richard Harrison, Rick Accomazzo and Ging Gingrich, March 1973.

411 RAINY DAY, DREAM AWAY 5.11b ★★★   (a serious lead)   FA: Dave Evans and Jim Angione, January 1978. FFA: John Bachar, Kevin Powell and Mari Gingery, spring 1979. First lead: unknown, 1984.

412 FISTICUFFS 5.10b ★★★   FA: John Long and Rick Accomazzo, March 1973.

SOLOSBY FACE

This overhanging, knobby and orange-colored face lies to the left (south) of the Tumbling Rainbow Formation and behind a series of blocks that face the trail. The descent from Tumbling Rainbow leads past this face. To reach it from below, scramble up between huge blocks to the left of the Tumbling Rainbow Face. Map, page 108.

413 SOLOSBY 5.10b   takes the crack on the left side of the face.   FA: Rick Cashner, 1979.

414 LATIN SWING 5.11b (TR) ★★   This route ascends the center of the face before traversing right to a thin crack.   FA: Rick Cashner, John Yablonski and Dale Bard, 1979.

415 BEBOP TANGO 5.11a (TR) ★★   Climbs buckets and holds on the right side of the face.   FA: John Bachar, John Yablonski and Mike Lechlinski, 1979.

TURTLE ROCK – SOUTH FACE

This large formation lies 150 yards south of the paved parking area for the Real Hidden Valley. Routes are listed from the south face (left) to the north face (right).

416 KIPPY KORNER 5.9   This route takes the crack system on the south face, up to a small roof, then up the crack and face above.   FA: Charles Cole and others, 1983.

417 BISKERING 5.9   This route takes the obvious crack system that diagonals up and left and lies to the right of route #416 and to the left of the corner crack of route #418.   FA: Charles Cole and others, 1983.

418 OK KORNER 5.9   This takes the obvious steep corner/crack system on the right edge of the south face.   FA: Cole and others, 1983.

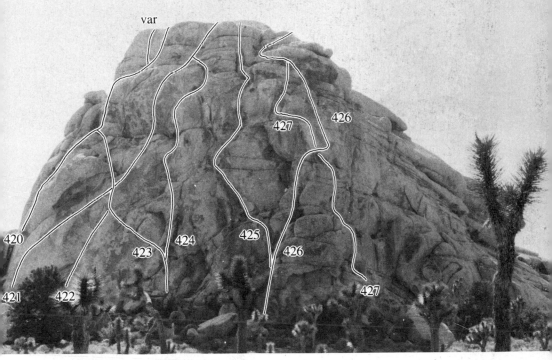

TURTLE ROCK – EAST FACE

419 SEXY SADYE 5.10c ★★★   This follows bolts up the face to the right of route #418.   FA: Charles Cole and Steven Anderson, 1983.

420 BISK 5.4   FA: John Wolfe and Rich Wolfe, 1965. **5.7 var.**   FA: Chris Gonzalez and John Wolfe, January 1976.

421 RIPPLES 5.7   FA: Gonzalez and Wolfe, February 1977.

422 LUMINOUS BREAST 5.8   FA: Dave Evans and Jeff Elgar, February 1977.

423 WANDERING TORTOISE 5.3   FA: unknown

424 BLISTERING 5.5   FA: Chris Perez and Nelson Smith, September 1976.

425 EASY DAY 5.4   FA: Gonzalez and Wolfe, February 1977.

426 TURTLE SOUP 5.3   FA: John Wolfe and others, 1967.

TURTLE ROCK – NORTH FACE
427 CORNERED 5.4   FA: Gonzalez and Wolfe, February 1977.
428 TOUCHE AWAY 5.9 ★   FA: Dave Evans and Jim Angione, 1979.
429 PILE IN THE SKY 5.10c   FA: Charles Cole and others, 1979.

THE PILLARS OF PAIN
These rocks lie just to the north of the western end of Turtle Rock and right next to the dirt road. Three pillars or towers can be seen. The eastern-most tower is Tower 1, the middle, Tower 2, and the western, Tower 3. Map, page 108.

TOWER 1 – EAST FACE
430 SUPER SPY 5.11d (TR) ★★   FA: John Bachar, February 1983.
431 SECRET AGENT MAN 5.11c (TR) ★★   FA: Bachar and others, 1980.

TOWER 2 – EAST FACE
432 ACID ROCK 5.11a ★   Takes the right-diagonalling hand crack on the left side of the east face of Tower 2.   FA: Mike Lechlinski, Gibb Lewis, Charles Cole, Marius Morstad and Dean Fidelman, November 1979.
433 DANNY GORE 5.10d   This is the first crack on the right side of the east face of Tower 2.   FA: Dan McHale, Joe Brown and Greg Bender, December 1969. FFA: unknown, 1979.

TOWER 3
434 WHATCHASAY DUDE 5.10b   This route takes the very short, overhanging finger crack on the upper east side of the the summit block of Tower 3.   FA: Mike Lechlinski and others, 1981.

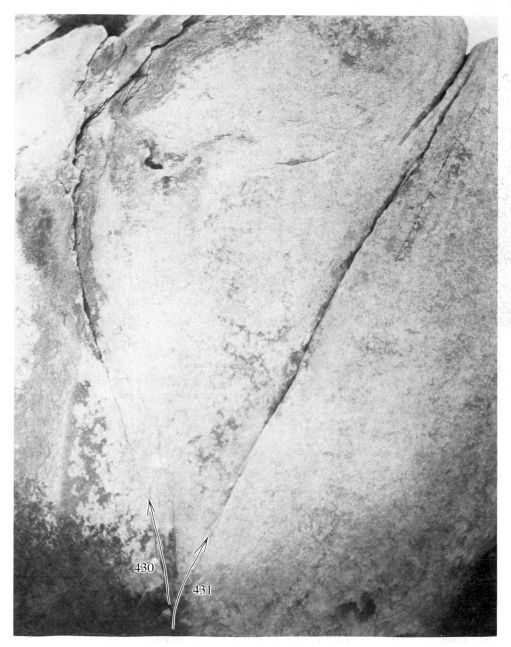

THE PILLARS OF PAIN – TOWER 1 – EAST FACE

THE CLUSTER

From the Pillars of Pain there is a dirt road which continues west about 150 yards. At the terminus of the road, walk between the boulders to the south into an open area with very large boulders and singular, small formations. To the east is a steep face with several solution holes on the east face.

There is excellent bouldering throughout this area, and further east toward the southwest corner of Turtle Rock.

435 GRIPPED UP THE HOLE 5.10a ★   FA: Dave Evans and Kevin Powell, February 1977.

436 FINGERS OF FRENZY 5.11b   FA: Rick Cashner and others, 1980.

HOUSER BUTTRESS AREA

From the western end of the Real Hidden Valley parking area, a dirt trail leads west along the outside perimeter of the Real Hidden Valley. This ridge of rocks and buttresses can be seen easily from the Pillars of Pain/Cluster area. A prominent buttress of rock (Houser Buttress) can be seen approximately 225 yards to the west. Map, page 108.

437 SMALL BUT SHORT 5.8   FA: unknown

438 SHORT BUT SWEET 5.9 ★★   RP's are helpful.   FA: Alan Bartlett and Alan Roberts, 1983.

HOUSER BUTTRESS
439 HIDDEN ARCH 5.11d ★★★   FA: Herb Laeger and Rick Smith, May 1977.
FFA: Mike Lechlinski, Lynn Hill and John Long, November 1979.
440 LOOSE LADY 5.10b ★★★★   FA: Dave Houser and Jan McCollum, November
1977.
442 DUMMY'S DELIGHT 5.9 ★★★   FA: Randy Leavitt and Mike Waugh, 1978.
443 DELIGHTFUL LADY 5.10b (TR) ★ Climbs the crack/face starting out of the
"pit" high on the east side.   FA: unknown, 1979.
444 LUCKY LADY 5.8 ★★   FA: Alan Bartlett and Alan Roberts, 1983.
445 DODO'S DELIGHT 5.10a ★   This climbs the right of two cracks.   FA: Bartlett
and Roberts, 1983.

ZOMBIE WOOF ROCK

From Houser Buttress, continue west for about 50 yards, where it is possible to turn north in a wash. Follow this wash for another 50 yards. Look back south and slightly east and you can see this small formation, facing a small clearing. Map, page 108.

446 POODLE WOOF 5.10b ★   FA: Charles Cole, Mike Lechlinski and Rob Raker, fall 1982.

447 ZOMBIE WOOF 5.12b ★★   FA: John Bachar (TR), January 1980. First lead: Jerry Moffat, spring 1983.

MILES OF PILES ROCK

This excellent rock lies approximately 150 yards northwest of *Zombie Woof,* in a narrow canyon. From *Zombie Woof,* stay just right of the open plains to the west, in a small valley. This narrows, and after a bit of scrambling leads to this west-facing rock.

448 FLARING RHOID 5.10b ★   FA: Perry Beckham and W. Ravitch, January 1984.

449 WINDS OF WHOOPEE 5.11a ★★★   FA: Rob Raker, Perry Beckham and Randy Vogel, January 1984.

BLUE NUBIAN WALL

This formation is about 250 yards northwest of Zombie Woof Rocks, on the east margain of the open plains to the west. This rock faces west and has several vertical crack systems and horizontal bands. Map, page 90.

450 BLUE NUBIAN 5.10a ★   The crack on the left.   FA: Mike Lechlinski and John Long, January 1980.

451 CONCEPTUAL CONTINUITY 5.11c (TR)   The crack on the right.   FA: Lechlinski and Long, January 1980.

Mari Gingery bouldering near Hidden Valley

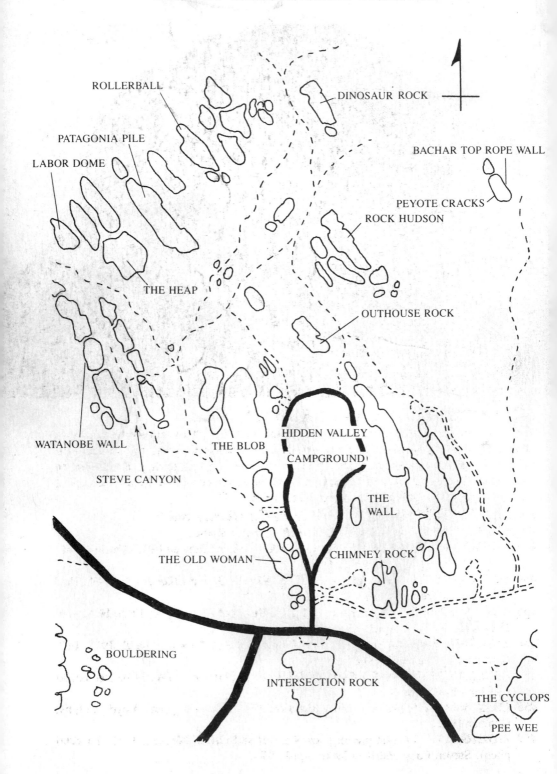

HIDDEN VALLEY CAMPGROUND

This campground is the true center of the Joshua Tree scene. Most climbers camp here, although a 14 day limit is variably enforced. The rocks surrounding the campground offer many good to excellent routes. The intersection of Quail Springs Road and the entrance to the campground has a parking lot at the south side of the road. The rock at the south side of the parking area is Intersection Rock.

INTERSECTION ROCK – NORTH FACE (facing road)

452 UPPER RIGHT SKI TRACK 5.3 ★★★ FA: unknown

453 LOWER RIGHT SKI TRACK 5.10b ★★★ FA: Al Ruiz and Rich Wolfe, 1966. FFA: John Long, September 1972.

454 OFF TRACK A4 FA: Steven Eddy, October 1973. *Variation* A3 5.8 FA: Pete Nystrom and James Barnett, May 1975.

455 LEFT SKI TRACK 5.11a ★★★ FA: Al Ruiz and Rich Wolfe, 1966. FFA: Tom Higgins and others, April 1968.

456 KOOL AID 5.10d A4 ★ FA: Tony Yaniro and Erik Burman, March 1977. FFA (2nd pitch): Lynn Hill, 1980.

457 IGNORANT PHOTONS FROM PLUTO 5.11a (TR) ★ FA: Mike Lechlinski and John Long, 1979.

458 HALF TRACK 5.10a ★ FA: unknown. FFA: John Long and Royd Riggins, October 1972.

459 ZIGZAG 5.7 FA (1st pitch): Dick Webster and Harold Webster, 1956. FA (2nd pitch): Steven Eddy and Rob Muir, April 1973.

INTERSECTION ROCK – EAST FACE
460 STATIC CLING 5.11a   FA: Charles Cole, Rusty Reno and John Long, 1985.
461 GOLDENBUSH CORNER 5.11a   FA: Dick James and John Wolfe, April 1969.
FFA: John Bachar, 1977.
462 SOUTHEAST CORNER 5.3   FA: unknown
463 JUNGLE 5.7   FA: John Wolfe, Don O'Kelley and Ken Stichter, October 1970.
464 SECOVAR 5.5   FA: Ed Zombro and John Wolfe, 1968.
465 THE WATERCHUTE 5.9   FA: John Wolfe, 1968.
466 MIKE'S BOOKS 5.6   FA: Mike Wolfe and John Wolfe, February 1967.
467 BONGLEDESH 5.10c   FA: John Long and Terry Goodykoontz, December 1973.

INTERSECTION ROCK – SOUTH FACE

INTERSECTION ROCK – WEST FACE

468 TRAVERSE OF NO RETURN 5.11a   FA: Bob Gaines and Jeff Batten, January 1985.

469 DRAWSTRING 5.7   FA: Woody Stark and DIck Webster, May 1969.

470 SOUTHWEST PASSAGE 5.8   FA: Howard Weamer and John Wolfe, May 1969.

471 PINNACLE STAND 5.7   FA: Weamer and Wolfe, May 1969.

472 LET IT ALL HANG OUT 5.10b   FA: Herb Laeger and Herb Saume, April 1978.

473 BAT CRACK 5.5   FA: John Wolfe and Rich Wolfe, December 1966.

474 SYMPATHY TO THE DEVIL 5.10b   FA: John Bachar 1976.

475 BILLABONG 5.10c ★★   FA: John Wolfe and Al Ruiz, March 1969. FFA: John Long, Bill Antel and Rick Accomazzo, December 1973.

476 SHOVLING-COLE 5.10b   FA: Charles Cole and Marjorie Shovlin, 1982.

477 OUTER LIMIT 5.6 A3   FA: John Wolfe, Dick James and Howard Weamer, May/June 1969.

478 WEST CHIMNEY 5.6   FA: unknown

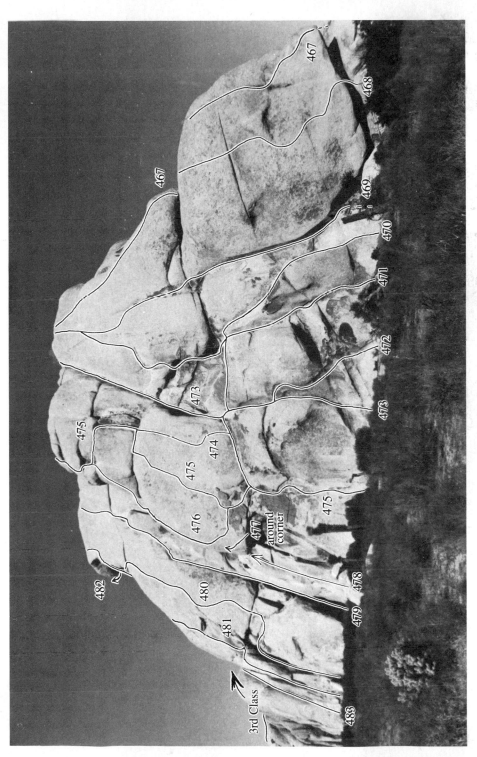

INTERSECTION ROCK – WEST FACE

INTERSECTION ROCK – NORTHWEST FACE

479 THE FLAKE 5.8 ★★   FA (to flake): Dick Webster and Woody Stark, 1967. FA (upper face): Jim Wilson and Dick Shockley, 1971.

480 WHEN SHEEP RAN SCARED 5.10c ★★   FA: Charles Cole, Dave Evans, Steven Anderson, Kelley Carignan and Craig Fry.

481 OVERHANG BYPASS 5.7 ★★★   Various variations exist to the first pitch, from 5.6 to 5.8.   FA: unknown. FFA: John Wolfe, Howard Weamer, June 1969.

482 NORTH OVERHANG 5.9 ★★★   This route starts off the ledge which leads up to **Upper Ski Track.** Climb a flake/crack to a ledge, just below the summit overhang. Climb out and left around the overhang, along a crack to the top.   FA: John Wolfe and Howard Weamer, May 1969. FFA: John Long and Rick Accomazzo, September 1972.

483 BEGINNER'S THREE 5.3   FA: unknown

John Yablonski on Bearded Cabbage

THE OLD WOMAN – EAST FACE

This is the first formation on the left (west) as you enter the campground. Map, page 140.

484 TOE JAM 5.7 ★★   FA: Kenn Smith and Dick Webster, 1959.

485 SPIDER 5.8   FA: John Svenson and George Karsh, 1968. FFA: Don O'Kelley, 1969.

486 JUDAS 5.10b ★   FA: John Wolfe, 1967. FFA: John Long and others, April 1972.

487 BEARDED CABBAGE 5.10c ★★★   FA: John Long and Richard Harrison, December 1973. *Schnurrenuff (var.)* 5.6 A3 This aids the thin horizontal cracks up and left to join the top of the route.   FA: John Wolfe and Steve Godshall, October 1970.

488 SPIDER LINE 5.11c ★★★★   FA: Woody Stark and Dick Webster, 1967. FFA: John Bachar (TR), January 1978. First lead: John Yablonski (free solo, after many top roped ascents), February 1978.

489 DEVIATE 5.10a   FA (to ledge): Dick Webster, April 1969. FA (up knobs): Dick James and John Wolfe, May 1969. FA *Geronimo* finish (5.7 roof): Phil Haney, John Mokri and Bob Dominick, November 1970.

490 JOINT EFFORT A4   FA: Tony Yaniro and Randy Leavitt, November 1977.

491 DYNAMIC PANIC 5.11d   FA: Bob Dominick and Phil Waner, December 1968. FFA: Tony Yaniro, March 1977.

492 CHURCH BAZAAR 5.10c   FA: Mike Waugh and Dave Houser, November 1977.

493 THE HINTERTOISER TRAVERSE 5.10c   FA: Charles Cole and Bob Gaines, 1985.

494 TABBY LITTER 5.8   FA: Phil Haney (free solo), 1969.

THE OLD WOMAN – EAST FACE

THE OLD WOMAN – WEST FACE

495 NORTHWEST CHIMNEY 5.2   FA: unknown

496 DOGLEG 5.8 ★★★   FA: unknown

497 THE FANG 5.11b   FA: John Wolfe and Ken Stichter, February 1970. FFA: Tony Yaniro, Mike Waugh and Dave Houser, December 1977.

498 DOUBLE CROSS 5.7+ ★★★★   FA: unknown

499 ROUTE 499 5.10c (TR) ★★   FA: Don O'Kelley and Dave Davis, 1971. FFA: unknown, 1976.

500 LOWER BAND 5.10b ★★   FA: John Wolfe and Al Ruiz, February 1969. FFA (5.9 1st pitch): unknown. FFA (second pitch): Randy Vogel and Charles Cole, 1983.

501 DOUBLE START 5.7   FA: Dick Webster and Woody Stark, February 1967.

502 BAND SAW 5.10c ★★   FA: Charles Cole and Gib Lewis, 1983.

503 MIDDLE BAND 5.10d   FA: John Wolfe, 1969. FFA: Bill Antel and Kim Cooper, 1973.

504 TREINTE ANOS 5.10b (TR)   FA: John Wolfe, June 1969. FFA: Bill Antel (TR), 1973.

505 ORPHAN 5.9 ★★★   FFA: John Wolfe and Al Ruiz, January 1970.

506 IRON MAN TRAVERSE A3 5.6   FA: Ken Rose and Rob Hershey, February 1972.

507 DANDELION 5.10a ★★   FA: Don O'Kelley and Dave Davis, September 1971. FFA: John Long, Richard Harrison, Kevin Worrall, Bill Antel, Rick Accomazzo, John Bald and America Pizzo, December 1973.

THE OLD WOMAN – WEST FACE

THE OLD WOMAN – WEST FACE

THE BLOB – EAST FACE

This formation is on the left (west) side of the campground, near its north end. Map, page 140.

508 BUISSONIER 5.7 ★★   FA: Mark Powell and Royal Robbins, 1965.

509 PAPA WOOLSEY 5.10b ★★★   FA: Mark Powell, 1972.

510 MAMA WOOLSEY 5.10a ★★   FA: Mark Powell, 1972.

511 PETE'S HANDFUL 5.9   FA: Craig Parsley and Mike Pope, November 1973.

THE BLOB – EAST FACE
512 SURREALISTIC PILLAR 5.10b ★   FA: Craig Parsley.
513 DISCO SUCKS 5.10c   FA: John Yablonski and Charles Cole, October 1979.
514 PERFIDIOUS A4 5.6   FA: John Wolfe and Ken Stichter, May 1970.
515 ZULU DAWN 5.10d   FA: Mike Law and Bob Gaines, May 1983.

THE BLOB – WEST FACE

516 BALLBURY 5.7   Lieback a right-facing flake 30 feet left of route #517.   FA: unknown

517 USE IT OR LOOSE IT 5.10a (two bolts)   FA: Rich Littlestone, Rick Booth and Rick Ledesma.

518 THE BONG 5.4 ★★   FA: unknown

519 HOBLETT 5.7   FA: Dave Stahl, Rob Stahl, John Wolfe and Mona Stahl, February 1972.

520 BEGINNER'S TWO 5.2   FA: unknown

521 SAFETY IN NUMBERS 5.10a   FA: Mike Waugh, Randy Vogel, Mike Lechlinski, Craig Fry, Dick Shockley and Jerry Garcia, January 1978.

522 SMEAR TACTICS 5.10c   FA: Alan Nelson and Alan Bartlett, 1984.

523 BERKELEY DYKE 5.8   FA: Nelson and Bartlett, 1984.

524 BEGINNER'S ONE 5.3   FA: unknown

525 BEGINNER'S TWENTY-SIX 5.10c   FA: Dave Davis and Don O'Kelley, December 1971. FFA: John Long, Rick Accomazzo and John Mokri, January 1973.

526 HOBBIT ROOF 5.10b ★★   FA: Steve Godshall, June 1971. FFA: John Long, 1975.

545

STEVE CANYON

This group of rocks lies 200 yards northwest of the gap between The Old Woman and the Blob. The formations form a canyon which runs in a north/south direction.

Routes #527 and #528 lie on the west face of the west side of the canyon and face Quail Springs Road. Map, page 140.

527 WATANOBE WALL 5.10a ★★★   FA: Tobin Sorenson, Jim Wilson and Guy
  · Keesee, 1975.

528 SEASON OPENER 5,8 ★★   FA: Alan Bartlett and Dave Black, January 1983.

STEVE CANYON – EAST FACE OF THE WEST WALL

529 GRAND THEFT AVOCADO 5.7   FA: Dave Evans, October 1978.

530 CANDELABRA 5.10a ★   FA: Dave Davis and Don O'Kelley, November 1971.
FFA: John Long, April 1972.

531 THE ORC 5.10a ★★   FA: Bob Dominick.

532 ORC SIGHS 5.10c (var)   FA: Mike Tupper and Craig Reason, January 1983.

533 TENNIS SHOE CRACK 5.8 ★   To the right of **The Orc** 100', and above a shelf
halfway up the rock is a hand crack which curves up and left.   FA: John Long,
June 1972.

The west side of Steve Canyon is broken in two parts. The upper formation is distinguished by large roofs located about halfway up.

534 LET'S GET HORIZONTAL 5.11c (TR) ★   25 feet left of **Super Roof** is a very steep face with horizontal cracks every few feet. Undercling out a large roof and climb the horizontals to the top.   FA: Mike Tupper, January 1983.

535 SUPER ROOF 5.9 ★★★   FA: Dave Ohlsen, Jon Lonne and Martin McBirney, April 1975.

536 COMFORTABLY NUMB 5.11 ★★   FA: Randy Leavitt and others, 1980.

STEVE CANYON – EAST SIDE (West Face)

537 FRIGID DARE 5.11c (TR) This strenuous route takes the overhanging and leaning lieback/groove across from *Super Roof.* FA: Matt Oliphant and Bill Lebens, 1984.

538 FEMALE MUD MASSACRE 5.10a (TR) Across from *Super Roof* is a wide, light colored, overhanging groove. Stem and chimney up the groove, then follow overhanging hand jams to the left. FA: Russ Eyles, John Strand and Tom Callaghan, October 1983.

539 GRAIN SURGERY 5.10b ★★★ FA: Randy Vogel and Brian Rennie, March 1980.

540 FIST FULL OF CRYSTALS 5.10a ★★ FA: Jonny Woodward, Mike Lechlinski and Randy Vogel, October 1982.

541 HOOPHARKZ 5.4 FA: Don O'Kelley and John Wolfe, December 1971.

542 DEFLOWERED 5.6 ★★ FA: Don O'Kelley and Dave Davis, October 1971.

543 THE DECOMPENSATOR OF LHASA 5.10d ★★★★ FA: Charles Cole and Randy Vogel, February 1980. FA (Direct Start): unknown, 1981.

544 PHINEAS P. PHART 5.10a FA: Andy Alper and others, 1979.

STEVE CANYON – EAST SIDE (West Face)

545 SKINNY DIP 5.7 ★★   FA: John Long and Phil Warrender, September 1972.

546 SKINNY PIN 5.4   FA: unknown

547 JUMPING JACK CRACK 5.11a ★★★   FA: John Long, November 1972.

548 VENUCIAN FECE 5.11a (TR)   FA: John Long and Eric Ericksson, March 1980.

549 SIDEWINDER 5.9+ ★★★★   FA: Kevin Worrall and Eric Schoen, June 1974.

STEVE CANYON – EAST SIDE (East Face)

~~550 ROCKWELL~~ 41C 5.10d ★★   FA: Rich Littlestone, Rick Booth and Rick Ledesma (TR). First lead: unknown.

551 *JACK GRIT* 5.10a   FA: Steve Emerson, 1978.

552 *ICE CLIMBING* 5.10a   FA: Alan Bartlett and Alan Roberts, November 1982.

553 *FREE CLIMBING* 5.10a   FA: unknown

554 *SLIPPERY WHEN WET* 5.7   FA: Craig Fry, 1978.

OUTHOUSE ROCK – WEST FACE

This formation lies in the Hidden Valley Campground, just right (north) of the apex of the Campground loop. Map, page 140.

555 NORTHWEST CHIMNEY 5.4   FA: unknown

556 PICKING UP THE PIECES 5.10a   FA: Hank Levine, December 1976.

557 FIVE-FOUR-PLUS 5.8   FA: unknown. FFA: John Wolfe and Dick Webster, April 1969.

558 FROSTLINE 5.10a   FA: Roger Linfield and Dave Woody, February 1979.

559 OUTHOUSE FLAKE 5.4   FA: Stew Harris and John Wolfe, 1965.

OUTHOUSE ROCK – EAST FACE
560 OUT FOR A BITE 5.10c (TR) ★★   FA: unknown, 1983.
561 STRAWBERRY JAM 5.9 ★★   FA: John Long, July 1972.
562 DIAGONAL CHIMNEY 5.6   FA: by many, 1965.
563 STRAIGHT FLUSH 5.8   FA: Joe Herbst and John Long, December 1971.
564 WISE CRACK 5.9   FA: Joe Herbst, February 1972.

THE WALL – NORTH END

This formation is a very long wall starting just south of Outhouse Rock and extending to a point just east of Chimney Rock. Map, page 140.

566 HANDS TO YOURSELF 5.11c (TR)   FA: Kurt Smith.

567 HANDS DOWN 5.11c (TR)   FFA: John Bachar, 1976.

568 TWO SCOOPS PLEASE 5.10c (TR) ★★   The original protection bolts were removed because they were placed on rappel.   FA: Herb Laeger and Dave Houser, November 1978.

569 HANDS OFF 5.8 ★★★   FA: John Long and Brian Portoff, October 1972.

THE WALL – MIDDLE SECTION

570 C.F.M.F. 5.8   FA: unknown

571 LAID BACK 5.8 ★   FA: Matt Cox, Dave Evans, Gary Ayres and Alan Lennard, December 1973.

THE WALL – SOUTH END

~~**572 GOOD TO THE LAST DROP**~~ 5.10a ★★   A serious route.   FA: Mike Waugh, Jan McCollum and Dave Houser, 1977.

573 FATTY WINDS HIS NECK OUT 5.10d (serious)   FA: Roger Whitehead and Roger (Strappo) Hughes, 1984. Top roped prior to being lead.

574 DON'T DIK WITH WALT 5.10c   FA: Dean Hart and Michael Dorsey, February 1985.

575 DAMN JAM 5.6   FA: Dick Webster, Bill Briggs and Woody Stark, February 1967.

576 CHALK UP ANOTHER ONE 5.9 ★★★   FA: Jan McCollum, Hank Levine and Dave Houser, January 1978.

~~**577 PUMPING EGO**~~ 5.10b ★★   FA: Alan Nelson and Mike Beck, December 1980.

CHIMNEY ROCK – WEST FACE

This rock is located at the east side of the campground, just east of where a dirt road heads off the paved loop road, leading to Echo Cove and Barker Dam. Map, page 140.

578 DYNO IN THE DARK 5.10b ★   FA: Charles Cole and Rusty Reno, January 1981.

579 LOOSE LIPS 5.11a ★★★   FA: Tobin Sorenson, Gibb Lewis and Dean Fidelman, November 1975. FFA: John Yablonski and Mike Lechlinski, October 1979.

580 WEST FACE OVERHANG 5.7 ★   FA: unknown

581 BALLET 5.10a ★ (serious)   FA: John Wolfe and Dick Webster, January 1970. FFA: Tobin Sorenson and Gib Lewis, 1975.

582 HOWARD'S HORROR 5.7 (**Direct** 5.10b)   FA: John Wolfe and Howard Weamer, January 1969. FFA: John Wolfe and Al Ruiz, January 1970.

583 DAMPER 5.9 ★   FA: Tom Higgins and others, April 1967.

584 PINCHED RIB 5.8+ ★★★   FA: Roy Naasz, March 1973.

CHIMNEY ROCK – EAST FACE

585 THE FLUE 5.8 ★★★   FA: John Wolfe and Dick James, February 1969.

586 FLUE RIGHT 5.10b ★★ (serious)   FA: Wolfe and James, January 1969. FFA: Gib Lewis and Tobin Sorenson, 1975.

587 RAVEN'S REACH 5.10a   FA: John Long and Larry Brown, March 1971. FFA: Long, 1979.

CYCLOPS ROCK – NORTHEAST FACE

This formation lies outside Hidden Valley Campground, about 300 yards east of the entrance. Map, page 140.

588 *OVERNIGHT SENSATION* 5.11b (TR) ★★   FA: John Wolfe and Rob Stahl, November 1970. FFA: Rick Cashner and Don Reid, 1979.

589 *FOUL FOWL* 5.6   FA: Woody Stark, Bill Briggs and Pat Wiedman, 1966.

590 *CAROLYN'S RUMP* 5.4   FA: John Wolfe, Carolyn Gilliland and Ed Zombro, 1967.

CYCLOPS ROCK – NORTHWEST FACE

591 ULYSSES' BIVOUAC 5.8   FA: Woody Stark and Dick Webster, February 1967.

592 THIN RED LINE 5.12 (TR)   FA: Ron Fawcett, 1985.

593 SURFACE TENSION 5.10c ★★★   FA: Charles Cole, George Willig, Randy Vogel and Steven Anderson, 1984.

594 OVERSIGHT 5.10a   FA: Alan Nelson and Randy Burks, March 1983.

595 THE EYE 5.1 ★★★   FA: Dick Webster and Harold Webster, 1957.

596 CIRCE 5.6 ★   FA: Webster and Webster, 1967.

597 FRACTURED FISSURE 5.10d (TR)   FA: John Long and Brian Pohorff, October 1971. FFA: Long (TR), 1981.

598 TELEGRAM FOR MONGO 5.10c ★★   FA: Randy Vogel and Rob Raker, 1982.

599 LEADER'S FRIGHT 5.8 ★★★   Poor protection.   FA: James Foote, Woody Stark and Dick Webster, 1966.

CYCLOPS ROCK – SOUTHWEST FACE

600 THE OFFICIAL ROUTE OF THE 1984 OLYMPICS 5.10c ★★★   FA: Randy Vogel, Charles Cole and Steven Anderson, 1984.

601 ARE WE OURSELVES 5.8   FA: Dave Evans, 1984.

602 PENELOPE'S WALK 5.4   FA: John Wolfe, Dick Webster and Woody Stark, April 1969.

THE POTATO HEAD

Immediately to the northeast of Cyclops Rock are two smaller formations. The northeast face of the second rock contains the following routes (from left to right).

603 SPUD PATROL 5.7   On the left of the face is a left-arching corner. Start 20' right of this where a horizontal crack courves down. Climb to the crack, traverse left to the corner, then up it and left to the top.   FA: Alan Nelson, March 1983.

604 TICKET TO NOWHERE 5.8   Climb a left-leaning crack in the center of the face to its end. Rappel off or down climb the route.   FA: Alan Nelson, March 1983.

605 MR. DNA 5.11 (TR)   Start at a flake six feet left of a patch of yellow lichen and continue straight up to the top.
FA: Alan Nelson and Randy Burks, March 1983.

606 KIDNEY STONE 5.10d (TR)   Start five feet right of the lichen patch and climb straight to the summit.   FA: Burks and Nelson, March 1983.

CYCLOPS BOULDERING

About 50 yards south from route #603 is a 15' high boulder with a cave on the southeast side. A hand crack in the roof of the cave leads to a thin crack above the lip. This boulder problem is known as "Bachar Cracker of the Desert."

Other good bouldering lies to the southwest about 100 yards.

PEEWEE ROCK – NORTH FACE

PEEWEE ROCK

This rather pathetic formation lies just southwest of Cyclops Rock. Map, page 140.

607 BELLY SCRAPER 5.4 FA: Dick Webster and Woody Stark, February 1967.

PEEWEE ROCK – SOUTH FACE

A large boulder at the south corner of the rock ha a large depression on its side. Route #608 is to the left, #609 to the right.

608 SPAN-NISH FLY 5.8 Climb a large water chute to a cave. FA: Woody Stark, Dick Webster and Bill Briggs, 1968.

609 TRI-STEP 5.8 Just left of the orang-colored face, climb a shallow water chute to a ledge; above, take the middle chute past a bolt to the top. FA: Greg Fumaro, Steve Godshall and Richard Zito, June 1971.

THE OUTBACK

This area covers territory starting to the north of Steve Canyon and continuing east in an arc to just west of the Echo Rock/Echo Cove area.

HIT MAN ROCK

This rock is actually a northern continuation of the western side of Steve Canyon. Hit Man Rock lies about 150 yards north of **Super Roof.** It can be easily reached via a trail which passes just east of the east side of Steve Canyon (**Slippery When Wet,** etc.). Hit Man Rock is the far north end of the formation, and the routes are on the east face.

610 THE ENFORCER 5.9 ★   FA: Alan Bartlett and Alan Roberts, 1983.

611 THE BRUISER 5.10c ★★★   FA: Bartlett and Roberts.

LABOR DOME

This small, dark colored formation lies directly opposite Hit Man Rock. Map, page 140.

612 WORKING OVERTIME 5.9 ★★   FA: Alan Bartlett and Alan Roberts, 1983.

613 A WOMAN'S WORK IS NEVER DONE 5.10c ★★★   FA: Maria Cranor, 1980.

LOOKING NORTH FROM HIDDEN VALLEY CAMPGROUND

THE HEAP   PATAGONIA PILE   ROLLERBALL

614
615

THE HEAP ❀

This blocky and square shaped rock lies to the right of Labor Dome about 75 yards and has two known routes on its west face. Map, pages 100, 140.

614 CHICAGO NIPPLE SLUMP 5.11c (TR) ★   FA: Mike Law, 1983.

615 BAD FUN 5.11a   FA: (with bolts placed on rappel) Mike Law, 1983.

PATAGONIA PILE – WEST FACE

Patagonia Pile is approximately 450 yards north-northwest of the appex of the Hidden Valley Campground loop. A trail leads from the deep campsite just east of the Blob (containing a large square-shaped boulder) out to an open area to the north of the campground. Patagonia Pile is the square looking formation with an overhanging east face. Map, pages 100, 140.

616 PEABODY'S PERIL 5.9 ★★ Two prominent cracks can be found near the right half of the south face. This route climbs the left crack, which has a fixed pin about 30 feet up.   FA: unknown

617 NOBODY'S RIGHT MIND 5.9   This is the right crack. It is a bit loose and has a bolt 30 feet up.   FA: unknown

PATAGONIA PILE – EAST FACE

618   WET ROCK DAY 5.10d (TR) ★   FA: unknown, 1981.

619   NO SHIRT NEEDED 5.10d ★★   FA: John Yablonski, Kevin Worrall, Mark Chapman and Ed Barry, 1979.

620   WET T-SHIRT NIGHT 5.11c (TR) ★★★★   FA: John Bachar, John Long, Lynn Hill and Mike Lechlinski, 1979.

620a JUGLINE Variation 5.11a

621   FAT LIP A3   85' right of *Wet T-Shirt Night*.   FA: unknown

ROLLERBALL FORMATION

This formation lies about 150 yards northeast of Patagonia Pile. Scramble up the valley located 100 yards to the east of Patagonia Pile. Map, pages 100, 140.

622 ROLLERBALL 5.10a ★★★★   FA: Jon Lonne and Dave Ohlsen, 1976.

DINOSAUR ROCK – WEST FACE

This small rock lies 500 yards directly north of the campground loop and Outhouse Rock. Map, page 140.

623 GO 'GANE 5.8   FA: unknown
624 TOO LOOSE TO TREK 5.10b ★   FA: Randy Vogel and Howard King, 1976.

DINOSAUR ROCK – NORTH FACE
625 NEGASAURUS 5.9   FA: John Bald and Hank Levine, November 1979.

ROOF ROCK
150 yards to the west-northwest is a very large roof, not very high above its floor. It extends back inside for about 30 feet.

626 THE LIVING CONJUNCTION 5.11d (TR) ★★   FA: Hank Levine, 1976. FFA: Dick Silly, 1981 (TR).

DUTZI ROCK

Dutzi Rock lies about 350 yards north of Dinosaur Rock. The hillside to the left (west) of Dutzi Rock is Mt. Dutzi (14,000 ft.). Map page 100.

627 SUZIE'S CREAM SQUEEZE 5.6   FA: Scott Stuemke, December 1976.

628 PINHEAD 5.9 ★   FA: Scott Stuemke and Howard King, December 1976. FFA: Dave Evans, Jeff Elgar and Randy Vogel, January 1977.

629 ELUSIVE BUTTERFLY 5.7 ★★★   FA: Dave Evans and Randy Vogel, December 1976.

630 PAPILLON 5.10b   FA: John Howe and Michael Dorsey, December 1984.

631 FINGERS ON A LANDSCAPE 5.11b   FA: Lynn Hill and Charles Cole, January 1980.

632 SHAKIN' THE SHIRTS 5.9   FA: Randy Vogel and Dave Evans, January 1977.

ROCK HUDSON

Rock Hudson is located about 150 yards north of Outhouse Rock. Map, page 140.

633 *DOING THAT SCRAPYARD THING* 5.10d ★★   This route is on the north end of the rock and follows a left-leaning crack just left of a crack beneath a right-facing corner.   FA: Tim Powell and Dan Ahlborn, 1977.

634 *NERELTNE* 5.7 ★★   FA: Craig Fry, 1978

635 *ABSOLUTE ZERO* 5.10c ★   FA: David Rubine, Don Mealing and Michael Wells, March 1980.

636 *LOONEY TUNES* 5.9 ★★★   FA: Tobin Sorenson, John Long and Eric Ericksson, June 1974.

637 *HOT ROCKS* 5.11b ★★★★★   FA: John Long, Richard Harrison and Ging Gingrich, February 1973. FFA (TR): John Bachar, 1978. First lead: John Bachar, 1979.

638 *A BOLT, A BASHIE AND A BOLD MANTLE* A4 5.8 ★★★   FA: Charles Cole, Dave Evans and Todd Gordon, 1984.

THE PEYOTE CRACKS – WEST FACE

This small but prolific formation is about 250 yards northeast of Rock Hudson. Its west face is less vertical and has three prominent cracks. The east face is overhanging and contains several Joshua Tree testpieces. Map, page 140.

639 BUTTON SOUP 5.2   FA: unknown
640 MATT'S PROBLEM 5.10b   FA: Matt Cox, 1974.
641 LEFT PEYOTE CRACK 5.10 ★★   FA: unknown
642 MIDDLE PEYOTE CRACK 5.9 ★★   FA: unknown
643 RIGHT PEYOTE CRACK 5.8 ★★   FA: unknown
644 FACE IT 5.10a (TR) ★★   FA: unknown

PEYOTE CRACKS – EAST FACE
(aka BACHAR TOP ROPE WALL)
645 PYGMY VILLAGE 5.9   FA: unknown
646 THE MOONBEAM CRACK 5.12d (TR) ★★   FA: John Bachar, 1983.
647 BABY APES 5.12b ★★★   FA: Bachar (TR), March 1980. First lead: Bachar, free solo, 1982.
648 THE WATUSI 5.11d (TR) ★★   FA: Bachar, 1980.
649 DIAL AFRICA 5.11c (TR) ★★   FA: Bachar, 1980.
650 DIMP FOR A CHIMP 5.11a ★   FA: Bachar, 1980.

PEYOTE CRACKS – EAST FACE

COMIC BOOK

ECHO COVE

To BARKER DAM

ECHO ROCK

LITTLE ROCK CANDY MTN.

SNICKERS

To RUSTY WALL

MOUNDS

LITTLE HUNK

BIG HUNK

HUNK ROCK

GUNSMOKE

photo by Dave Houser

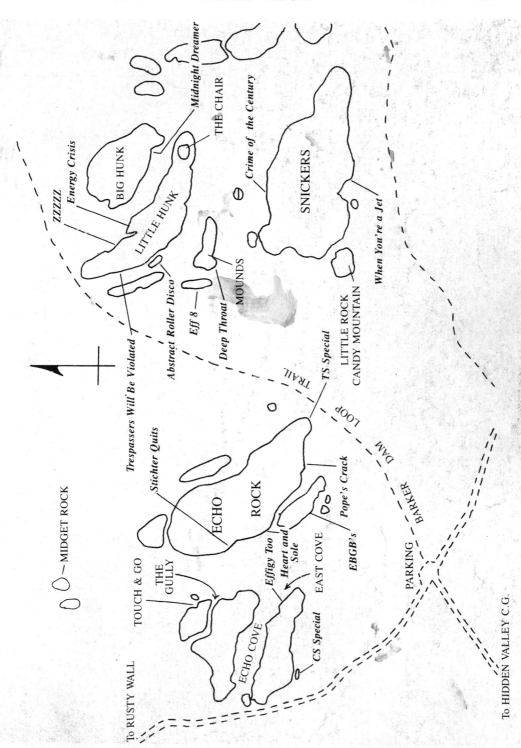

ECHO ROCK AREA

This area lies about .7 mile to the northeast of Hidden Valley Campground. The dirt road leading to it heads out just south of Chimney Rock. A large parking area is found where the road "tee s" (Echo Tee). The road is called the Big Horn Pass Road. To the northwest the road leads to Key's Ranch, an area off limits to all but guided tours of this old ranch site. Heading right (east) from Echo Tee takes one past parking areas for the Comic Book Area, The Barker Dam and Wonderland of Rocks parking areas, and eventually back to the main, paved Monument road. Map, page 183.

RUSTY WALL

Drive north from Echo Tee for one mile to the gate at Key's Ranch. A parking lot is located on the left (west) side of the road. A short hike west (of about 400 yards) leads to the base of this orange-ish, overhanging wall. Two cracks are located on the wall.

651 WANGERBANGER 5.11c ★★★★   This is the left crack.   FA: Tobin Sorenson, March 1975.

652 O'KELLEY'S CRACK 5.10c ★★★★★   This is the right crack.   FA: Don O'Kelley, 1974. FFA: Tobin Sorenson, Jim Wison, Dean Fidelman and Gary Ayres, March 1975.

653 RIDDLES IN THE DARK 5.11c ★★   This route takes a right facing corner (1" flake) past two bolts up an arête to top.   FA: Tony Yaniro, 1980.

ECHO COVE

This little "cove" lies about ¼ mile northwest from Echo Tee, on the right (east) side of the road. Routes are described as they lie on either wall of the cove. Right and left is used in reference to how you would view the walls as facing east into the cove.

ECHO COVE – LEFT SIDE

654 FUN STUFF 5.8   FA: Herb Laeger and Howard Doyle, December 1977.

655 CHUTE UP 5.2   FA: unknown

656 W.A.C. 5.8 ★   FA: Tom Higgins and others, 1967.

657 HELIX 5.2   FA: unknown

658 R.A.F. 5.9 ★★   FA: Dave Houser and Alan Winter, January 1976.

659 PINKY LEE 5.10d ★   FA: unknown. FFA: Matt Cox, 1976.

660 PORKY PIG 5.11b (TR) ★   FA: Herb Laeger and others (TR), 1977.

661 HOT KNIFE 5.10d   FA: Paul Piana and Todd Skinner, March 1981.

662 TOFU THE DWARF 5.9   FA: David Rubine, Don Mealing, Michael Wells and Martin Wensley, March 1980.

663 PALM-U-GRANITE 5.7   FA: Bob Elledge and Charlie Schreck, November 1978.

664 HANG TEN 5.8   FA: Howard Doyle and Herb Laeger, December 1977.

ECHO COVE – LEFT SIDE

ECHO COVE – RIGHT SIDE

ECHO COVE – RIGHT SIDE

665 OUT TO LUNGE 5.10d (TR)   Originally two protection bolts were placed on rappel; these have been removed and should not be replaced.   FA: Herb Laeger and others.

666 OUT FOR LUNCH 5.11a (TR)   FA: unknown, 1981.

667 BIG MOE 5.11a ★★★   FA: John Bachar, Mike Lechlinski and Mari Gingery (TR), 1980. First lead (solo): Bachar, 1981. First lead: Jerry Moffett, 1983.

668 BOULDER DASH 5.9   FA: Howard Doyle and Herb Laeger, February 1977.

669 DECEPTIVE CORNER 5.7   FA: Herb Laeger and Howard Doyle, February 1977.

670 OUT TO GRUNGE 5.10a   FA: unknown

ECHO COVE ROCKS – SOUTH FACE

The Echo Cove Rocks form the cove itself, and the outer faces of these rocks contain many fine routes. The south face faces the Big Horn Pass Road. Map, page 183.

671 ATARI 5.10c ★★   FA: Alan Nelson and Alan Bartlett, January 1984.

672 BONZO DOG BAND 5.7 ★   FA: Randy Vogel and Charles Cole, 1982.

673 ASS OF DOG 5.9   FA: Rick Sumner and Don Reid, January 1980.

674 AXE OF DOG 5.10a ★   (#4 Crack n' up protects crux)   FA: Dan Ahlborn, Dave Evans, Randy Vogel, Kevin Powell and Tim Powell, November 1976.

675 R.M.L. 5.8 ★★   FA: Paul Neal and Charlie Saylan, December 1976.

676 C.S. SPECIAL 5.10a ★★★   FA: Dave Houser, Ed Ehrenfeld and Bob Molloy, November 1974.

677 FLAKE AND BAKE 5.8   FA: Alan Nelson, Eben Strongquist and Richard Gottlieb, 1978.

671   672 673   674

descent

675 676   677

ECHO COVE ROCKS – SOUTH FACE

ECHO
ROCK

#678-679

ECHO COVE ROCKS
SOUTH FACE

ECHO COVE ROCKS
EAST FACE

676

681

697

ECHO ROCK AREA

EAST COVE/ECHO COVE ROCKS
This small cove is actually a continuation of Echo cove itself; a pile of boulders separates the two areas. A trail connects the two. Map, page 183.

EAST COVE – LEFT SIDE
678 HALFWAY TO PARADISE 5.10a ★★★ This is a serious lead; the protection bolt placed on rappel by the first ascent party has been removed.   FA: Herb Laeger, Mike Waugh, Jan McCollum and Dennis Knuckles, February 1978.

679 EFFIGY TOO 5.9+ ★★★   FA: Matt Cox and Dave Evans, 1975.

Misfits. 11b Right of 679 Tracy & Paul Bora

↖ 5.11c

EAST COVE – RIGHT SIDE

680 MAKE THAT MOVE OR SIX FOOT GROOVE 5.10c ★   FA: Andy Alper and others, 1983.

681 NO MISTAKE OR BIG PANCAKE 5.10d-5.11c ★★   Difficulty varies with climbers' height; the taller, the easier.   FA: Marius Morstad, Gib Lewis and Charles Cole, 1979.

681.5   <u>Solo Dog</u>   11C

ECHO COVE FORMATIONS – EAST SIDE

To the right of East Cove about 100 yards is a very narrow side canyon/gully. Several routes lie on the left side of this fissure. This gully also serves as the descent route for routes #686-690. Map, page 183.

THE GULLY

682 THE D.E.CHIMNEY 5.6 ★★   FA: Dave Evans and others, 1984.

683 THE SNATCH 5.10a ★   FA: Roger Linfield, March 1979.

684 THE ASHTRAY 5.6   FA: Luke Strong and Roger Linfield, March 1979.

685 JUGHEAD 5.10a (3 bolts up a knobby face)   FA: Luke Strong, Jim Thoen and Ken Marsh, April 1979.

TOUCH AND GO FACE

To the right of the Gully is an east facing part of the Echo Cove Rock, an excellent looking, left facing corner. This corner is *Touch and Go*, route #687. Map, page 183.

686 THE CORNERSTONE 5.10a   FA: Luke Strong and Roger Linfield, March 1979.

687 TOUCH AND GO 5.9 ★★★★   FA: Matt Cox, Bobby Kessinger and Dan Ahlborn, January 1976.

688 BROWN OUT Λ3   FA: Jeff Morgan and Dick Richardson, 1976.

689 THE GOLD HUNK 5.11a (TR)   FA: John Long, Mike Lechlinski and John Bachar, March 1980.

690 CREDIBILITY GAP 5.9   FA: Luke Strong and Jim Thoen, 1979.

691 THRASH OR CRASH 5.9   FA: Linfield and Strong, March 1979.

ECHO ROCK

706

697

709

720

ECHO ROCK
This rock lies nearly straight ahead (northeast) from the parking area at Echo Tee. The Left End lies directly across from the east side of the Echo Cove formation. The Right End is best reached via an excellent trail (a continuation of the road heading from the Hidden Valley Campground) which starts at the Echo Tee parking lot. This trail (Barker Dam Loop Trail) also gives easy access to the Candy Bar Area. Map, page 183.

ECHO ROCK – NORTH END – WEST FACE
692 THE TROUGH 5.0   This takes the easy gully left of route #693.   FA: unknown

693 DOUBLE DIP 5.6 ★★   FA: Chris Gonzalez and Mona Stahl, October 1973.

694 TRY AGAIN 5.10c ★★   FA: Bill Antel, Darrell Hensel and Bobby Kessinger, 1976.

695 MINUTE MAN 5.10d   FA: Roger Whitehead and Dave Lanman (top roped first), 1985.

696 GONE IN 60 SECONDS 5.10a ★   FA: Matt Cox, Randy Vogel and Steve Emerson, 1976.

697 STICHTER QUITS 5.7 ★★★   FA: John Long and others, November 1972. (Ken Stichter and John Wolfe had placed several bolts on this route and left to finish later; Long and others climbed the route before it was "finished.)

698 LEGOLAS 5.10c   FA: Paul Piana, December 1976.

699 STICK TO WHAT 5.9 ★★★   FA: Mike Jaffe and Larry Thaxton, April 1974.

700 TEN CONVERSATIONS AT ONCE 5.10a   Bolt has no hanger.   FA: Randy Vogel and Charles Cole, February 1980.

701 QUICK DRAW MCGRAW 5.10a ★★   FA: Gary Geraths and Paul Piana, December 1976.

702 THE FALCON AND THE SNOWMAN 5.10c ★★   FA: unknown, 1984.

703 HEART AND SOLE 5.10a ★★★★   FA: Herb Laeger, Rich Smith and Jai Watts, January 1978.

704 EFF FOUR 5.6   FA: unknown

705 COLE-EVANS 5.10a ★   FA: Charles Cole and Dave Evans, 1981.

ECHO ROCK – NORTH END – WEST FACE

Routes #706-708 lie on a large block high and right of previous routes. Descent is down a chimney on the back(east) side. Map, page 183.

706 EBGB'S 5.10c ★★★★   FA: Dave Houser, Mike Waugh, Jan McCollum and Nick Badyrka, April 1977.

707 CORNER OF FOREIGNER 5.10c   FA: unknown, 1982.

708 ZONDO'S PERKS 5.10a ★   This route is located just left of the descent chimney.   FA: unknown

709 LIFE IN THE FAST LANE 5.10c ★★   FA: Bob Gaines and Dave Katz, March 1982. Some form of aid was used in the placement of some of the protection.

710 SINNER'S SWING 5.10b (TR) ★   This takes the first dike system to the right of route #709.   FA: Mike Tupper and Greg Mayer (TR), December 1982.

ECHO ROCK – SOUTH END

711 FRETS DON'T FAIL ME NOW 5.9 ★ Located on the brown face left of the descent route for #712-714; past two bolts but runout at top. FA: Dave Evans and Randy Vogel, 1979.

712 MOMENT'S NOTICE 5.6 ★ FA: Randy Vogel, Charles Cole and Steven Anderson, 1983.

✔ **713 POPE'S CRACK** 5.9 ★★★ FA: Craig Parsley and Mike Pope, 1975.

714 BRITISH AIRWAYS 5.10c ★★★ FA: Vogel, Cole and Darryl Nakahira, fall 1982.

715 RAKED OVER THE COLES 5.10d ★★★ FA: Rob Raker and Charles Cole, 1983.

716 NUTS ARE FOR MEN WITHOUT BALLS 5.9 FA: Charles Cole, 1983.

717 PRIMAL SCREAM 5.10c FA: Anderson and Cole, 1983.

718 SOLE FUSION 5.12a ★★★★ FA: John Bachar, 1983.

719 THE ROOF 5.10a FA: Cole, 1978.

720 SWEPT AWAY 5.11a ★★★★ FA: Dave Evans and Randy Vogel, November 1977.

721 T.S. SPECIAL 5.8+ ★★★ A scary route that goes over the roof. FA: Mike Graham, Rick Accomazzo, Tobin Sorenson, Peter Wilkening and Jim Wilson, December 1973.

ECHO ROCK – EAST FACE
722 SECOND THOUGHTS 5.10a ★   FA: Herb Laeger and Dick Saume, December 1977.

723 AMAZING GRACE 5.11a ★   FA: Herb Laeger, January 1977.

724 CLOSED ON MONDAYS 5.10a ★   FA: unknown

725 BAMBI MEETS GODZILLA 5.8+ ★★★   FA: Ben Townsend and Mingo Morvin, April 1982.

THE CANDY BAR

To the east of Echo Rock is a group of formations; these are the Candy Bar. Just south of Echo Rock the main trail proceeds northeast, passing just north of a large dome with a right-diagonalling dike system on the west face. This is Little Hunk. Map, page 183.

LITTLE HUNK

MOUNDS

741

729 730

LITTLE HUNK – WEST FACE

726 TOP 40 TO MIDDLE TOILET 5.9   This route lies on the left end of the west face. Climb a face/flake past a bolt before easy climbing leads to a bolt at the top.   FA: Randy Vogel, 1976.

727 GO FOR BROKE 5.8   To the right of route #726, climb from the top of a triangular shaped block past three bolts to the top of the face.   FA: Randy McDonald and Ron Overholtz, 1978.

728 TRESPASSERS WILL BE VIOLATED 5.10c ★★★   This is the right diagonalling dike system.   FA: Matt Cox and Spencer Lennard.

729 THE COMPASSION OF THE ELEPHANTS 5.10c ★★★   Eighty feet right of route #728, this route climbs off a 10' boulder past four bolts to grey flakes. Two more bolts protect face climbing to the summit.   FA: Maria Cranor and Randy Vogel, November 1979.

730 ABSTRACT ROLLER DISCO 5.11a ★★★   This climbs past four bolts on the large slab 100' right of route #729.   FA: Gib Lewis, Charles Cole and Marius Morstad, November 1979.

731 FEELING GROOVY 5.10a   Climbs a water groove 30' right of the flake containing route #729.   FA: Dag Kolsrud and Hank Levine, 1978.

732 EXHIBIT A 5.10a   Approximately 75 yards right of route #731 is a crescent shaped arch. Climb up and right on a ramp to above the middle of the ramp. Climb straight up on mantles past a bolt to the top.   FA: Alan Nelson, Bob Van Belle and Mike Paul, December 1978.

LITTLE HUNK – EAST FACE

733 CASHEWS WILL BE EATEN 5.8   FA: Randy Vogel, Charles Cole and Marjorie Shovlin, October 1983.

734 ENERGY CRISIS 5.10b   FA: Dean Fidelman, Guy Kesse and Mike Pope, February 1974.

735 ZZZZZ 5.8+ ★★★★   FA: Vogel, Cole and Shovlin, October 1983.

736 POWER LINE 5.7   FA: Randy Vogel and Bob Dominick, August 1976.

737 POWER DROP 5.10b ★   FA: Kevin Powell and Darrel Hensel.

738 FUNCTIONAL ANALYSIS 5.11d (TR)   FA: John Bachar and Mike Lechlinski, 1983.

ZZZZZ

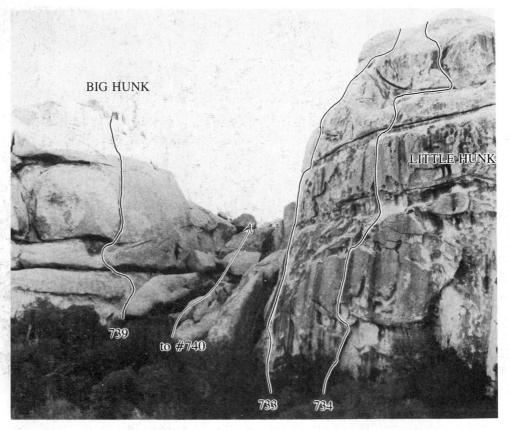

BIG HUNK

This formation parallels and is east of Little Hunk. Map, page 183.

739 TOBIN BIAS 5.6   FA: Fish and Bullwinkle, February 1974.

740 MIDNIGHT DREAMER 5.9   About 150 yards right of **Tobin Bias** and up the talus gully, through the high rock valley, is a 100' high black buttress on the left. Climb up to a small roof, around to the left, and up a crack to the top.   FA: Tony Yaniro and Randy Leavitt, December 1978.

MOUNDS

Map, page 183.

741 DEEP THROAT 5.9   FA: John Bachar, Tobin Sorenson, Bill Antel and Craig Parsley, 1975.

742 EFF EIGHT 5.8   This climbs the short crack which faces west of the small formation located just north of Mounds.   FA: unknown

THE CHAIR

749

746   747   748

LITTLE HUNK – RIGHT SIDE

The right end (southeast) of Little Hunk has several prominent roofs. Directly above this is a large boulder (The Chair) sits atop the rock. Map, page 183.

743 ROAST LEG OF CHAIR 5.7   FA: Steve Godshall, John Wolfe and Mona Stahl, October 1971.

744 ORDINARY ROUTE 5.10b ★★   This lies on the west corner of The Chair. A bolt and very poor bashie protect the lead.   FA: Godshall and Wolfe, October 1971. FFA: unknown

745 LADDER BACK 5.10b   This route lies about 25' left of route #744.   FA: unknown, 1984.

746 ROOFING COMPANY 5.10a ★★   FA: Tony Yaniro, 1974.

747 MONKEY BUSINESS 5.8 ★★   FA: Yaniro, 1974.

748 WAGE AND PRICE CEILING 5.10d (TR) ★   FA: Rick Accomazzo, Kevin Powell and Randy Vogel, 1977.

749 SPACE SLOT 5.10a   FA: Chick Holtkamp and John Lakey, February 1978.

750 POINT OF NO RETURN 5.10c ★   One hundred feet around the corner and right of route #748 is an offwidth crack in a chimney, topped with a roof. The crux is underclinging the roof.   FA: Tony Yaniro, Mike Waugh and Randy Leavitt, January 1978.

SNICKERS – NORTH FACE

This formation lies directly east of Echo Rock, south of Little Hunk. The north face of Snickers faces the right end of Little Hunk. Map, page 183.

751 NORWEGIAN WOOD 5.9   FA: Dag Kolsrud, Trond Ornhoi and Hank Levine, December 1978.

752 FRANKENWOOD 5.7   FA: unknown, 1979.

753 FUNNY BONE 5.8   FA: Dave Evans and Steve West, March 1978.

754 DON'T THINK JUST JUMP 5.10a ★   FA: Dave Evans, October 1978.

755 CRIME OF THE CENTURY 5.10c ★★★   FA: Tony Yaniro, Mike Waugh and Nick Badyrka, January 1978.

756 TWO FLEW THE COOP 5.11a (TR)   FA: John Bachar, 1978.

LITTLE ROCK CANDY MOUNTAIN

This small, roundish formation is located at the southwest end of Snickers. Map, page 183.

757 KENDAL MINT CAKE 5.6   This climbs the easy crack on the left side of the north end of Little Rock Candy Mountain. Face climb up to the crack (Can also be used as a down climb).   FA: Bob Yoho and Chick Holtkamp, February 1978.

758 SUGAR DADDY 5.9 ★   FA: Chick Holtkamp and John Lakey, February 1978.

759 NESTLE CRUNCH 5.10c ★   FA: Holtkamp, Forrest and Dan, December 1978.

760 CHICKEN BONES 5.4   FA: Holtkamp and Lakey, 1978.

761 JOLLY RANCHER FIRESTIX 5.10d   FA: Holtkamp and Lakey, December 1978.

762 CHICK FLAKEY 5.11b ★   FA: Marius Morstad and Charles Cole, November 1979.

763 FLAKE HICKY 5.3   FA: unknown

764 M & M'S PEANUT 5.10a   FA: Holtkamp and Lakey, February 1978.

765 M & M'S PLAIN 5.9 ★★   FA: Holtkamp and Lakey, 1978.

766 LITTLE ROCK CANDY CRACK 5.7   FA: Holtkamp and Lakey, 1978.

LITTLE ROCK CANDY MOUNTAIN – WEST & SOUTH FACES

LITTLE ROCK CANDY MOUNTAIN – EAST FACE

SNICKERS – SOUTH FACE
About 100 yards east of Little Rock Candy Mountain and on the south face of Snickers is a small canyon. The right wall has a couple routes. Map, page 183.

767 HENNY PENNY 5.10d (RP's useful)   FA: Kevin Powell, Darrell Hensel and Alan Roberts, spring 1985.

768 WHEN YOU'RE A JET 5.11c (TR) ★★★   FA: Dick Silly, 1980.

WONDERLAND VALLEY

LAKESIDE ROCK

HUNK ROCK

BARKER DAM

RAT ROCK

ESCAPE ROCK

BED ROCK

ROCKWORK ROCK

BIG HUNK

Gunsmoke

More Monkey Than Funky

BIG HORN PASS ROAD

photo by Dave Houser

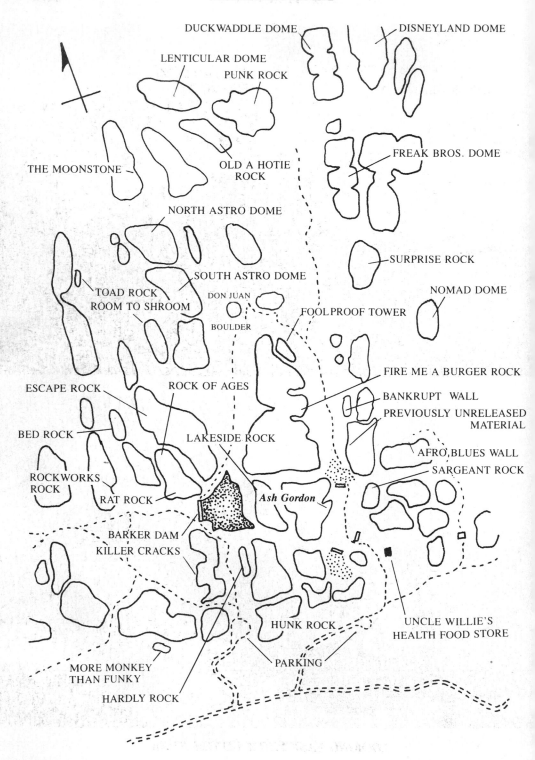

DUCKWADDLE DOME

DISNEYLAND DOME

LENTICULAR DOME

PUNK ROCK

FREAK BROS. DOME

THE MOONSTONE

OLD A HOTIE ROCK

NORTH ASTRO DOME

SURPRISE ROCK

SOUTH ASTRO DOME

DON JUAN

NOMAD DOME

TOAD ROCK
ROOM TO SHROOM

BOULDER

FOOLPROOF TOWER

ESCAPE ROCK

ROCK OF AGES

FIRE ME A BURGER ROCK

BANKRUPT WALL

PREVIOUSLY UNRELEASED
MATERIAL

BED ROCK

LAKESIDE ROCK

AFRO,BLUES WALL

SARGEANT ROCK

ROCKWORKS
ROCK

RAT ROCK

Ash Gordon

BARKER DAM
KILLER CRACKS

UNCLE WILLIE'S
HEALTH FOOD STORE

MORE MONKEY
THAN FUNKY

HUNK ROCK

PARKING

HARDLY ROCK

NORTH ASTRO DOME
LENTICULAR DOME
SOUTH ASTRO DOME
BED ROCK

790 789

TO ROCKWORK ROCK

BARKER DAM LOOP TRAIL

805

804

TO
ROCKWORK ROCK

BARKER DAM

TO GUNSMOKE AREA

LOOKING EAST FROM LITTLE HUNK

BARKER DAM AREA

From Echo Tee, turn right and follow the Big Horn Pass Road as it heads east. After about one mile there is a side road that heads north. This road ends after about 300 yards at a large parking area. A trail (which connects with the Barker Dam Loop Trail) heads straight north to Barker Dam, about 600 yards away. Map, page 208.

MORE FUNKY THAN MONKEY

This small formation lies about 200 yards west of the Barker Dam road and about 200 yards north of the Big Horn Pass Road. The low formation is marked by a 20' roof about 30' off the ground.

769 MORE MONKEY THAN FUNKY 5.11b ★★★   This route can be lead, but because of severe rope drag is usually top roped.   FA: John Bachar, 1976.

BARKER DAM PARKING AREA
From the Parking Lot, a formation with light colored faces can be seen about 100 yards to the east. This is Hunk Rock. Map, page 208.

HUNK ROCK – WEST FACE
770 ON THE AIR 5.8   FA: Alan Nelson and Bob VanBelle, December 1979.

771 GUT REACTION 5.6   This is a smooth, deep squeeze chimney 100' left of route 770.   FA: Nelson and VanBelle, 1979.

HUNK ROCK – EAST FACE
772 HUNKLOADS TO HERMOSA 5.9   Climb past two bolts on the east face, 40' left of the obvious dihedral.   FA: unknown

773 DEATH OF A DECADE 5.10a   Climb the dihedral past one bolt.   FA: VanBelle and Nelson, 1979.

GUNSMOKE AREA

From the Barker Dam Parking Area head north for about 25 yards to a point where a trail heads west through some small boulders. This leads to a large open basin extending to the west and north. The trail continues in a northwest direction and joins up with the Barker Dam Loop Trail. Map, page 208.

THE KILLER CRACKS

From a point where the trail enters this basin head straight north about 150 yards. Directly east is a small formation with several wide cracks. These are the Killer Cracks.

774 DIE-HEDRAL 5.7   FA: Tony Yaniro and Dario Gambretta. 1978.
775 FISTS OF FURY 5.10a   FA: Tony Yaniro, 1978.
776 ENTER THE DRAGON 5.9   FA: Yaniro and Gambretta, 1978.
777 JACK THE RIPPER 5.8   FA: Yaniro and Gambretta, 1978.

GUNSMOKE

This lies about 30 yards north of the Killer Cracks.
778 GUNSMOKE 5.11 ★★★★   (an excellent boulder traverse)   FA: unknown

ROCKWORK ROCK – SOUTH END

This long, narrow formation lies about 650 yards northwest of the Gunsmoke area. A flared, overhanging, orange colored dihedral at the south end of the rock distinguishes this crag. Map, page 208.

779 ROCKWORK ORANGE 5.11c ★★★   FA: Tony Yaniro, Mike Waugh and Nick Badyrka, January 1978.

780 SNOW FALLS 5.9   FA: Alan Roberts and Jill Lawrence, 1982.

781 A-JILL-ITY 5.10a   FA: Alan Roberts and Tim Hansen, 1982.

782 EASY LOOKER 5.6   FA: unknown, 1980.

783 FLAMING ARROW 5.9+ ★ (serious)   FA: John Bachar and Mike Lechlinski, 1980.

ROCKWORK ROCK – NORTH END

784 RAIN DANCE 5.10d ★ (serious)   FA: John Bachar and Mike Lechlinski, 1980.

785 KICKOFF 5.8   FA: Alan Roberts and others, 1980.

786 EL BRUJO 5.10d ★★   FA: Erik Ericksson and John Bachar, 1980.

787 EL BLOWHOLE 5.10c ★   FA: unknown, 1981.

BED ROCK

This crag lies about 200 yards up the canyon from **Rockwork Orange**, and is on the right hand (east) side. Map, page 208.

788 HARD SCIENCE 5.8 ★   FA: unknown

789 SOFT CORE 5.9 ★★   FA: Randy Vogel and Darryl Nakahira, 1980.

790 BARNIE RUBBLE 5.10b ★★   FA: Alan Roberts, Maria Cranor and Darryl Nakahira, 1980.

ESCAPE ROCK

This face lies about 500 yards northwest of Barker Dam. It can be easily reached from Bed Rock, which lies directly west of Escape Rock. Map, page 208.

791 EXIT STAGE RIGHT 5.9 ★★   FA: Jan McCollum and Dave Houser, January 1978.

792 PSORIASIS 5.9 ★   FA: Rob Mulligan and Bill Odenthal, September 1985.

793 BALLBEARINGS UNDER FOOT 5.10a   FA: unknown. FFA: Odenthal and Mulligan, September 1985.

TOAD ROCK

This formation is located 300 yards north of Escape Rock and on the west side of the next valley to the east. Map, page 208.

794 TOAD CRACK 5.9   FA: John Long, Craig Fry and Randy Vogel, September 1978.

← TO ESCAPE ROCK

To Forsaken Mein-key →

ROCK OF AGES

This formation is about 225 yards south of Escape Rock. Map, page 208.

795 HALLOW FRICTION 5.10c   FA: Bill Odenthal and Rob Mulligan, September 1985.

BARKER DAM

This reservoir was constructed in the 1930's to supply much needed water for nearby Key's Ranch. Water is almost always standing behind this concrete dam. However, drinking from or swimming in this lake should be considered very hazardous. Map, page 208.

796 NO FALLS 5.10d   This obscure route lies on a small, northeast facing wall containing several overhangs on its left. It is located on the left (west) side of the Barker Dam Trail, just before the lake can be seen. A thin crack on the right leads up and over this roof.   FA: Herb Laeger, January 1978.

HARDLY ROCK

This is a small, long face on the opposite side of the trail from *No Falls*. A large dike system ascends the wall. Several very short routes (5.0 to 5.7) have been done on this face. Map, page 208.

LAKESIDE ROCK

Just as you get to Barker Dam, a large, low angled dome will be seen to the right (east). This is Lakeside Rock. Map, page 208.

797 FAT MAN'S FOLLY 5.8   FA: Darrell Hensel and Bobby Kessinger, 1976.

798 THIN MAN'S NIGHTMARE 5.9   FA: unknown

799 AN EYE FOR AN EYE AND A ROUTE FOR A ROUTE 5.10b ★★★   FA: Dave Houser, Jan McCollum and Bob Malloy, 1978.

800 X-RATED TITS 5.9 ★   FA: Matt Cox, Randy Vogel and Shawn Curtis, 1976.

801 PARENTAL GUIDANCE SUGGESTED 5.8 ★   FA: Mike Orr and Brad Johnston, 1976.

RAT ROCK

This formation lies at the north end of the dam wall. To get across the dam, walk across the top of the wall. From here you can scramble northeast to where the trail starts again. The dam ends right at the start of route #802. Map, page 208.

802 RAT LEDGE 5.8 ★   FA: Kim Cooper and Mike Zatto, March 1973. FFA: unknown

803 THE ARRAIGNMENT 5.10a   This very contrived and overbolted line is immediately left of route #802.   FA: Richard Jensen and Mark Smith, April 1982.

804 BAD LIZARDS 5.10a ★★   This can be done in one pitch; it has 3 unnecessary bolts.   FA: Smith and Jensen, April 1982.

805 THE FORSAKEN MEIN-KEY 5.10   FA: Frank Noble, Dave Jones and Martha L. Uber, March 1978.

Route #806 lies about 200 yards northeast of the dam. It is located under a roof on the left (west) side of the valley.

806 EMOTIONAL RESCUE 5.12a ★★   This route is a finger to offwidth crack in a 15' roof.   FA: Randy Leavitt, 1980.

RAT ROCK

ROOM TO SHROOM

This formation is about 700 yards north of Barker Dam. As you walk north from the dam you can see very large formations. These are the Astro Domes. The right hand part of the valley takes you to the east face of the Astro Domes.

A left (northwest) turn into a narrow gully leads to the Room to Shroom rock. Map, page 208.

807 ROOM TO SHROOM 5.9 ★★★★   FA: Dave Evans and Jim Angione, 1978.

808 CHEMICAL WAREFARE 5.10b ★★★ (This is a variation to #807.)   FA: Drew Bedford, George Zamelis and Skunk, March 1983.

UNCLE WILLIE'S HEALTH FOOD STORE

SUPER DOME

BIGHORN DOME

LOST IN THE WONDERLAND TRAIL

NOMAD DOME

DISNEYLAND DOME

WONDERLAND VALLEY TRAIL

LAKESIDE ROCK

SURPRISE ROCK

THE SHOULDER

FREAK BROS.

SOUTH ASTRO DOME

BIG BROWN EYE

PUNK ROCK

LENTICULAR DOME

BARKER DAM

BARKER DAM TRAIL

N. ASTRO DOME

ROOM TO SCHROOM

RAT ROCK

photo by Dave Houser

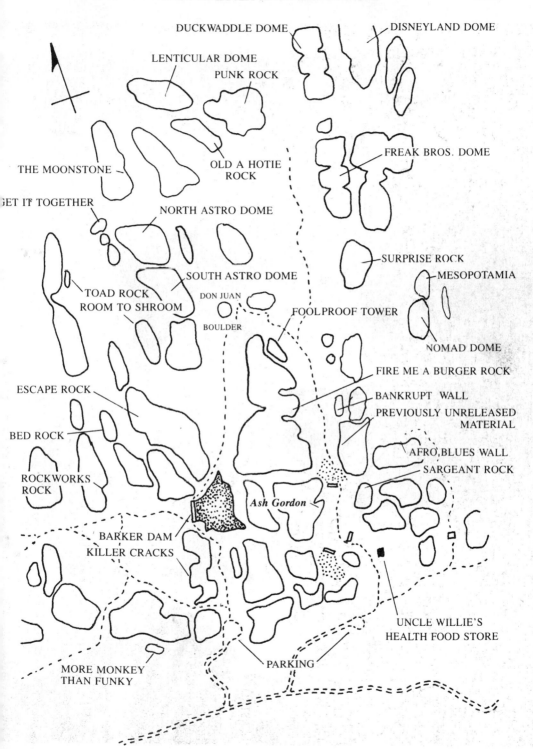

WONDERLAND OF ROCKS

The Wonderland of Rocks lie to the north and east of Barker Dam. Although you can approach the Wonderland from Barker Dam, the most common way to get into this vast area is from the Wonderland Ranch Trailhead.

Drive 200 yards on the Big Horn Pass Road past the Barker Dam turnoff. Another turn off to the north will be found at this point. Follow this until it ends at a parking area. Map, page 223.

WONDERLAND VALLEY

From the parking area you head north to an old burned out building (Uncle Willie's Health Food Store). A wash located to the left (west) of Uncle Willie's leads past a small dam to a valley which runs in a north-south direction. This is the southern end of the Wonderland Valley.

Approximately 400 yards north along the Wonderland Valley wash is a small dam.

809 ASH GORDON 5.10a   This crack lies to the southwest of the dam.   FA: Darryl Nakahira, Jim Ducker and Maria Cranor, 1980.

SARGEANT ROCK

This lies directly east of the dam mentioned as for route #809. Map, page 223.
810 WAR GAMES 5.10a ★★   FA: Alan Bartlett and Dave Black, January 1983.
811 ROCK STAR 5.10d (TR) ★★★   FA: unknown
812 39 STEPS 5.4 ★★   FA: Maria Cranor and Charles Cole, 1983.

PREVIOUSLY UNRELEASED MATERIAL

This large formation lies northeast of the flat sandy area lying behind (north) of the dam. Map, page 223.
813 KNIGHT MARE 5.7   FA: Kurt Shanebecka and Don Gangwere, February 1978.

FIRE ME A BURGER ROCK

This rock lies almost directly opposite Previously Unreleased Material. It is distinguished by the roof cracks on the upper right hand side. Map, page 223.

814 RED HEADED STRANGER 5.11a ★★   FA: Randy Vogel, Darryl Nakahira and Dan Leichtfuss, 1980.

815 HO MAN! 5.11b   FA: unknown

816 IT DON'T MEAN A THING IF IT AIN'T GOT THAT SWING 5.11d ★★★   FA: John Bachar (TR), 1978. First lead: unknown

817 SOLSTICE 5.10c ★   FA: Larry Friend, 1979.

BANKRUPT WALL

This small crag is on the right side of the wash, just a little north of Previously Unreleased Material, and nearly opposite Fire Me A Burger Rock. Map, page 223.

818 INSOLVENT 5.10b ★★   FA: Greg Bender and others, 1979.
819 CHAPTER 7 5.5   FA: unknown
820 CREDITOR'S CLAIM 5.6   FA: unknown
821 WASTING ASSETS 5.6   FA: unknown

FOOLPROOF TOWER

About 450 yards north of Bankrupt Wall, the Wonderland Valley widens out. An outcrop can be seen with a large flake/block, capped by a roof, lying against its face. This is Foolproof Tower. Map, page 223.

822 HIGH STRUNG 5.9 ★★   FA: Herb Laeger and Rich Smith, March 1977.

823 RICE CAKE ROOF 5.10c ★   FA: unknown

824 YOGI THE OVERBEAR 5.10a   FA: Phil Broscovak, Jim Angione and Sibylle Hechtel, November 1978. *Direct Start* 5.10c   FA: unknown

NOMAD DOME – WEST FACE

Nomad Dome lies approximately 600 yards northeast of Foolproof Tower and approximately 300 yards east of the nearest approach from the Wonderland Valley. Several approaches are possible; however, a wash just south of Surprise Rock, if followed southeast, then east, is the easiest. Map, page 223.

825 *BEN* 5.10b ★★   FA: Dave Houser, Darryl Nakahira, Doug Ziesner, Kelly Vaught, Todd Gordon and Ian Carter, November 1980.

826 *LAST ANGRY ARAB* 5.6   FA: John Wolfe, Rob Stahl and Bob Dominick, 1972.

827 *WILLARD* 5.7 ★   FA: Houser, Nakahira, Ziesner, Vaught, Gordon, Carter, with Paul Quinn, November 1980.

828 *RICOCHET* 5.5 ★   FA: Jonny Woodward et al, 1983.

MESOPOTAMIA DOME

Walk east along the south end of Nomad Dome and then head north along a canyon. A white slab will be seen on the left side of the canyon. This slab faces east. Map, page 223.

829 *MESOPOTAMIA* 5.10b ★★★   This route starts behind several large boulders. Climb the face past four bolts up a faint water streak.   FA: Bob Gaines and Dan Scdoris, December 1982.

THE ASTRO DOMES

The two domes offer some of Joshua Tree's finest face climbing routes. The rock on the northeast faces of both the North and South Astro Domes is uncharacteristically smooth. Most routes climb sharp edges or flakes on excellent rock.

At a point where the Wonderland Valley widens (near Foolproof Tower) the Astro Domes can be seen about 350 yards to the northwest. A very large boulder (Don Juan Boulder) will be encountered about halfway between Foolproof Tower and the South Astro Dome. One aid route on the southeast corner (bolt ladder) is the only known way to the summit. This bolt ladder was established about 1972. Map, page 223.

RODEO ROCK

This rock is really the southern end of the chain of domes of which the North and South Astro Domes are a part. It lies about 100 yards south of the South Astro Dome.

830 SERIOUS FASHION 5.10c ★   This route is on the southeast corner of Rodeo Rock. Climb up the corner past 5 bolts.   FA: Mike Beck and Mike Guardino, 1982.

831 BEVERLY DRIVE 5.10c (TR)   This route climbs the face left of route #830, and starts on a small flake.   FA: Mike Beck, December 1982.

SOUTH ASTRO DOME – EAST FACE

The easiest descent from South Astro Dome is down the northwest shoulder. This is Class 3.

832 PRIMAL FLAKE 5.9+   On the southeast shoulder of the South Astro Dome climb a 60' 5.9 face past two bolts. Above, hand traverse the "Primal Flake" to a bolt. Climb right and up to an overhang/corner, then continue to the summit.   FA: David Rubine, Michael Wells, Martin Wensley, Sheri and Jeff, March 1980.

833 HEX MARKS THE POOT (aka *Lightning Bolt Crack*) 5.7 ★★★   FA: unknown, 1971. A second pitch can be done (5.8), up an obvious lieback flake.   FA: unknown, 1977.

834 STRIKE IT RICH 5.10b ★★   FA: Herb Laeger, Ed Ehrenfeld and Eve Uiga, December, 1976.

SOUTH ASTRO DOME – NORTHEAST FACE

835 BOLT HEAVEN 5.10 A1   FA: Jack Roberts and others, 1977.

836 MY LAUNDRY 5.9 ★★★   FA: Jim Wilson and Herb Laeger, November 1976.

837 SOLID GOLD 5.10a ★★★★   FA: Herb Laeger, Jon Lonne, Jim Wilson and Mike Jaffe, March 1977. (Aid may have been used to place a couple bolts.)

838 MIDDLE AGE CRAZY 5.11b ★★★   FA: Herb Laeger, Mike Jaffe and Dave Houser, February 1980. (Aid used on a bolt.)

839 SUCH A SAVAGE 5.11a ★★★★★   FA: Spencer Lennard and Craig Fry, November 1977. (A couple bolts were placed on aid.) *Direct Start* 5.10   FA: unknown, 1976.

840 WALKING PNEUMONIA 5.11b ★★★   (serious lead)   FA: Jonny Woodward and Randy Vogel, November 1982.

841 BREAKFAST OF CHAMPIONS 5.8+ ★   FA: Ed Ehrenfeld, Herb Laeger and Eve Uiga, December 1977.

842 PIGGLE PUGG 5.10c ★★★   Climbs a lieback flake to right of route #841 and joins that route.   FA: Spencer Lennard and Chris Robbins, December 1977.

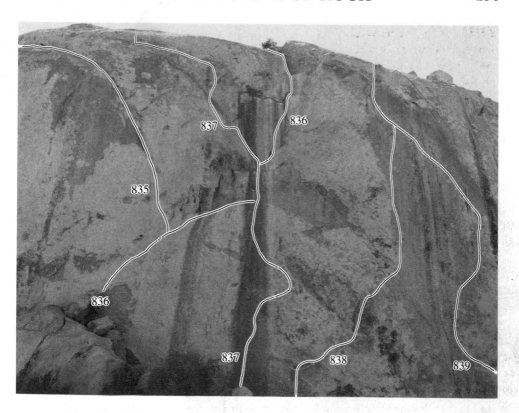

SOUTH ASTRO DOME – NORTHEAST FACE

NORTH ASTRO DOMES

837

836

834

833

SOUTH ASTRO DOME – EAST FACE

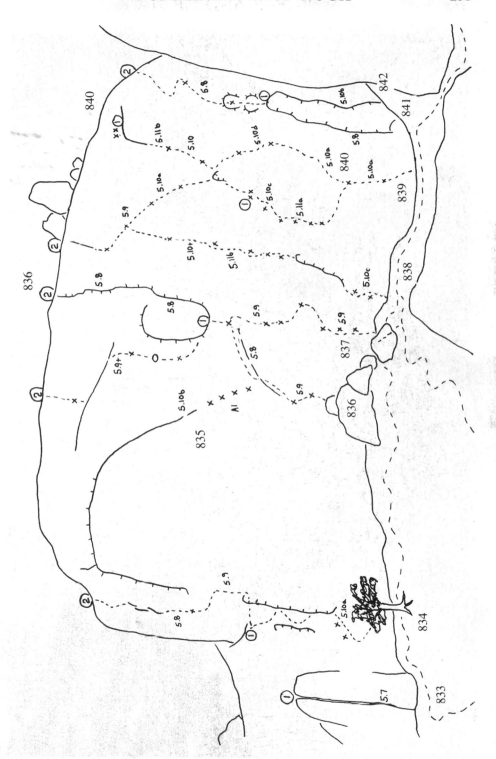

SOUTH ASTRO DOME – NORTHEAST FACE

NORTH ASTRO DOME – NORTHEAST FACE

The easiest descent off the North Astro Dome is down the northwest shoulder (5.4). It is possible to rappel from the belay bolts of a West Face route, but two ropes are required. Map, page 223.

843 THROAT WARBLER MANGROVE 5.9 (dirty; serious, with poor pro.) FA: Dan King and Ron Overholtz, October 1976. FFA: Dave Evans and Mike Lechlinski, April 1978.

844 ZION TRAIN 5.10d ★★ FA: Craig Fry and Paul Tear, March 1984.

845 POWER FINGERS 5.11d FA: Ed Kaufer and Keith Cunning, 1981. This route stands as a monument to sick ambition. The first ascent team not only placed bolts on rappel and with other aids, but "improved" numerous holds with hammers and other unknown devices. This potentially excellent route has been butchered by victims of the overly competitive climbing scene. There is also some doubt whether the climb was entirely free climbed on the first ascent.

846 FIGURES ON A LANDSCAPE 5.10b ★★★★★ FA: Randy Vogel and Dave Evans, November 1978. (Belay bolts were drilled off a hook.)

847 THE UNKNOWN ROUTE 5.10a ★★ (poor protection) FA: unknown, around 1972.

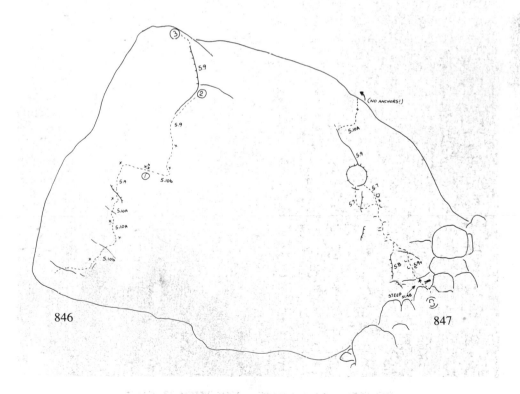

up corner
to top

845

846

843

844

NORTH ASTRO DOME – NORTHEAST FACE

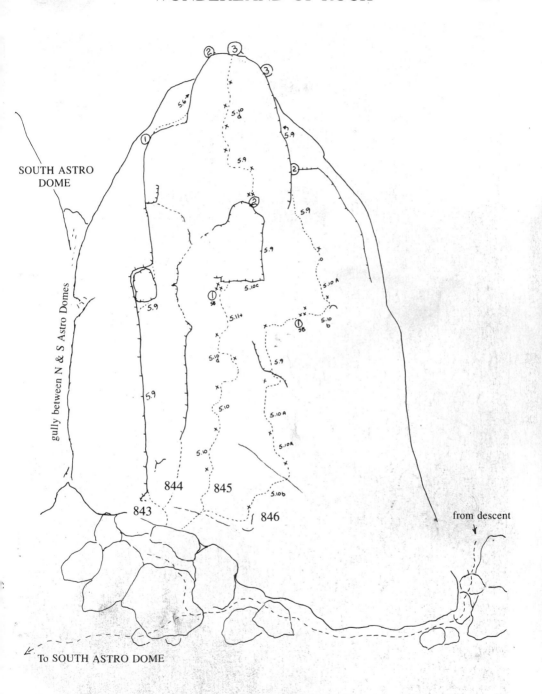

SOUTH ASTRO
DOME

gully between N & S Astro Domes

844

845

843

846

from descent

To SOUTH ASTRO DOME

NORTH ASTRO DOME – NORTHEAST FACE

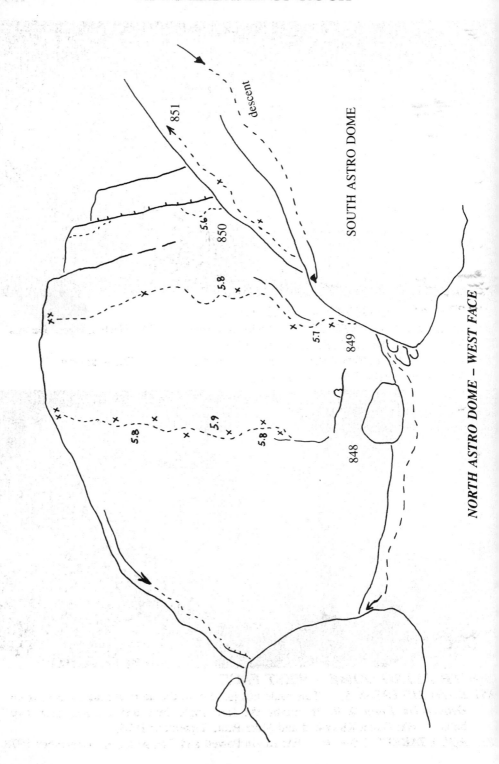

851

descent

850

5.6

5.8

5.7

849

SOUTH ASTRO DOME

5.8

5.9

5.8

848

NORTH ASTRO DOME – WEST FACE

NORTH ASTRO DOME – WEST FACE

848 LEAD US NOT INTO TEMPTATION 5.9 ★★★ FA: Herb Laeger, Dennis Knuckles and Jan McCollum, January 1978.

849 DELIVER US FROM EVIL 5.8 ★ (runout for a 5.8) FA: unknown

850 HUSH PUPPIES 5.6 FA: unknown

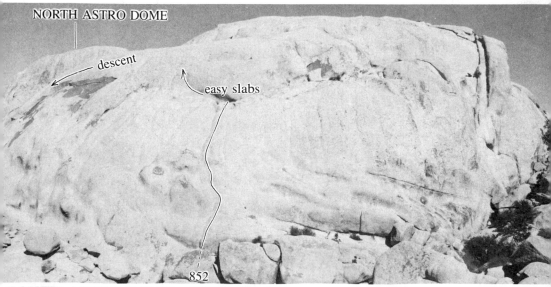

SOUTH ASTRO DOME – WEST FACE

851 BOZO BUTTRESS 5.1 This route lies just left of the descent route, across from *Deliver Us From Evil*. It climbs the low angle face and buttress past two bolts. FA: Galen Kirkwood and Mike Paul, September 1976.

852 AQUA TARKUS 5.9+ ★ FA: Kevin Powell and Dan Ahlborn, December 1978.

LOOKING NORTH FROM THE ASTRO DOMES

LOOKING SOUTHEAST FROM THE ASTRO DOMES

GET IT TOGETHER ROCK

This is the north facing wall which lies west of the north face of the North Astro Dome (route #844) and across from the south end of the Moonstone. Map, page 223.

853 I GOT IT 5.9   To the left of several large, rust-colored roofs is an obvious left arching flake/crack. Climb an easy chimney up to this crack and continue to the top.   FA: Kenny Morrell and Dave Harden, December 1982.

THE MOONSTONE – NORTHEAST FACE
(as seen from Lenticular Dome)

This dome lies northwest of the North Astro Dome and across a small gully which runs east-west. The best approach to the Moonstone is via the Lenticular Dome approach, before heading southwest 300 yards. Map, page 223.

This dome has excellent potential; a roof on the left hand side of the northeast face has been tried, and seems definitely possible.

854 COSMIC DEBRIS 5.10a ★   Climb up a corner and discontinuous cracks to a bolt; face climb to the summit.   FA: Randy Vogel and Maria Cranor, 1979.

LENTICULAR DOME

This attractive rock lies about 450 yards north of the North Astro Dome. However, it is best approached via the main trail in the Wonderland Valley. Eventually you must cut into a wash which heads northwest and passes directly below the southwest face of Lenticular Dome. A trail that heads north from near Don Juan Boulder leads directly into this wash and offers an alternative route. Descent is to the left, then down slabs into a gully. Map, page 223.

855 UNCONSCIOUS OBSCENITY 5.9   This follows five bolts on the face left of #853.   FA: Davis Rubine and Gwyn Cattrell, December 1980.

856 HAND WOBLER DELIGHT 5.9   FA: Ken Black and J. Bruce, November 1982.

857 DAZED AND CONFUSED 5.9 ★★★   FA: Bud Bruce, Brad Johnston, Mike Orr and Randy Vogel, January 1977.

858 MENTAL PHYSICS 5.7+ ★★★★   FA: unknown

OLD A HOTIE ROCK

This rock is the small ridge forming the gully along the southern end of Lenticular Dome. The following routes lie on the north side. This formation may also be approached as for Punk Rock. Map, page 223.

859 LAID BACK AND DOING IT 5.10c   This route lies directly across from the descent route for Lenticular Dome. A large, arching roof is located on the right side of a straight 2" crack. Layback up a right arching fingertip crack to the hand crack, which is followed more or less straight up to the top.   FA: Dan Harrow, Jay Marmo and Mike McMullen, 1981.

860 NIHILISTIC PILLAR 5.11c ★★   (small to 3½" nuts)   FA: Paul Schweizer and Randy Vogel, spring 1985.

PUNK ROCK   (aka Beagle Rocks) – SOUTHWEST FACE

This prominent pile of rocks lies squarely in the middle of the northern part of the
Wonderland Valley. It is easily approached via the main trail. Just before reaching Freak
Brothers Domes, head northwest. Route #858 can easily be seen from the approach.
Map, page 223.

861 PUNKED OUT PORPOISE 5.8+ ★★ (loose and poor pro.)   FA: Craig Fry,
   Dave Evans and Jim Angione, November 1979.

862 SCAR WARS 5.11a This route ascends a finger crack to a very obvious offwidth
   crack on the east end of Punk Rock. It is best seen and approached from Freak
   Brothers Domes.   FA: Charles Cole and Maria Cranor, 1982.

SURPRISE ROCK – WEST FACE

This small dome lies on the eastern side of Wonderland Valley, to the northeast of the Astro Domes. If you hike straight out the main Wonderland Valley trail, you will pass just west of it. Map, page 223.

863 TREMBLING TOES 5.9 ★   This can be done in one pitch.   FA: Richard Jensen and Mark Smith, April 1982. (The route is overbolted and aid was possibly used to place some of the bolts.)

864 DIRTY SURPRISE 5.9   FA: Herb Laeger, December 1977.

FREAK BROTHERS DOMES – WEST FACE

This distinctive trio of domes is just north of Surprise Rock and is recognizable by the three roofs which run through the domes. Map, page 223.

865 I CAN'T BELIEVE IT'S A GIRDLE 5.9 ★★★★   FA (1st pitch): Randy Vogel and Charles Cole, 1982. (2nd pitch): Phil Broscovak, Randy Vogel and Jim Angione, November 1978. (3rd pitch): Randy Vogel, Dave Houser and Maria Cranor, December 1979. (4th pitch): Alan Bartlett and others, 1980.

866 THE SOUND OF ONE HAND SLAPPING 5.11c ★★★★   FA: Gib Lewis and Charles Cole, 1981.

867 SAFE MUFFINS 5.8   FA: Randy Vogel and Dave Evans, December 1977.

868 FAT FREDDIE'S ESCAPE 5.8   (The upper part is "the escape," 5.6)   FA: Randy Vogel, Phil Broscovak and Jim Angione, November 1978.

869 ZAP #4 5.6   FA: unknown

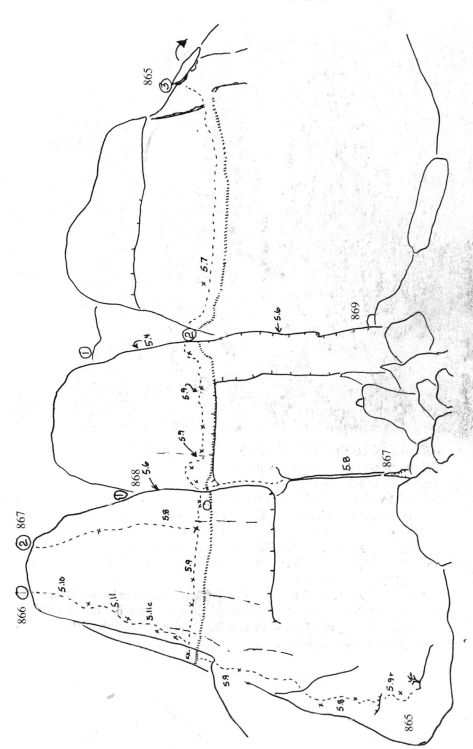

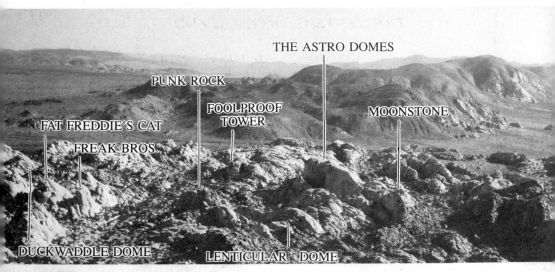

THE WONDERLAND OF ROCKS – LOOKING SOUTH photo by Dave Houser

THE WONDERLAND OF ROCKS – LOOKING SOUTHEAST photo by Dave Houser

THE CENTRAL WONDERLAND

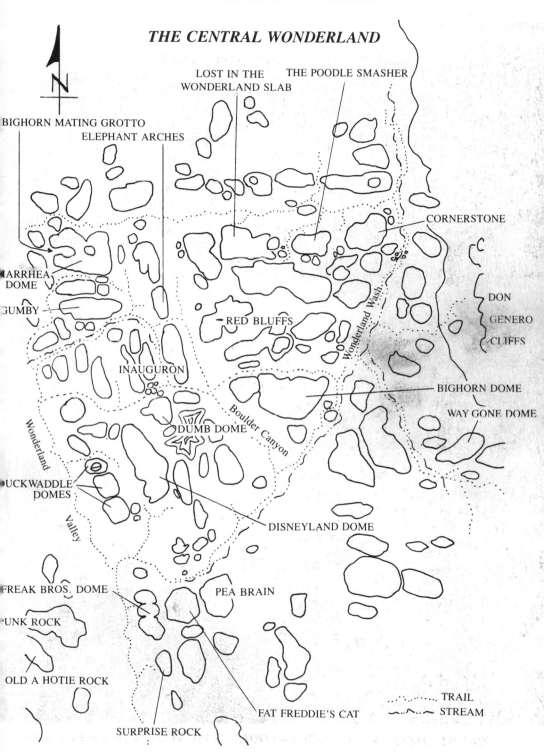

LOST IN THE
WONDERLAND SLAB

THE POODLE SMASHER

BIGHORN MATING GROTTO
ELEPHANT ARCHES

CORNERSTONE

ARRHEA
DOME

GUMBY

DON
GENERO
CLIFFS

RED BLUFFS

Wonderland Wash

INAUGURON

BIGHORN DOME

WAY GONE DOME

DUMB DOME

Boulder Canyon

Wonderland

UCKWADDLE
DOMES

Valley

DISNEYLAND DOME

FREAK BROS. DOME

PEA BRAIN

UNK ROCK

OLD A HOTIE ROCK

TRAIL
STREAM

FAT FREDDIE'S CAT

SURPRISE ROCK

FAT FREDDIE'S CAT

This is the long dome which lies parallel and immediately east of Freak Brothers Domes. A very narrow canyon separates those formations. Map, page 249.

870 THE NORTH FACE 5.2 ★★ (no pro) FA: Charles Cole and Maria Cranor, 1983.

Several routes lie on the east and northeast faces of Fat Freddie's Cat.

871 FIELDS OF LAUGHTER 5.6 ★★   This climbs the low angle northeast face, with no pro.   FA: Craig Fry and Greg Epperson, April 1985.

872 EARLY BIRD 5.9+ ★★   This is a two pitch crack route opposite *Joan Jetson*, route # 874.   FA: Charles Cole and Kelly Carignan, 1984.

873 LUST IN THE WONDERLAND 5.9 ★   100 feet left of route #872, this follows discontinuous cracks.   FA: Craig Fry and Dave Evans, February 1985.

PEA BRAIN

This dome is just east and parallel to Fat Freddie's Cat. Map, page 249.

874 JOAN JETSON 5.9 ★   FA: Dave Evans, Kelly Carignan, Margy Floyd and Charles Cole, spring 1985.

THE RED OBELISK

This is the red pillar of rock just north of Fat Freddie's Cat and Pea Brain. It sits in the east-west running wash that is the main trail to the Lost in the Wonderland Valley.

875 BOOGERS ON A LAMPSHADE 5.10a   This is on the east face.   FA: Dave Evans, 1985. FFA (TR): Margy Floyd.

DISNEYLAND DOMES

This formation lies northeast of Freak Brothers Dome. Map, pages 223, 249.

876 THRUTCHER 5.7   FA: Dave Evans and Mike Lechlinski, March 1978.

877 TRAGIC KINGDOM 5.8 A1   FA: Dave Evans and Jeff Elgar, February 1977.

878 ENCHANTED STAIRWAY 5.9 ★★   FA: Mike Pope, Hanke Levine and Russ Yeoman (via variation), December 1975.

879 JUNGLE CRUISE 5.10b ★★★   FA: Craig Fry and Bob Robach, February 1981.

880 MENTAL BANKRUPTCY 5.10b ★★   This route climbs the left diagonalling dike on the main face of Disneyland Dome. Three pitches.   FA: Charles Cole, Maria Cranor and Dan Leichtfuss, 1982.

DUCKWADDLE DOMES

This long formation has three distinct summits and parallels Disneyland Dome, but just to the west. The last summit has a summit block that is split in four sections. On the east side of the formation, facing route #880, is *Innervisions*. Map, page 249.

881 INNERVISIONS 5.9   Climb a crack up to the base of the summit block. Follow the wide crack in the block to the summit.   FA: John Bald and Mike Jaffe, 1974.

DISNEYLAND DOME – NORTH FACE

Hike along the Wonderland Valley past Duckwaddle Domes and head right (east) into an open area which lies north of Disneyland Dome. This can also be used as an approach to the Inauguron Formation. Map, page 249.

882 *THE WEAK FORCE* 5.10a ★   This route climbs the northeast face of Disneyland Dome, up a series of ramps and cracks.   FA: Randy Vogel and Paul Schweizer, April 1985.

883 *GRAIN AND BEAR IT* 5.9   This climbs the left (east) side of a detached flake near the summit of the north face.   FA: Vogel and Schweizer, 1985.

INAUGURON

descent

888

889

alternate approach to Inauguron

884

DUMB DOME

This rock lies just northeast of Disneyland Dome. Several good lines remain to be climbed. Map, page 249.

884 MONUMENT MANOR 5.8 ★   FA: Dave Evans, Craig Fry, Margy Floyd and Kelly Carignan, February 1985.

GUMBY DOME

This formation is located north of Disneyland Dome about 500 yards. It lies on the north side of an east-west canyon which leads to Secret Valley. Secret Valley contains the following formations: Inauguron, Elephant Arches, and Hard Rock. The Inauguron Dome may also be reached via the boulder-choked gully just left (north) of Dumb Dome. Map, page 249.

885 GUMBY GOES TO WASHINGTON 5.8   FA: Randy Vogel and Paul Schwiezer, April 1985.

886 POKIE'S BIG CHANCE 5.4   This route is the easiest way down Gumby Dome.   FD: Vogel and Schweizer.

LOOKING NORTH TO SECRET VALLEY

SECRET VALLEY

This canyon runs in a north-south direction, parallel to the Wonderland Valley, but about 450 yards to the east. Several large west facing rocks lie on the east side of Secret Valley. From south to north they are the Inauguron, Elephant Arches and Hard Rock. Map, page 249.

INAUGURON DOME

This lies just south of the junction of Secret Valley and the canyon with Gumby Dome. Best approach may be from the Dumb Dome area. Map, page 249.

887 THE INAUGURON 5.10c A1 ★★   FA: Dave Evans, Todd Gordon and Margy Floyd, January 1985.

888 YARDY-HOO AND AWAY 5.10a ★★★   FA: Evans and Floyd, spring 1985.

889 WHITE BREAD FEVER 5.11b ★★★   FA: Randy Vogel and Paul Schweizer, April 1985.

ELEPHANT ARCHES

This formation is north of Inauguron Dome. Map, page 249.

890 TRUE DEMOCRACY 5.9 ★   FA: Craig Fry, March 1985.

891 VICE PRESIDENT 5.10b ★★★ (runout)   FA: Dave Bruckman, Dave Evans and Craig Fry, December 1984.

892 BLACK PRESIDENT 5.10d ★★★★★   FA: Fry, Evans and Bruckman, December 1984. (The route was apparently attempted by unknown climbers around 1979).

893 UNDER SECRETARY A2 5.7   FA: Kelly Carignan and Margy Floyd, 1985.

HARD ROCK

This "layered" rock lies to the north of Elephant Arches, in the Secret Valley. Map, page 249.

894 SOLAR WIND 5.8 ★★   FA: Randy Vogel and Paul Schweizer, March 1985.

895 HAWK WIND 5.10c ★★★   (poor protection)   FA: Schweizer and Vogel, March 1985.

DIARRHEA DOME

This very large dome lies about 300 yards north of Gumby Dome. The best approach is to walk north along The Wonderland Valley, past the canyon with Gumby Dome. The next canyon on the right (east) is followed a short distance until you can head north (by scrambling) to the base of Diarrhea Dome. Map, page 249.

The main (south) face of the Dome has one recorded route. If you head north along the western (right) end of the dome, a narrow canyon on the right (east) leads you into the amazing Bighorn Mating Grotto.

896 BIG BROWN EYE 5.10d ★★★   FA: Dave Evans, Todd Gordon, Craig Fry and Charles Cole, February 1985.

BIGHORN MATING GROTTO

Routes are described from left to right. Map, page 249.

897 TAKE TWO THEY'RE SMALL 5.9   This is a fist crack, offwidth, on the left.   FA: Kelly Carignan and Margy Floyd, April 1985.

898 DANGLING WOO LI MASTER 5.10a ★★★★   This is the second crack on the left, and climbs red colored rock before exiting up a hand/fist crack, on the left.   FA: Craig Fry, Dave Evans, Alan Roberts, Margy Floyd and Kelly Carignan, February 1985.

899 BOOK OF CHANGES 5.10b (direct start is 5.10d) ★★★★   This is the third crack on the left. Climb up and left to a 5.10b crack or straight up (5.10d). Two fixed pins and one bolt are at the top.

900 MORNING THUNDER 5.10d ★★★   This route is the longest route in the Grotto, and climbs an overhanging chimney system. It is hard to protect; angles are helpful.   FA: Craig Fry and Dave Evans, February 1985.

901 CAUGHT OUTSIDE ON A BIG SET 5.10b ★★★★★   This lies on the right wall of the Grotto, up discontinuous crack systems. FA: Herb Laeger and others.

OWL PINNACLE

This pillar of rock lies on the top of Diarrhea Dome.

902 OWL 5.9 ★   FA: Craig Fry and Dave Evans, February 1985.

BIGHORN MATING
GROTTO

896

DIARRHEA DOME

THE FAR EAST photo by Dave Houser

THE FAR EAST

The Far East is an area of the Wonderland of Rocks which lies northeast of the Freak Brothers Domes and the Secret Valley. It is best reached via the wash just north of the Freak Brothers complex (passing just by the Red Obelisk). A wash (Wonderland Wash) heads from there in a northeasterly direction. A canyon which heads northwest from the open area located past the Freak Brothers complex can be used to connect up with Secret Valley Domes (Boulder Canyon). Map, page 249.

BIGHORN DOME – NORTH FACE

This rock forms the southern border of a canyon that runs east-west, the east entrance of which lies about 650 yards northeast along the Wonderland Wash from the Freak Brothers complex. The south face of Bighorn Dome actually faces out into the open area past the Freak Brothers complex. Map, page 249.

903 THE TUBE 5.10b   This takes the obvious tube-shapped chimney.   FA: Charles Cole and others, April 1985.

904 POACHING BIGHORN 5.11b ★★★★   FA: Craig Fry, February 1985.

905 GREENHORN DIHEDRAL 5.10c ★★★   FA: Craig Fry, Dave Evans, Kelly Carignan, Margy Floyd and Alan Roberts, February 1985.

906 RUSTY PIPES 5.2 ★   This crack lies northeast of the north face of Bighorn Dome, taking a reddish crack up a small face.   FA: Craig Fry, February 1985.

RED BLUFFS

These obscure cliffs lie in a canyon which is north of the western end of Bighorn Dome. From the Bighorn Canyon hike west until Boulder Canyon is encountered. Follow this for about 150 yards to another small canyon (Choke Canyon), which heads east. It is easiest to hike straight northwest up Boulder Canyon to Choke Canyon. Red Bluffs lie on the north side of Choke Canyon. Map, page 249.

907 SLIP SKRIG 5.10c ★★★   This route lies on the far side of Red Bluffs.   FA: Craig Fry and Alan Roberts, May 1985.

DON GENERO CLIFFS

DON GENERO BOULDER

DON GENERO CLIFFS *(from the Cornerstone)*

This outcrop lies on the hillside about 500 yards northeast of Bighorn Dome and about 250 yards east of the Wonderland Wash. The outcrop has several unclimbed crack routes. Below the cliffs is a very large, rectangular boulder (Don Genero Boulder) that has a clean, overhanging aid crack located on the west face. Map, page 249.

908 MEXICAN HAT OF JOSH A2 5.4   FA: Dave Evans, Todd Gordon and Margy Floyd, January 1985.

LOST IN THE WONDERLAND VALLEY

This valley lies about 600 yards further along Wonderland Wash from Bighorn Dome. It is necessary to hike up a small rise to enter Lost In The Wonderland Valley. The east face of Cornerstone, which is visible from Wonderland Wash, has two thin flakes on it. Map, page 249.

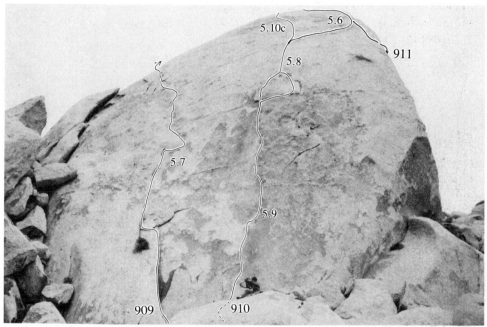

THE CORNERSTONE

909 AS THE CRAGS TURN 5.7 ★★★ (a little loose) FA: Randy Vogel and Charles Cole, January 1985.

910 GENERAL HOSPITAL 5.9 ★★★ FA: Cole and Vogel, January 1985. 5.10c Variation at top has no pro.

911 ONE MOVE LEADS TO ANOTHER 5.10c ★★ FA: Dave Evans and Craig Fry, January 1985.

First Ascent of General Hospital

POODLE SMASHER AREA

This lies 100 yards west of the Cornerstone. Map, page 249.

912 THE POODLE SMASHER 5.11a ★★★ FA: Charles Cole, Randy Vogel and Paul Schweizer, January 1985.

913 IN ELKE'S ABSENCE 5.10a ★ 50 feet left of route # 914, this goes up a layback crack/flake to a wide crack, then out face to left and the top. FA: Tom Lindner and John Hayward, October 1985.

914 MENTAL SIEGE TACTICS 5.10c ★ FA: Paul Schweizer, Randy Vogel, Randy Leavitt and Tom Lindner, October 1985.

915 DEFOLIATION 5.9 ★ FA: Vogel, Schweizer, Leavitt and Hayward, October 1985.

LOST IN THE WONDERLAND SLAB

This large slab lies about 175 yards west of the Poodle Smasher. Map, page 249.

916 EYES WITHOUT A FACE 5.10b ★   FA: Dave Evans, Randy Vogel and Charles Cole, January 1985.

917 DESERT DELIRIUM (aka Lost In The Wonderland) 5.10a ★★★   FA: Dave Houser and Jon Lonne, January 1981.

THE NEAR EAST TO WAY GONE DOME

Hook & Ladder

Poodle Boy

Fishing Trip

City H

HILLSIDE

NOMAD DOME

W.B.M.D

TO ASTRO DOMES
WONDERLAND VALLEY

Squid of My Desire

OLD MINE WORKS

BANKRUPT WALL

PREVIOUSLY

UNRELEASED MATERIAL

AFRO BLUES WALL

SARGEANT ROCK

Ash Gordon

PUMP

FIRE ME A BURGER ROCK

UNCLE WILLIE'S

TO PARKING LOT

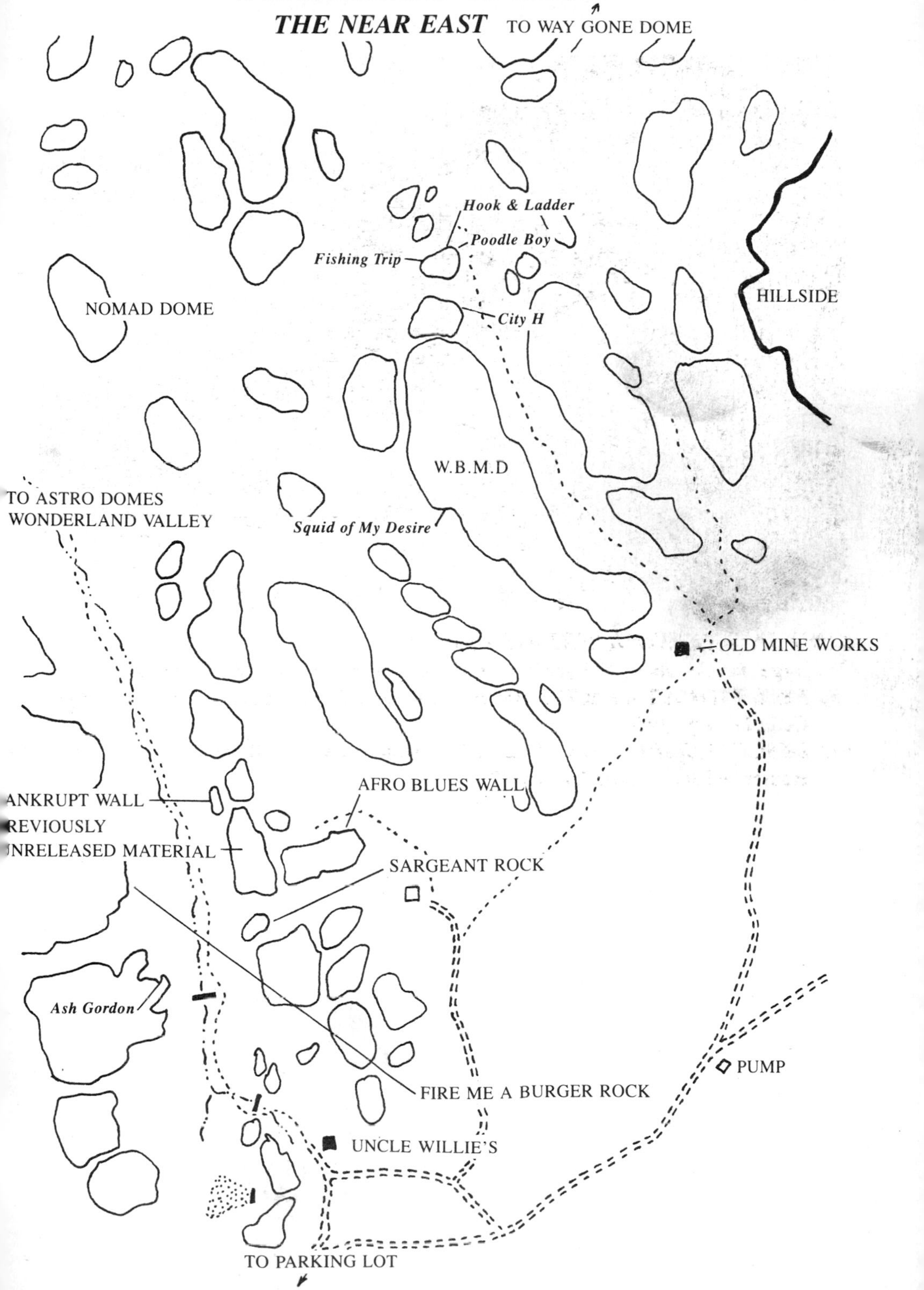

THE NEAR EAST

This area lies east of the Wonderland Ranch Parking Area. From the parking area do not head north toward Uncle Willie's, but head straight east along the southern end of the Wonderland.

An old dirt road heads into the first open area on the north. A cement slab marks an old homesite at the end of this road. The dome on the left (northwest) is the Afro Blues Wall. One route has been recorded on the pocketed north face. Map, page 267.

AFRO BLUES WALL

918 MY FAVORITE THINGS 5.10b (TR) ★★★   Start climbing below a conspicuous crack in the middle of the face which starts some 60 feet above the ground. Interesting face climbing past two overhangs leads to that crack.   FA: Randy Vogel and Alan Roberts, 1978.

THE MILL AREA

About ½ mile northeast of the parking area is an old mining operation, consisting of an ore crushing facility (mill). The canyon just west of the mill has a large formation on its east side known as the Worth Bagly Memorial Dome (W.B.M.D.) Map, page 267.

919 NAKED REAGAN 5.11a ★★★   This climbs a finger crack in a flare on the south face of the W.B.M.D.   FA: Dave Evans, Mike Paul, Alan Roberts and Ken Gordon, 1985.

920 BIVO SHAM 5.8   This route lies on the east face of the W.B.M.D., near the right side of the solution-pocketed face. It is easily approached by walking by route #919 into the next small canyon to the east.   FA: Kevin Powell and Alan Roberts, March 1985.

921 WORTH BAGLY DIHEDRAL 5.10b ★★   Across the canyon (northeast) from route #920 are two obvious cracks. *Worth Bagly Dihedral* climbs the left crack. Hand traverse up and right to gain the right facing dihedral which is followed to the top.   FA: Kevin Powell, Darrell Hensel and Alan Roberts, March 1985.

922 SQUID OF MY DESIRE 5.10a   This route climbs the left facing dihedral on the right end of the face with *Worth Bagley Dihedral.* Climb a thin diagonal crack to a ledge, then lieback the diheral. A few face moves above the dihedral lead to a thin crack which is climbed to the top.   FA: Jeff Bosson and Royce Carlson, 1981.

HOOK AND LADDER AREA

From the Mill hike to the next canyon northeast, which is followed for about 400 yards between two large domes. At the northern end of the western dome is a large rock split by an offwidth crack. Map, page 267.

923 CITY H 5.8 ★   FA: Mike Lechlinski, Mari Gingery and John Bachar, January 1981.

924 POODLE BOY 5.10b   FA: unknown

925 HOOK AND LADDER 5.11a (with ladder), 5.12b (w/o ladder) ★★   FA: Mike Lechlinski and Randy Vogel, 1981. FFA (no ladder): John Bachar, 1981.

926 FISHING TRIP 5.9   Offwidth on the back of route #923   FA: Mike Lechlinski, 1981.

WAY GONE DOME

This formation lies about 500 yards northeast of *Hook and Ladder*. Consult the photo for reference. Map, page 267.

927 CRYSTAL VOYAGER 5.9 A1 ★★   FA: Dave Evans and Craig Fry, December 1979.

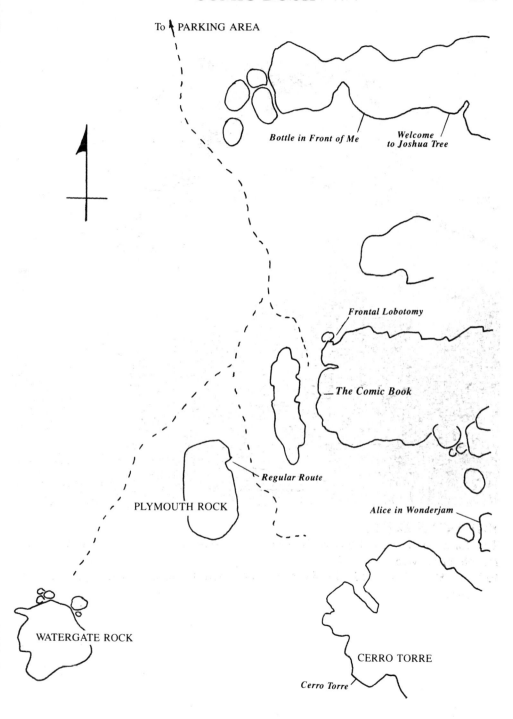

To ↑ PARKING AREA

Bottle in Front of Me

Welcome
to Joshua Tree

Frontal Lobotomy

_ The Comic Book

Regular Route

PLYMOUTH ROCK

Alice in Wonderjam

WATERGATE ROCK

CERRO TORRE

Cerro Torre

THE COMIC BOOK AREA

The Comic Book Area lies to the south of Big Horn Pass Road and is most easily approached at a point about 600 yards west of the Barker Dam turnoff. Two small parking areas on the south side of the road are located about 100 yards apart. The main climbing area is located on the hillside about ½ mile from the road. Map, page 271.

HERMAN ROCKS

This small group of rocks lie about 500 yards south of the Big Horn Pass Road and west of the trail leading to the main Comic Book Area.

928 HERMAN 5.9   FA: This route lies on a large boulder on the left. Two bolts protect steep face climbing up the northeast face.   FA: Scott Elrer and Jack Marshall, November 1982.

929 CONTROVERSIAL 5.9   Lies to the left of **Herman**.   FA: Dave Tapes, Jack Marshall, Dave Evans and Bruce Pottenger, December 1983.

The main Comic Book area is about ½ mile south of Big Horn Pass Road.

930 BOTTLE IN FRONT OF ME 5.10a ★★   FA: Charles Cole, Dave Houser and Alan Winter, May 1978.

931 WELCOME TO JOSHUA TREE 5.10c ★★   This is a two pitch face climb; belay on dike.   FA: Herb Laeger, Dave Houser and Jan McCollum, February 1977.

932 FROTAL LOGRANITY 5.10a   FA: Gib Lewis, Charles Cole and Marjorie Shovlin, 1982.

933 TAKE IT FOR GRANITE 5.10c ★★★   FA: Cole and Lewis, 1982.

934 TUBULAR BALLS 5.10b ★   FA: Matt Cox, Gary Ayres and Alan Lennard, January 1975.

THE COMIC BOOK AREA

935 FRONTAL LOBOTOMY 5.10a ★★★   FA: Matt Cox, Dave Evans, Spencer Lennard and Alan Lennard, January 1975.

936 CRUISING FOR BURGERS 5.10c ★   This is a two pitch face climb; belay on dike.   FA: Mark Goldsmith and Robert Critchfield, 1983.

937 FULL FRONTAL NUDITY 5.10a ★★★   This is a two pitch face climb. Start up crack of **Comic Book,** traverse left on dike to belay, and climb straight up to top.   FA: Randy Vogel and Dave Evans, February 1975.

938 COMIC BOOK 5.9+ ★★★   This follows an obvious crack for two pitches. Belay in "hole." Crux is starting the second pitch.   FA: Richard Harrison, John Long, Don Watson and Rick Accomazzo, December 1972.

939 CHARLIE BROWN 5.9   To the right of the previous route, this climbs left and up a ramp until a crack which parallels **Comic Book** is reached. Follow it straight up and over a small roof to the top.   FA: unknown

THE COMIC BOOK AREA

940 ALICE IN WONDERJAM 5.9 ★★★   FA: Dick Shockley, Peter Wilkening and Jim Wilson, December 1974.

941 WHITE RABBIT 5.10a ★★   FA: Pete Wilkening, Dick Shockley, Jim Wilson, Chris Wegener and Pete Steres, December 1974.

942 URINE TROUBLE 5.8   FA: unknown

There are four cracks on the right (west) side of a small box canyon which lies just right of **Urine Trouble**.

943 JAMBURGER 5.10a   (left-most crack)   FA: Matt Cox and Gary Ayres, 1975.

944 HAM & SWISS 5.10b   (crack 2nd from left)   FA: unknown

945 B.L.T. 5.10b   (crack 2nd from right)   FA: unknown

946 BRAIN DEATH 5.12a ★★★   FA: Spencer Lennard (TR), 1978. First lead: Dale Bard, 1981.

947 DRANO 5.10a ★★   FA: Jon Lonne and Dave Ohlsen, 1975.

CERRO TORRE

This is the tower that is up and right (southwest) of **Drano**. Map, page 271.

948 SW FACE 5.8 ★   Climb a chimney on the southwest face. Rappel to descend.   FA: Dave Evans and Jim Angione, January 1975.

PLYMOUTH ROCK

This small rock is west of the part of the Comic Book area with **Drano** and **Urine Trouble**. One route has been recorded on the northeast face. Map, page 271.

949 THE REGULAR ROUTE 5.10c   FA: Marius Morstad, Gib Lewis and Charles Cole, November 1979.

WATERGATE ROCK

This lies about 300 yards southwest of the main Comic Book Area. Map, page 271.

950 I AM NOT A CROOK 5.8   This route is about 75' left of **H.R. Hardman,** on a perched pinnacle of rock. Climb this up to a smooth face with two bolts.   FA: unknown

951 WHITE COLLAR CRIME 5.8   FA: unknown

952 H.R. HARDMAN 5.8 ★   FA: unknown. FFA: Dave Houser, Alan Winter and Bob Malloy, November 1977.

953 FIFTEEN MINUTE GAP 5.6   FA: Dave Houser and Kendall Downing, April 1976.

954 DIRTY TRICKS 5.11d (TR)   This can be lead, but protection at the top is wanting; no complete ascent of the route has been made.   FA: Kevin Powell and others did the crux (TR), 1981.

955 DEJA VU 5.10a ★   FA: Charles Cole and Marius Morstad, November 1979.

WATERGATE ROCK

956

ASTEROID BELT

This small formation lies about ½ mile west of the main Comic Book Area. It also is about ½ mile east of Cyclops Rock, in Hidden Valley Campground. One route has been recorded on the southwest face. Much bouldering can be found nearby.

956 ASTEROID CRACK 5.12+ (TR)   FA: unknown French climbers, 1984.

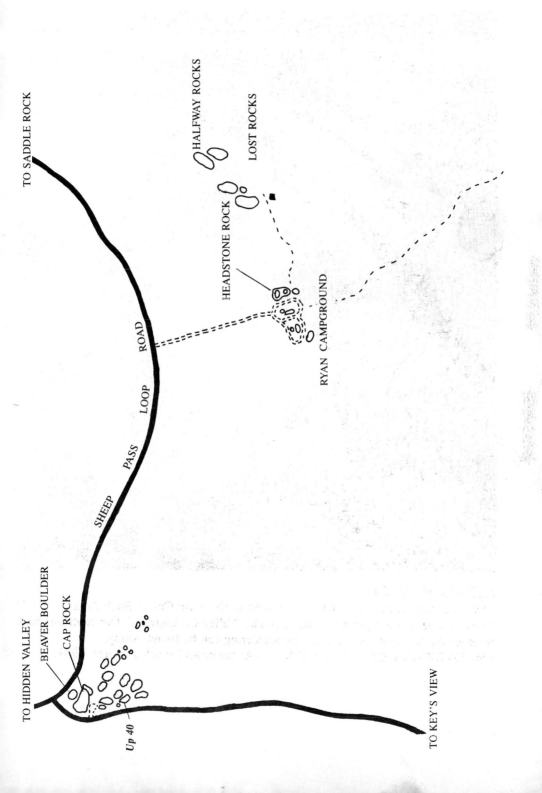

TO SADDLE ROCK

HALFWAY ROCKS

LOST ROCKS

HEADSTONE ROCK

ROAD

LOOP

PASS

SHEEP

RYAN CAMPGROUND

TO HIDDEN VALLEY

BEAVER BOULDER

CAP ROCK

Up 40

TO KEY'S VIEW

RYAN AREA

The remainder of this part of the guide continues to "encounter" crags as would be encountered along the Quail Springs Road. From Hidden Valley Campground head south for about two miles to a point where the Key's View Road branches off right. The Quail Springs Road curves east and then northeast from here. From the point of intersection with the Key's View Road, Quail Springs Road changes names (probably just to confuse people). For about the next 11 miles the main road is called Sheep Pass Road.

CAP ROCK

Cap Rock is situated at the southeast corner of the intersection of Quail Springs Road and Key's View Road. A large parking area is located south of the main formation and is reached by driving south on Key's View Road for a short distance. Map, page 279.

BEAVER BOULDER

Beaver Boulder is the very large boulder located in front of Cap Rock's north side. It is quite obvious from Quail Springs Road. Several aid routes climb the boulder.

957 RURP ROMP A3+ ★   FA: John Wolfe and Howard Weamer, May 1969.

958 LOST LID A4 5.9 ★   FA: Hugh Burton, John Long, Fred East and Billy Westbay, December 1975.

959 BOLT LADDER A1   This short bolt ladder is located on the east face of Beaver Boulder.   FA: unknown

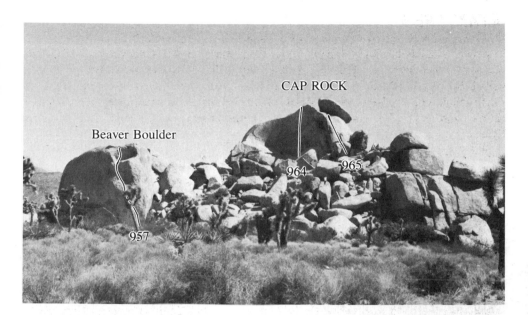

CAP ROCK – NORTHEAST AND NORTH FACES

960 EVENT HORIZON 5.10b ★★   FA: Dan Ahlborn, January 1976.

961 NUTCRACKER 5.2   FA: Rob Stahl, Dave Stahl, John Wolfe and Mona Stahl, March 1971.

962 SPACE ODYSSEY 5.10b ★   FA: Dan Ahlborn and Kevin Powell, January 1976.

963 FALSE LAYBACK 5.4   FA: John Wolfe and Dick James, December 1968.

964 THE AYATOLLAH 5.11a (TR) ★★   FA: Mike Waugh and others, 1979.

965 CIRCUS 5.2 ★   FA: Dick James and John Wolfe, December 1968.

CAP ROCK – SOUTH FACE

966 VISUAL NIGHTMARE 5.10a   FA: Alan Nelson, January 1985.

967 SLIM PICKINGS 5.10b (direct start: 5.10c)   FA: Herb Laeger and Dennis Knuckles, March 1978.

CAP ROCK – SOUTHEAST FACE

968 CATCH A FALLING STAR 5.8 ★★   FA: Laeger and Knuckles, March 1978.
969 NOBODY WALKS IN LA 5.8+ ★   FA: Gary Cobb, Greg Rice and Robert
Yucknat, November 1982.

CAP ROCK AREA

970 UP 40 5.11b ★★ *(can't* be top roped) This short route/boulder problem lies
about 100 yards south of the parking area and just off Keys View Road.   FA:
John Bachar, 1979.

RYAN CAMPGROUND

Ryan Campground is located about ¾ mile east of Cap Rock, along the Sheep Pass
Loop Road. A dirt road is taken about ¼ mile south to the actual campground. A few
routes are located in the campground, while the balanced pillar to the east (Headstone
Rock) and other formations found further east provide additional climbing.

971 SLIGHTLY AHEAD OF OUR TIME 5.12a ★   This is the bolt ladder route on
a large boulder behind campsite #27.   FA: unknown. FFA: Kevin Powell and
Darrell Hensel, May 1976.

BEHIND CAMPSITE #18

972 MIGHTY HIGH 5.11c (TR)   FA: Alan Nelson, November 1981.

973 TOM BOMBADIL 5.7   FA: Paul Piana, 1976.

974 BARELY CRANKIN' 5.7   FA: Mike Beck, February 1975.

975 DECEPTION 5.10a   FA: Jim Thoen and Susan Hurst.

976 BABY ROUTE 5.9   This route lies behind campsite #19. A small roof is passed before a right facing corner and crack lead to the summit.   FA: Mingo Morvin and Bill Antel, 1976.

HEADSTONE ROCK – SOUTH FACE

This pillar of rock sits on top of a jumble of rocks and boulders about 200 yards east of the campground. The first ascent of Headstone Rock was made in 1956 by Bob Boyle and Rod Smith. A rope, tossed over the summit, was climbed to reach the top. Map, page 279.

977 SW CORNER 5.6+ ★★★   FA: Mark Powell, 1958.
978 SOUTH FACE CENTER 5.9 (TR) ★★   FA: unknown
979 CRYPTIC 5.8 ★★★   FA: Mark Powell, March 1971.

HEADSTONE ROCK – NORTH FACE

980 NORTH FACE A1   bolt ladder   FA: unknown
981 JAM CRACK 5.8   This short hand crack leads up to the northeast corner of
Headstone Rock.   FA: unknown

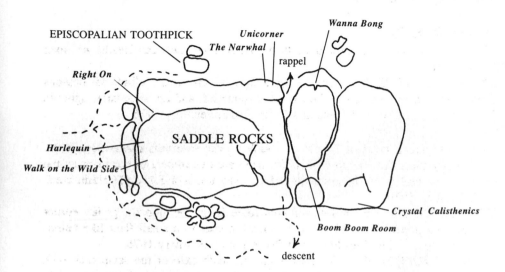

EPISCOPALIAN TOOTHPICK

Unicorner

The Narwhal

Wanna Bong

rappel

Right On

SADDLE ROCKS

Harlequin

Walk on the Wild Side

Crystal Calisthenics

Boom Boom Room

descent

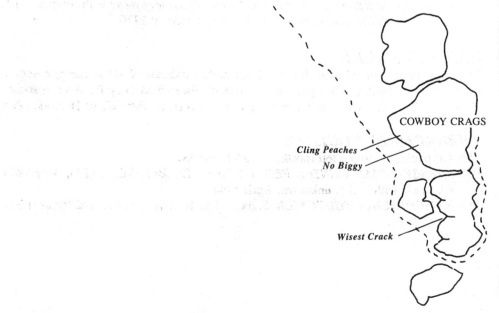

COWBOY CRAGS

Cling Peaches

No Biggy

Wisest Crack

LOST ROCKS
These rocks lie east of Balance Rock. The first and southern formation has two routes. Map, page 288.

982 M.F. DIRTY RAT 5.7   Near the south side of this clump is a small corridor. Climb a clean hand crack on the left (north) side of this corridor.   FA: Alan Nelson, November 1981.

983 DIRTY CAT 5.10c (TR)   This is a thin crack just right of **M.F. Dirty Rat**.   FA: Mike Beck, November 1981.

HALFWAY ROCKS
Further east and slightly north is a whittish colored dome between Headstone Rock and Saddle Rocks.

984 ANCIENT FUTURE 5.9   On the west face of this rock, climb an obvious depression to a bolt and on to the top (or traverse left and up, then back right via 5.7 climbing).   FA: Paul Piana and Bruce Franz, February 1976.

A band of cliffs which lie right (south) of Saddle Rocks continues down towards the road (southwest). Near the bottom of this cliff band are two routes. In a canyon on the north side of this cliff band, about a third of the way up, is a 5.11c (TR) thin crack (FA: Rick Cashner, 1979).

985 HEFFALUMP 5.5   (no protection) This route is on the smooth, grainy corner that faces the road (west). Climb up a smooth corner to a small flake-like bump, then to the top.   FA: Paul Piana and Bruce Franz, February 1976.

986 BOOM BOOM O'HARA 5.5   This is on the south face of the same rock with **Heffalump.** Climb a slanting gully to the top. (The entry move is the crux.)   FA: Paul Piana, Bruce Franz and Margie O'Hara, February 1976.

SADDLE ROCKS
This very large slab of rock lies about one mile northeast of Ryan Campground. A series of car pullouts on the right and left sides of Sheep Pass Loop Road leave about a ½ mile walk to the rock. On the west side of the road is The Hall of Horrors. Map, page 288.

THEORETICAL BOULDER
This tall boulder is to the left (north) of Saddle Rocks.

987 PRESBYTERIAN DENTAL FLOSS 5.10d   FA: Bob Gaines (TR), May 1983. FA (lead, with bolts): unknown, April 1984.

988 EPISCOPALIAN TOOTHPICK 5.10c   FA: Rick Accomazzo and Richard Harrison, 1976.

SADDLE ROCKS

Saddle Rocks has three distinct summits (Lower, Middle, Upper). However, the routes on Saddle Rocks will be described left (north) to right (south) around the entire rock. **Wanna Bong** is the route furthest to the right and lies on the north face.

989 **'WANNA BONG** 5.9+ This route climbs the obvious wide crack and corner system on the middle formation. It is the furthest left route. FA: Mike Jaffe and Greg Cloutier, April 1973.

990 **UNICORNER** 5.8 ★★ This route climbs a giant left facing open book on the northeast corner of the lower formation. This is just below the rappel route from the north end of the lower formation. FA: Charles Cole and Gib Lewis, January 1980.

991 **THE NARWHAL** 5.10b ★★ Start at the **Unicorner**, but follow a traversing crack which heads up and right. It joins the top of **Orange Flake** after two pitches. FA: unknown. FFA: Randy Vogel and Charles Cole, February 1980.

992 **ORANGE FLAKE** 5.8+ ★★ FA: Roy Naasz and Ron Osborn, April 1969.

993 **R & R** 5.8 FA: Steve Godshall and Richard Canning, February 1972.

994 **RIGHT ON** 5.5 ★★ FA: John Wolfe and Rob Stahl, June 1971.

995 **THE HIGH COST OF LIVING** 5.11a to 5.12b (depending on height) ★★★★ FA: Gib Lewis, Herb Laeger and Charles Cole, February 1980.

996 **A CHEAP WAY TO DIE** 5.10d ★★★ FA: Cole, Lewis and Laeger, February 1980.

997 **HARLEQUIN** 5.10c ★★★★ (runout sections) FA: Jim Wilson and Tobin Sorenson, November 1974.

998 **WALK ON THE WILD SIDE** 5.7+ ★★★★ FA: Roy Naasz and Chris Wegener, January 1970.

999 **HAM SANDWICH** 5.8 FA: unknown

1000 **A2** FA: unknown

1001 **RAKER MOBILE** 5.8 FA: unknown

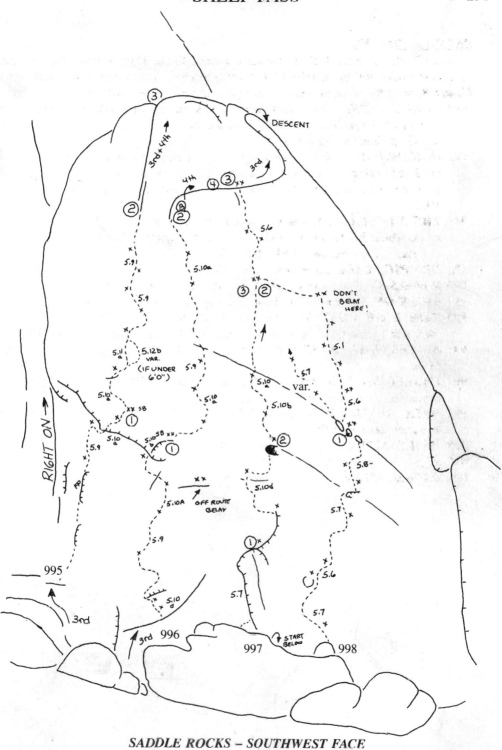

SADDLE ROCKS – SOUTHWEST FACE

SADDLE ROCKS

The lower formation has a gully/chimney (the descent route) splitting the upper south side. To the right (east) of this chimney is a low angled face. The top of this face is the end of *Right On.* Map, page 288.

1002 **PRESTO IN C SHARP** 5.7   This climbs a water streak on the low angled face, past two bolts.   FA: Charles Cole and Hank Levine, April 1978.

1003 **SULLIVAN FROM COLORADO** 5.9   This climbs up and right past two horizontal cracks from a chockstone in the corridor to the right (east) of *Presto in C Sharp.*   FA: Sullivan from Colorado (who else?), 1978.

1004 **BOOM BOOM ROOM** 5.9 ★★   Named after a bar in Joshua Tree (which has changed names more often than can be counted), this route climbs past five bolts on the south face of the middle formation.   FA: Randy Vogel, Dianne Brown and Charles Cole, December 1977.

1005 **MORE HUSTLE THAN MUSCLE** 5.8   This climbs a left leaning, overhanging crack which is located about 90' right and around the corner from *Boom Boom Room.*   FA: Hank Levine and Dag Kolsrud, December 1978.

1006 **CRYSTAL CALISTHENICS** 5.10a ★   Climb a crack left of a black streak, and traverse right past a bolt to a dihedral and ledge. From the ledge climb up and left along a crystal ridge and past a bolt to a shallow crack.   FA: Herb Laeger, Charles Cole and Hank Levine, April 1978.

1007 **THE GOOD BOOK** 5.9   This climbs up to the ledge mentioned in route #1006, then climbs a huge, left leaning dihedral.   FA: Kevin Powell and Alan Roberts, 1982.

COWBOY CRAGS

These slabs lie up and right of Saddle Rocks. Map, page 288.

1008 **CLING PEACHES** 5.9 ★★   Start at a big pine tree, climb up a flake to a bolt, and climb up and left past another bolt to an arching thin crack.   FA: Randy Vogel, Matt Cox and Steve Van Meter, 1976.

1009 **NO BIGGY** 5.10b ★   (serious) Climb straight up past the first bolt on *Cling Peaches*. One more bolt and poor nuts protect this long pitch.   FA: Randy Vogel, 1976.

1010 **IMMUNO REACTION** 5.10a ★   This climbs a crack over a small roof 40' left of *Wisest Crack,* and continues up a dihedral to the top.   FA: Brain Povolny and Todd Gordon, November 1984.

1011 **WISEST CRACK** 5.7 ★★★   This climbs a very clean crack in a dihedral to the top.   FA: Matt Cox and Randy Vogel, 1976.

1012 **BABY FAE** 5.10c ★★   This climbs the face right of *Wisest Crack* past two bolts.   FA: Dave Evans, Charles Cole, Todd Gordon and Brian Povolny, November 1984.

Spencer Lennard on Brain Death – Comic Book Area

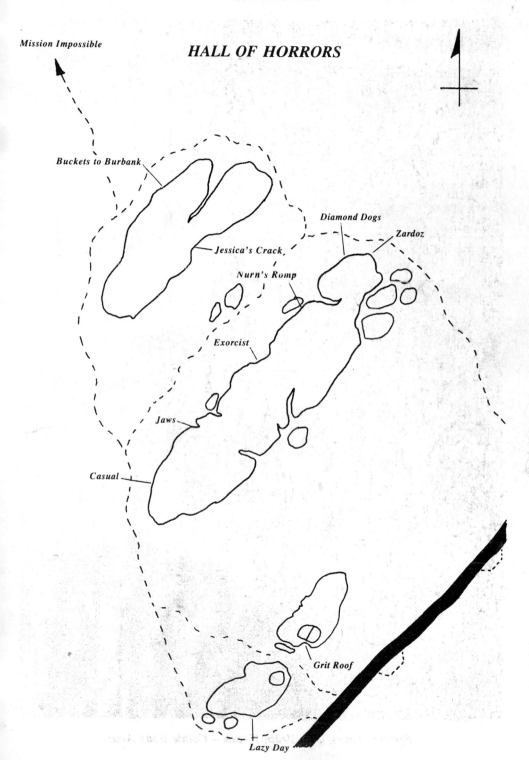

Mission Impossible

HALL OF HORRORS

Buckets to Burbank

Diamond Dogs

Zardoz

Jessica's Crack

Nurn's Romp

Exorcist

Jaws

Casual

Grit Roof

Lazy Day

HALL OF HORRORS

This fine area is located just west of the Sheep Pass Loop Road, where you park for Saddle Rocks. Map, page 295.

The following routes lie on the southern-most rock, closest to the road.

1013 LAZY DAY 5.7 ★★   FA: Jim Wilson, Mike Kaeser and Phil Warrender, November 1971.

1014 PERHAPS 5.9   FA: Dave Wonderly and Jeff Elgar, October 1983.

1015 DOG DAY AFTERNOON 5.10b ★★★   This route lies opposite *Grit Roof,* and on the Lazy Day rock. Five bolts protect good, steep face climbing.   FA: Dave Houser and Charles Cole, February 1979.

1016 GRIT ROOF 5.10c ★★   FA: Tobin Sorenson, Rick Accomazzo and Jim Wilson, December 1973.

1017 GLUMPIES 5.9   FA: Mike Pope and Hank Levine, 1974.

1018 ZARMOG THE DRAGON MAN 5.10a ★   FA: Jim Wilson and Bill Squires, January 1974.

1019 QUIVERING LIPS 5.8   FA: Matt Cox, Dave Evans, Gary Ayres, Spencer Lennard and Allan Lennard, November 1974.

HALL OF HORRORS – EAST FACE (seen from Sheep Pass Loop Road)

HALL OF HORRORS – EAST WALL (West Face)

The main "Hall" lies west of the formation that is next to the road. Most of the established routes lie within the canyon formed by two long domes. Map, page 295.

1020 ZARDOZ 5.8 ★★ (runout)   FA: Matt Cox and Shawn Curtis, 1974.

1021 LICKETY SPLITS 5.7 ★★★ (upper face unprotected)   FA: Gary Ayres and Steve Skinner, November 1974.

1022 DIAMOND DOGS 5.10a ★★★   FA: Jim Wilson and Gib Lewis, November 1974.

1023 UNCERTAINTLY PRINCIPAL 5.9+   FA: Milt Strickler, Dean Parker and Ben Valdez, December 1980.

1024 NURN'S ROMP 5.8 ★★   FA: Dave Evans and Mike Raab, November 1974.

1025 DOUBLE JEOPARDY 5.10c ★★   FA: Dave Evans, Todd Gordon, Charle Cole, Jim Angione and Margy Floyd, January 1985.

1026 EXORCIST 5.10a ★★★★   FA: Tobin Sorenson, Dick Shockley, Jim Wilson and Dean Fidelman, February 1974.

1027 IT 5.9   FA: Dick Shockley, Tobin Sorenson and Jim Wilson, March 11974.

1028 THAT 5.10b   FA: Mike Graham and John Bachar, November 1974.

1029 CAT ON A HOT TIN ROOF 5.10c   FA: Paul Roseman and Rob Mulligan, September 1985.

1030 WHAT 5.8   FA: unknown

1031 AERO SPACE 5.10a   FA: Matt Cox, 1974.

1032 THIN AIR 5.9   FA: Matt Cox, 1974.

1033 BUENOS AIRES 5.10a ★   FA: Pat Cooper and Dick Richardson.

1034 JAWS 5.6 ★★★   FA: Dave Jones, November 1975.

1035 CASUAL 5.9 ★   FA: Dick Richardson and Pat Cooper, 1974.

1036 HEMROIDIC TERROR 5.7 ★   FA: Matt Cox and Dave Evans, November 1974.

HALL OF HORRORS – WEST WALL (East Face)

1037 JESSICA'S CRACK 5.6   Almost directly across from *Exorcist* is a short hand crack on a knobby face.   FA: Dave Evans, December 1974.

1038 RAY'S CAFE 5.10a (loose and short) This loose crack lies about 80' right of *Jessica's Crack*. Climb up a loose hand crack, traverse left under a loose roof, and up a finger crack to top.   FA: Jessica, Charles Cole and Gib Lewis, 1981.

1039 FIRST ELEVEN 5.10c   This route lies 150' right of *Jesscica's Crack*. Approach via a hidden corridor which lies behind the main east face. This route climbs a left leaning, flared crack, with jugs on the face. The crux is reaching a bush in the crack.   FA: Rob Mulligan and Paul Roseman, February 1985.

around side to descend

descent

1020

1021

1022

leap across to descend

chimney behind

1023

1024

1025

1026

1027

1028

1029

1030

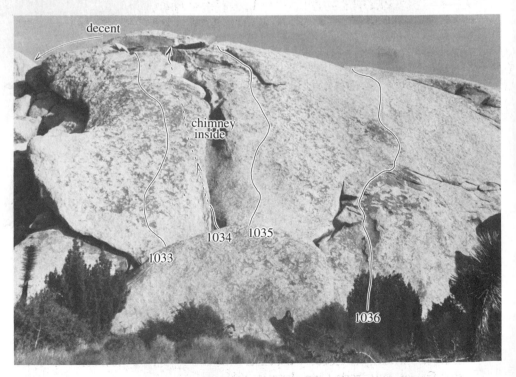

HALL OF HORRORS

HALL OF HORRORS – WEST WALL *(West Face)*

This steep wall has two obvious horizontal cracks running across it and is full of large buckets.

1040 HOLDS TO HOLLYWOOD 5.4   FA: Todd Swain and Paul Trapani, March 1985.

1041 LEDGES TO LAUNDALE 5.10a ★   FA: Todd Swain and Dan Wirth, March 1985.

1042 BUCKETS TO BURBANK 5.8 ★   FA: Matt Cox, Dave Evans and Darrell Hensel, November 1975.

1043 PULLUPS TO PASADENA 5.10c   FA: Todd Swain and Dan Wirth, March 1985.

KING DOME

This is the large rock which lies about 250 yards northwest of the west wall of the Hall of Horrors. All known routes lie on the east face. Map, page 295.

1044 AZTEC TWOSTEP 5.7   This route starts just left of the chimney system left of *Arturo's Special*. Climb up a crack for 30' and move right up another crack, exiting left where it fades at the top.   FA: Jonny Woodward, January 1983.

1045 ARTURO'S SPECIAL 5.8 ★   This face route climbs the left margin of the main face of King Dome. Three bolts protect the climbing which lies just right of a deep crack/chimney.   FA: unknown, 1978.

1046 MISSION IMPOSSIBLE 5.11b ★★★   This improbable line climbs the center of the main face on knobs. The running start and jump to the first knob is the crux; its difficulty is probably dependent on the height of the climber.   FA: Bob Gaines and Charle Cole, January 1980.

1047 TRASHMAN ROOF 5.9 ★   This is the short roof crack which lies at the base of the center of the main face of King Dome.   FA: unknown, 1974.

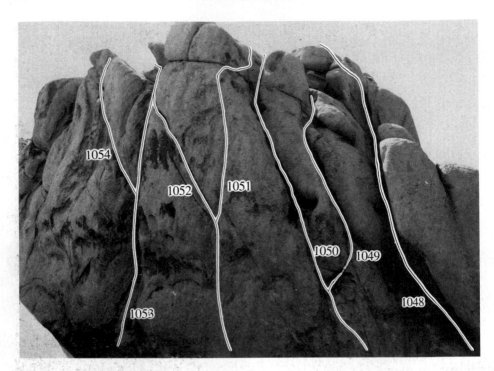

CAVE CORRIDOR

Cave Corridor is located about .6 mile northeast of the Hall of Horrors/Saddle Rocks Parking Area. A large parking area on the right (south) side of Sheep Pass Loop Road is located just next to the rocks. This parking area is used for a trailhead for the Ryan Mountain Trail. (Ryan Mountain is the large hill upon which Saddle Rocks lie.)

Most of the climbing is located on the two rocks which form a narrow canyon just south of the parking lot.

CAVE CORRIDOR – SOUTH SIDE

1048 RESURRECTION 5.7   FA: Bob Dominick and Chris Gonzalez, May 1976.

1049 UNWED MUDDERS 5.7   FA: Bob Dominick, Diana Duham, Ron Tharp, Cliff Ketcham, Melanie Killian and Craig Heinselman, November 1978.

1050 LUST WE FORGET 5.9   FA: Bob Dominick, Chris Gonzalez and John Wolfe, November 1978.

1051 Y KNOT 5.10b ★   FA: Charles Cole and Dave Wonderly, October 1983.

1052 WORKOUT AT THE Y 5.9+ ★   FA: Charles Cole, Herb Laeger, Dick Saum and Steven Anderson, 1982.

1053 REJUVENATION 5.6   FA: John Wolfe and Mona Wolfe, May 1976.

1054 WHAT'S LEFT 5.9   FA: Chris Gonzalez and John Wolfe, June 1976.

1055 CHOCOLATE CHIPS 5.9   This route is on the west face, around and right of *Resurrection.* (two bolts)   FA: Dave Houser and Charles Cole, February 1979.

1056 ROUTE 1056 5.9+   This face climb is just left of the southwest corner and right of *Chocolate Chips.* Climb past five bolts to a 2-bolt belay.   FA: Kurt Smith, Dave Hague and Mart Hirt, 1983.

1057   1058   1059

CAVE CORRIDOR – NORTH SIDE

The following routes lie on the north formation which forms the Corridor.

1057 CARAMEL CRUNCH 5.10a   FA: unknown. FFA: Dennis Richards, Charles Cole, Dave Houser, Herb Laeger and Eve Uiga, February 1979.

1058 BANANA SPLITS 5.10d ★★   FA: Cole, Houser and Laeger, February 1979.

1059 ROCKY ROAD 5.10d ★   FA: Cole and Houser, February 1979.

1060 ROUTE 1060 5.11b   FA: Jon Lonne and Dave Ohlsen.

CAVE CORRIDOR – NORTH SIDE

JUNK CLUMP

This clump of rocks lies southeast of Cave Corridor.

1061 SOMA 5.8   This 2-bolt face route lies on the grainy southwest face of Junk Clump. Finish up a chimney.   FA: Alan Nelson and Janine Rubinfier, 1984.

1062 BIG BROTHER 5.9   A short distance left of *Soma,* follow a right diagonalling groove past one bolt to the upper chimney on that route.   FA: Nelson and Rubinfier, 1984.

SHEEP PASS CAMPGROUND

Sheep Pass Campground lies about ¾ mile further east of Cave Corridor along the Sheep Pass Loop Road. This is a group campground. A road leads about ⅓ mile off the Sheep Pass Loop Road to the the campground.

TIMELESS VOID CLUMP

Just south of campsite #3 is a boulder with three problems on its west face. West of this boulder is a short wall with several problems. Left of this is an east facing wall.

1063 VAINO'S RENEGADE LEAD 5.10a   This is a right facing corner. The crux is at a steep section. RP's are handy.   FA: Hans Lippuner and Vaino Kodas, 1981.

1064 BULLOCKS FASHION CENTER 5.8   This route is on a wall left and behind *This Puppy.* Follow a lieback crack which is located to the left of a block in the center of the face.   FA: Kodas and Lippuner, 1981.

1065 THIS PUPPY 5.6   Climb a crack/flake up and right to a steep thin crack with jugs.   FA: Mike Beck and John Yeggy, December 1981.

1066 HOLY CROSS 5.10a   On the west side of Timeless Void Clump (the east side of the guly behind campsite #2) is this obvious short crack that leads to a horizontal crack.   FA: Mike Beck and Hans Lippuner, November 1982.

1067 TIPPLES IN RIME 5.10a (TR)   Thirty feet left of *Ripples in Time* climb an arête/face to a small roof; continue up, face climbing to the top.   FA: Mike Beck, November 1982.

1068 RIPPLES IN TIME 5.6   Climb up a face to a finger crack just left of the notch in the gully behind campsite #2.   FA: Mike Beck and others, November 1982.

1069 TURKEY TERROR 5.9 (TR)   Walk south from campsite #1 through a pass. Southeast of the pass is a small buttress. This route climbs the south face of this buttress.   FA: lots of people, November 1982.

1070 PUMPKIN PIE 5.8   This route climbs a thin crack 15' right of *Turkey Terror.*   FA: Hans Lippuner and others, November 1982.

1071 PRIME TIME 5.10a (TR)   From campsite #1, one can see a vertical arête about halfway between the pass to the south and the summit to the southwest. Climb directly up the arête past a partially detached knifeblade block near the top.   FA: Alan Nelson and others, November 1982.

1072 HOB NOB 5.6   An obvious wall with several cracks in it can be seen southwest of campsite #1. Climb the second crack from the right.   FA: Mike Beck and Kim Lathrop, December 1982.

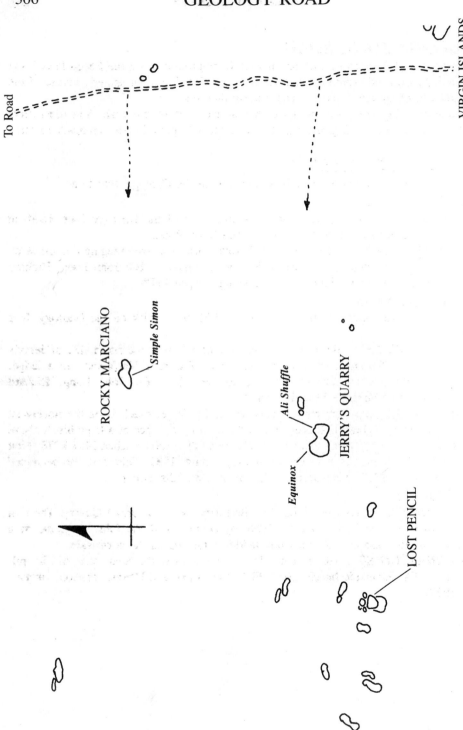

VIRGIN ISLANDS

To Road

ROCKY MARCIANO

Simple Simon

Ali Shuffle

JERRY'S QUARRY

Equinox

LOST PENCIL

LOST PENCIL AREA

GEOLOGY TOUR ROAD

Approximately 2½ miles east of Sheep Pass Campground along the Sheep Pass Loop Road a dirt road heads south. This is the Geology Tour Road, so named because of the self-guided geology tour which proceeds down this road.

Several climbing areas are located both east and west of this road. You must drive about 3¾ miles south along the road to reach spots to park for the approach to these areas.

LOST PENCIL AREA

This loose conglomeration of rocks lie to the west of the Geology Tour Road.

ROCKY MARCIANO

This formation is located approximately ⅔ mile west of the Geology Tour Road, at about the 3.1 mile mark south of the Sheep Pass Loop Road.

1073 SIMPLE SIMON 5.11c ★★★   This route climbs an overhanging thin crack on the very overhanging east face of Rocky Marciano.   FA: John Long, Richard Harrison, Mike Lechlinski and Mike Waugh, April 1978.

JERRY'S QUARRY

Jerry's Quarry lies about ¾ mile west of the 3.75 mile mark on the Geology Tour Road.

1074 ALI SHUFFLE 5.10b ★★   This crack climb lies on the north side of Jerry's Quarry. An S-shaped crack on the left side of a large block ends on a ledge. Above climb a squeeze chimney up to the left.   FA: John Long, Richard Harrison and Mike Lechlinski, April 1978.

1075 EQUINOX 5.12d ★★★★★   This wonderful finger crack is on the northwest side of Jerry's Quarry. It goes up and then left up the face of a large block above the talus.   FA: Dennis Johnson, 1972. FFA (TR): John Bachar, May 1978. First lead: Tony Yaniro, after rehearsals and top roping, 1981. This route has been lead on sight, in 1983, when Jerry Moffat made a no-falls ascent.

LOST PENCIL

This balanced pillar of rock lies about ½ mile further west of Jerry's Quarry. The first ascent of the Lost Pencil was made in 1956, by Don Cornell and John Merriam, via a bolt ladder on the east side. Another bolt ladder is located on the north side.

1076 INDIAN GIVER 5.10c ★★★   This route climbs the west face of the pillar.   FA: Riverside bunch, 1967. FFA: Jon Lonne and Dennis Johnson, January 1977.

Jonny Woodward on Equinox

Rob Raker leading Indian Giver

EAST VIRGIN ISLANDS

VIRGIN ISLANDS

VIRGIN ISLANDS and EAST VIRGIN ISLANDS

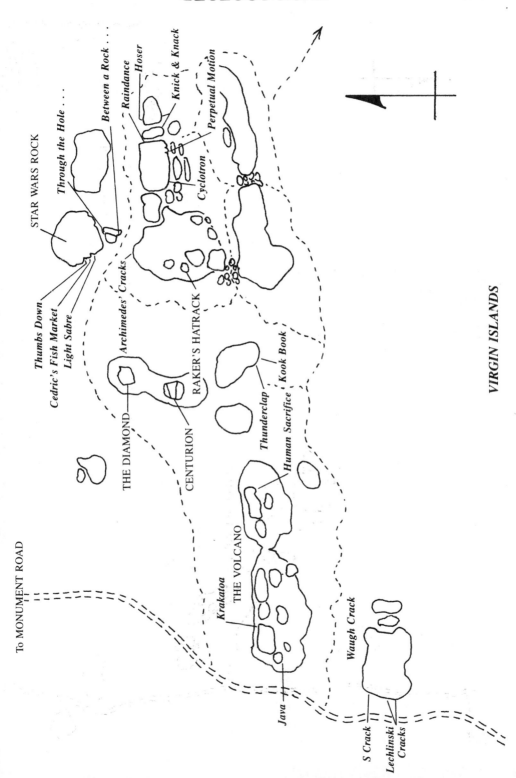

STAR WARS ROCK

Between a Rock . . . .

Raindance

Hoser

Knick & Knack

Perpetual Motion

Through the Hole . . . .

Cyclotron

Thumbs Down

Cedric's Fish Market

Light Sabre

Archimedes' Cracks

RAKER'S HATRACK

THE DIAMOND

CENTURION

Thunderclap

Kook Book

Human Sacrifice

Krakatoa

THE VOLCANO

To MONUMENT ROAD

Java

Waugh Crack

S Crack

Lechlinski Cracks

VIRGIN ISLANDS

VIRGIN ISLANDS AREA

About ¼ mile further south on the Geology Tour Road from the parking spot for the Lost Pencil Area (4 miles south of the Sheep Pass Loop Road) are several piles of rocks to the east. These are the Virgin Islands. About 1¼ mile further east of these are the East Virgin Islands.

The formation furthest to the south has two parallel crack/flakes on the west face; these are the **Lechlinski Cracks.**

1077 RIGHT LECHLINSKI CRACK 5.9 ★   FA: unknown

1078 LEFT LECHLINSKI CRACKS 5.9 ★   FA: unknown

1079 S CRACK 5.11a ★   FA: unknown

1080 WAUGH CRACK 5.10b ★★   FA: Mike Waugh and others

1081 ROBERTS CRACK 5.9 ★   This climbs the left hand thin crack.   FA: Alan Roberts, Bob Harrington and Joe Rousek, 1984.

1082 KIDDIE CORNER 5.9   Climbs a nice 30' long dihedral hidden down low.   FA: Bob Harrington and Alan Roberts, 1984.

THE VOLCANO

This large rubble pile is northeast of the formation with the Lechlinski Cracks. Map, page 311.

1083 JAVA 5.9+   This is the chimney/slot just above the Volcano Boulder. It is just west of the large summit boulder.   FA: Tony Yaniro and Vaino Kodas, 1981.

1084 KRAKATOA 5.9   This route climbs a flake/crack/chimney system on the north side of the large summit block.

VOLCANO BOULDER

1085 HOT LAVA 5.11a ★   FA: Vaino Kodas and Tony Yaniro, 1981.

1086 OBSIDIAN 5.12   (need small wires)   FA: Yaniro and Kodas, 1981.

1087 MAGMA 5.11c (TR)   FA: Yaniro and Kodas, 1981.

1088 HUMAN SACRIFICE 5.11c   This climbs an overhanging hand and fist crack on the southeast face of the summit boulder on the adjacent rubble pile.   FA: Yaniro and Kodas, 1981.

The following two routes lie on the south end of a rubble pile north east of the Volcano. Map, page 311.

1089 THUNDERCLAP 5.10a (***Direct Finish*** 5.10d)   FA: Alan Nelson (TR), October 1982.

1090 KOOK BOOK 5.10c   FA: Alan Nelson and Scott Lewis, October 1982.

East of Volcano about 400 yards are a conglomeration of rubble piles. In the midst of this is a high, level valley. Two approaches are possible into this valley (see photo). On the northwest side of these rubble piles is a pillar called Raker's Hatrack.

1091 RAKER'S BLARING HAT RACK 5.10d ★★   This face climb acends the northwest side of the pillar, up a left leaning dike system and past a black knob to the top. Rappel off—with no anchors—by stringing a rope over the top.   FA: unknown

1092 EDGE OF THE KNIFE 5.8 ★   This climbs the northeast arête of the pillar, with no protection.   FA: unknown

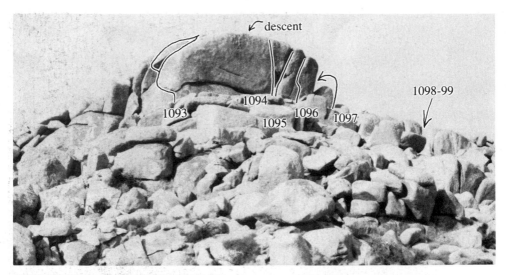

PERPETUAL MOTION WALL

This wall lies on the north side of the high valley mentioned previously. Map, page 311.

1093 CYCLOTRON 5.8 to 5.10d   (The entry move is height dependent.) Turn roof on the left (5.10c), or to the right (5.7).   FA: Tony Yaniro and Vaino Kodas, 1981.

1094 PERPETUAL MOTION 5.10d ★★★★   FA: Kodas and Yaniro, 1981.

1095 GROSS CHIMNEY 5.10a   FA: unknown

1096 I EAT CANNIBALS 5.10d ★   FA: Tony Yaniro, 1982.

1097 RAINDANCE 5.8   Climb the overhanging corner to the top of the Perpetual Motion Wall.   FA: Mike Beck and Alan Bell.

The next two routes lie in the corridor about 75' east of the Perpetual Motion Wall.

1098 KNICK 5.10a   Climbs a dihedral on the west (left) side of the corridor.   FA: Vaino Kodas and Toney Yaniro, 1981.

1099 KNACK 5.10c ★★   This is the finger crack on the right (east) side of the corridor.   FA: Yaniro and Kodas.

North through the corridor leads to an open area. This forms the north side of the Perpetual Motion Rubble Pile. Map, page 311.

1100 LEAN TWO (left 5.8; right 5.10; both 5.9)   These twin cracks lie east on the north side of the Perpetual Motion Piles.   FA: Rob Muchnicki and Vaino Kodas, 1982.

1101 HOSER 5.6   This is a right facing corner located to the right of *Lean Two*.   FA: Rob Muchnicki, 1982.

1102 LEFT ARCHIMEDES' CRACK 5.10a   This route is the left hand crack of two short cracks directly opposite (south) of route #1109, and they lie on the western end of the north side of the Perpetual Motion Rubble Pile.   FA: Tony Yaniro, Vaino Kodas and Gregg Davis, 1981.

1103 RIGHT ARCHIMEDES' CRACK 5.9   FA: Yaniro, Kodas and Davis, 1981.

Rob Raker starting Perpetual Motion

STAR WARS ROCK

This rock lies north of the Perpetual Motion Rubble Pile and is easily distinguished by its overhanging south face and the presence of a large split boulder to its south. Map, page 311.

1104 THUMBS DOWN LEFT 5.9 ★★   FA: Konrad Hughen, Alan Bell and Vaino Kodas, 1982.

1105 CEDRIC'S DEEP SEA FISH MARKET 5.10d ★   FA: Vaino Kodas, Toivo Kodas and Alan Bell, 1982.

1106 LIGHT SABRE 5.10b ★★   FA: Vaino Kodas, Toivo Kodas and Tony Yaniro, 1981.

1107 APOLLO 5.12b (TR) (no fixed protection)   FA: Dan Goodwin, 1985.

1108 THROUGH THE HOLE AND UP THE WALL 5.2   FA: Vaino Kodas, 1982.

1109 BETWEEN A ROCK AND A HARD PLACE 5.10b   FA: Tony Yaniro, Toivo Kodas and Vaino Kodas, 1981.

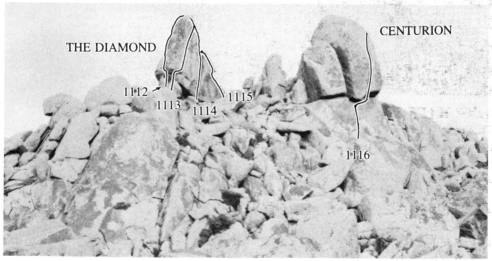

DIAMOND CLUMP

The Diamond Clump is the large pile of rocks which lies west of Star Wars Rock and the Perpetual Motion Piles. Two large blocks sit atop the piles. The first (northern) block is the Diamond; the southern block is the Centurion. Map, page 311.

1110 GEMSTONER 5.10a   (2 bolts)   FA: Alan Nelson and Mike Beck, October 1982.

1111 SPARKLE 5.8 (TR)   FA: Beck and Nelson, 1982.

1112 TEENAGE ENEMA 5.9 (TR)   FA: Beck and Nelson.

1113 KILLER PUSSY 5.11a (TR)   FA: Nelson and Beck.

1114 NURSES IN BONDAGE 5.9 (TR)   FA: Nelson

1115 CLEARASIL (left 5.8; center 5.7, right 5.2) (TR)   FA: Mike Beck, Alan Nelson and Denise Cox, October 1982.

1116 CENTURION 5.10d   FA: Tony Yaniro and Vaino Kodas, 1981.

EAST VIRGIN ISLANDS

EAST VIRGIN ISLANDS FROM PERPETUAL MOTION WALL

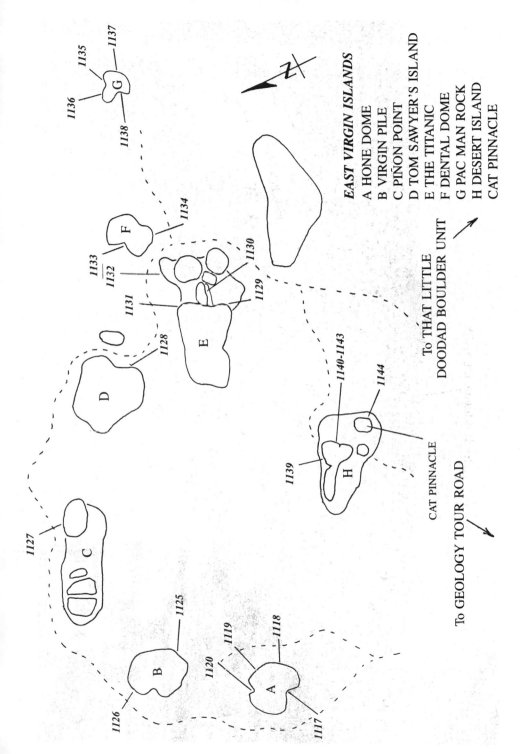

EAST VIRGIN ISLANDS

A HONE DOME
B VIRGIN PILE
C PIÑON POINT
D TOM SAWYER'S ISLAND
E THE TITANIC
F DENTAL DOME
G PAC MAN ROCK
H DESERT ISLAND
CAT PINNACLE

To THAT LITTLE
DOODAD BOULDER UNIT

CAT PINNACLE

To GEOLOGY TOUR ROAD

EAST VIRGIN ISLANDS

The East Virgin Islands lie almost directly east (and a little bit south) of the Virgin Islands. They lie about one mile east of the Geology Tour Road. Map, page 321.

HONE DOME

Map, page 321.

1117 HAWKS RETREAT 5.10a   FA: Mike Beck and Mike Guargino, December 1982.

1118 V CRACKS 5.8 (both)   FA: unknown

1119 NO HOLDS BARRED 5.9+ (TR) Climbs the face between #1118 and 1120.   FA: Beck and Guardino, 1982.

1120 SAME AS IT EVER WAS 5.9   FA: Beck and Guardino, 1982.

VIRGIN PILE

Map, page 321.

1121 ONE WAY UP 5.7   FA: Alan Nelson, December 1982.

1122 GNARLY 5.10a (TR)   FA: Mike Beck and Alan Nelson, December 1982.

1123 RAD 5.9 (TR)   FA: Nelson and Beck, 1982.

1124 BITCHIN' 5.10b (TR)   FA: Nelson and Beck

1125 EASY OFF 5.6   FA: Alan Nelson, 1982.

1126 BUSTER HYMEN 5.9   This route climbs the left slanting crack which starts near a small roof.   FA: Nelson and Beck, 1982.

PIÑON POINT

1127 DEFIBRILLATION 5.10a Climbs a short ugly crack on the back side of a boulder. FA: Vaino Kodas, 1981.

TOM SAWYER'S ISLAND

1128 CARRIBEAN CRUISE 5.11c FA: Tony Yaniro and Vaino Kodas, 1981.

THE TITANIC

Map, page 321.

1129 *SINBAD THE SAILOR* 5.10c (TR) FA: Alan Nelson and others, November 1982.

1130 *CASTAWAY* 5.11c Climbs the roof crack formed by split boulders. FA: Vaino Kodas and Tony Yaniro, 1981.

1131 *DOS DEDOS* 5.4 Climbs a low angled crack above and to the right of *Castaway*. FA: Alan Nelson, November 1982.

1132 *SCOPE & HOPE* 5.10b Climbs a crack on the lower northeast side of Tom Sawyer's Island. FA: Mike Beck, Hans Lippuner and Alan Nelson, November 1982.

DENTAL DOME

Map, page 321.

1133 SURREALISTIC COLGATE 5.10d (TR) Climbs the dihedral.   FA: Vaino Kodas, Rob Muchnicki, Alan Bell and Konrad Hughen, 1982.

1134 BURIED TREASURE 5.11c A very thin crack on the south face of Dental Dome.   FA: Tony Yaniro and Vaino Kodas, 1981.

PAC MAN ROCK

This small rock lies on the hillside about 150 yards east of Dental Dome. Map, page 321.

1135 WIND SPRINT 5.9 Climbs a leaning offwidth on the north side of the rock.   FA: Tony Yaniro and Vaino Kodas, 1981.

1136 FLAKES OF GRASP 5.10c (TR)   Ascends right facing flakes just right of route #1135.   FA: Mike Beck, November 1982.

1137 SHIP WRECKED 5.12+ (boulder problem) This is the thin crack directly opposite *Marathon Crack* (which passes all the way through the formation).   FA: Yaniro and Kodas, 1981.

1138 THE MARATHON CRACK 5.12 This is the thin crack on the southwest side of Pac Man Rock.   FA: Kodas and Yaniro, 1981.

DESERT ISLAND
Map, page 321.

1139 LOST AND FOUND 5.7 This rather inobvious route climbs a thin crack just left of the chimney/gully system on the north side of Desert Island.   FA: Rob Muchnicki and John Johnston, November 1982.

1140 THE THUMB 5.6   FA: Muchnicki and Johnston, 1982.

1141 MIDDLE FINGER 5.7   FA: Mike Beck, Denise Brown and Frank Brown, December 1982.

1142 SPLIT MITTEN 5.6   FA: Muchnicki and Johnston, November 1982.

1143 FUMBLERS BELOW THE ROOF 5.10c   FA: Mike Beck, December 1982.

1144

CAT PINNACLE
This is a large flat top boulder just southeast of Desert Island. Map, page 321.

1144 MEMORIAL MEOWZER 5.10c Face climb past two bolts on the southeast face.   FA: Alan Nelson and Mike Beck, December 1982.

THAT LITTLE DOODAD BOULDER UNIT
This boulder lies on the hillside about 200 yard west of Pac Man Rock.

1145 DIKE DA DOODAD 5.10c Climb a dike past two bolts.   FA: Mike Guardir Mike Beck and Doug Munoz, December 1982.

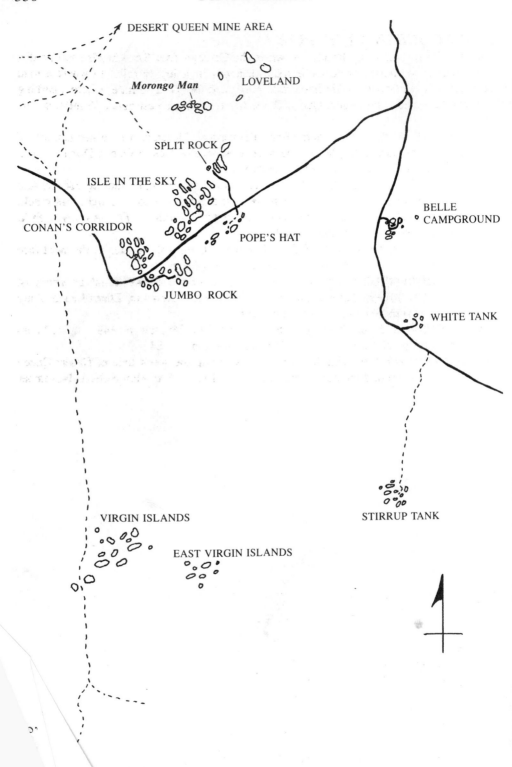

DESERT QUEEN MINE AREA

LOVELAND

Morongo Man

SPLIT ROCK

ISLE IN THE SKY

CONAN'S CORRIDOR

BELLE
CAMPGROUND

POPE'S HAT

JUMBO ROCK

WHITE TANK

VIRGIN ISLANDS

EAST VIRGIN ISLANDS

STIRRUP TANK

DESERT QUEEN MINE AREA

From the Sheep Pass Loop Road, just where the Geology Tour Road heads south, a dirt road heads to the north. Follow this road for approximateley ¾ mile, to where a road splits off right. Follow the right hand fork in the road for about ½ mile, where a parking area will be found. The Desert Queen Dome lies to the northeast about ½ mile, on the hill top.

1146 THIN IS IN 5.9   This route climbs the vertical thin crack which lies just left of a large chimney, lying left of the main west face of Desert Queen Dome.   FA: Mike Guardino and Mike Ayon, January 1983.

1147 MOTHER LODE 5.10a ★★★   This route climbs a right slanting dike system on the west face until a difficult move past a bolt leads to a straight thin crack. At the crack's end, climb up and right to the summit.   FA: unknown. FFA: Guardino and Ayon, January 1983.

1148 GET THE BALANCE RIGHT 5.10 ★★★   Climbs the center of the west face past three bolts.   FA: Vaino Kodas and Diana Leach.

1149 ALL-REET ARÊTE 5.8   Down and right from route #1148, climb an arête past two bolts.   FA: Alan Nelson, Vaino Kodas, Hans Lippuner, Diana Leach, Amy Lippuner and Lori Leach, November 1984.

1150 FACE RACE 5.10a (TR)   Climb the face 15' left of route #1149.   FA: Vaino Kodas, Alan Nelson and Hans Lippuner, November 1984.

1151 RUSH HOUR 5.9   Climb a thin crack/seam on the south face of Desert Queen Dome, just around the corner and right of #1150.   FA: Alan Nelson, November 1984.

To 1155-56

1153

1154

JUMBO ROCKS CAMPGROUND

Although Jumbo Rocks Campground has a fair amount of rock, most of it is very grainy and rough (even by Joshua Tree standards) and few worthwhile climbs have been done here. The entrance to the campground is located approximately 1¾ miles further southeast along the Sheep Pass Loop Road from the Geology Tour Road turnoff. A very sharp turn in the road is encountered just before the campground.

A large east facing escarpment can be seen about ½ mile south of the campground. This cliff has been used by Sierra Club groups for climbing practice and several moderate routes have been established. No records are available which give more specific information.

1152 NOT A HOGAN 5.10a   This route climbs the teepee-shaped crack/cave system on the west face of the formation just north of the campground road, near the end of the loop.   FA: John Long and others, 1979.

JUMBO ROCKS CORRIDOR

From the very end of the Jumbo Rocks Campground Loop, a narrow corridor can be seen 100 yards to the northwest. Many cracks lie on the left (west) side of the corridor. Map, page 330.

1153 FINGERS OF FRENZY 5.12a (TR)   On the left side of the corridor, just before it severely narrows is a dihedral system. To the right of the dihedral is a right diagonalling thin crack. Climb this until another crack/ramp diagonalling left is reached. Follow this to a vertical hand crack and the top.   FA: unknown, 1980.

1154 HANDSAW 5.10b   This route climbs the dihedral mentioned in the previous description. From the top of the dihedral, climb a hand crack to the top.   FA: Keith Cunning and Ed Kaufer, 1980.

1155 CARNAGE 5.10c   Walk into the narrow part of the corridor about 50-60 feet, passing several crack systems on the left wall. *Carnage* takes a hand crack which lies just left of *Mere Illusion.* It is loose at the bottom; a concave section about 25' up is the crux, and the rock improves above.   FA: Cunning and Kaufer, 1980.

1156 MERE ILLUSION 5.11a ★★   Near the deepest section of the corridor is this route. Follow steep face climbing past three bolts until a move up and left gives access to a crack system. Climb the crack until an exit left is necessary to reach the top.   FA: Cunning and Kaufer, 1980.

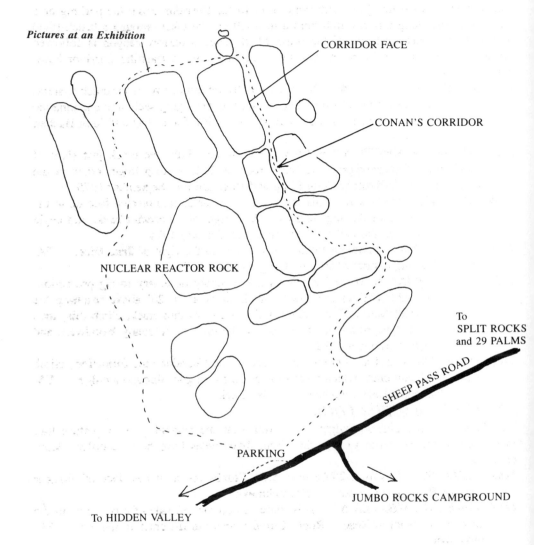

Pictures at an Exhibition

CORRIDOR FACE

CONAN'S CORRIDOR

NUCLEAR REACTOR ROCK

To
SPLIT ROCKS
and 29 PALMS

SHEEP PASS ROAD

PARKING

JUMBO ROCKS CAMPGROUND

To HIDDEN VALLEY

CONAN'S CORRIDOR

This conglomeration of rocks lies almost directly acros the road (north) from the entrance to Jumbo Rocks Campground. Unlike Jumbo Rocks Campground, the rock tends to be quite good. Several excellent crack climbs are located on the east face of the Corridor Face.

CORRIDOR FACE

Corridor Face is situated just north (and through) the Corridor. From the parking area walk northeast along a nature trail until a turn left can be taken through a brush-filled valley. At the northwest end of the brush-filled valley a narrow canyon is followed north, through Conan's Corridor, until the widening valley reveals the Corridor Face. Map, page 334.

1157 SPIDERMAN 5.10a ★★   This route climbs the left of two major crack systems on the left side oft the Coridor Face. A short overhanging section is encountered near the bottom. Protection is difficult above.   FA: John Long and John Bachar, September 1975.

1158 COLORADO CRACK 5.9 ★★★★   This route climbs the crack just right of *Spiderman.* Excellent grey and black rock leads to a steep finger crack at the top.   FA: Billy Westbay, John Long and Hugh Burton, September 1975.

1159 TRUE DICE 5.10a ★★   This serious lead climbs an unprotected face up to the center of three right slanting cracks which lie right of *Colorado Crack,* and begin about half-way up the face.   FA: John Bald, January 1974.

1160 GEM 5.8 ★★   Climb an obvious hand crack to the right of *True Dice.*   FA: John Bald, Hugh Burton and John Long, January 1974.

1161 WINTER WINE 5.10c ★★★   RP's are probably necessary to rig protection. Just to the right of *Gem* is a crack which starts about 20' above reaching the ground. Start at *Gem* and face climb right to a short thin crack; climb this, then go right to the base of a crack that leads to the top.   FA: Jonny Woodward and Randy Vogel, November 1982.

1162 RUFF STUFF 5.10c   On the north face of the Corridor Face formation, climb a steep incipient crack which turns to hand size as it goes through a bulge.   FA: Louis Sheppard, Hans Lippuner and Mike Beck.

NUCLEAR REACTOR ROCK

This large rock lies almost straight north from near the beginning of the nature trail mentioned in the approach to Corridor Face. Two routes have been recorded. Map, page 334.

1163 WE'LL GET THEM LITTLE P'S 5.8   Climbs the southwest face of Nuclear Reactor Rock past one bolt.   FA: unknown

1164 NUKE THE WHALES 5.9   This route lies on the left side of a corridor on the east side of Nuclear Reactor Rock. Climb a finger to fist crack to the top.   FA: unknown

1165 PICTURES AT AN EXHIBITION 5.10a   This dike system lies on the north end of the formation just west of the Corridor Face formation and directly north of Nuclear Reactor Rock. Climb past three bolts to the top.   FA: Mike Paul, Todd Gordon and others, October 1978.

Two parallel cracks lie to the left of route #1165; the left is 5.6 and the right is 5.8.

THE WEDGE

THE WEDGE

This large triangular rock is .8 miles past Jumbo Rocks Campground and about 350 yards north of the Sheep Pass Loop Road.

1166 WEDGE 5.4   This route climbs the chimney on the northwest side of the Wedge. The chimney ends on a ledge below the top, and a bolt protects face moves to the summit.   FA: Jack Davis, Bruce Fortine and Rod Smith, June 1956.

1167 HEX 5.7   Climb a hand crack on the west face to the top.   FA: Chris Gonzalez and Dave Stahl, September 1976.

LIVE OAK PICNIC AREA   POPE'S HAT

LIVE OAK AREA

Approximately 1.2 miles northeast on the Sheep Pass Loop Road past Jumbo Rocks Campground is a road which heads north to Split Rocks and south to Live Oak Picnic Area. The road heading south curves to the southwest and gives access to the Pope's Hat. The Pope's hat can also be easily reached from the Sheep Pass Loop Road near the one mile mark from Jumbo Rocks Campground. This is about a 200 yard walk from the Sheep Pass Loop Road. Map, page 330.

POPE'S HAT

This distinctive formation has the characteristic shape of what else . . . ?

1168 POPE'S HAT 5.9   Climb the short north face past three bolts.   FA: Don Cornell and Rod Smith, 1956. FFA: John Long, 1976.

1169 TODD SQUAD 5.9   Climb the southeast face of the Pope's Hat, starting above a 30' roof boulder.   FA: Todd Gordon and others, 1985.

1170 PAPAL PLEASER 5.4   From the large boulder at the base of the northeast face scramble up easy slabs to vertical cracks. These are followed to the second horizontal crack. Then, head left, then up and right over a bulge to the top.   FA: Larry DeAngelo and R. Kyle Horst, November 1979.

LIVE OAK PICNIC AREA

Several routes lie on the various short formations around the Picnic Area road. A particularly good boulder problem is *Big Bob's Big Wedge,* which climbs a 30' roof crack.

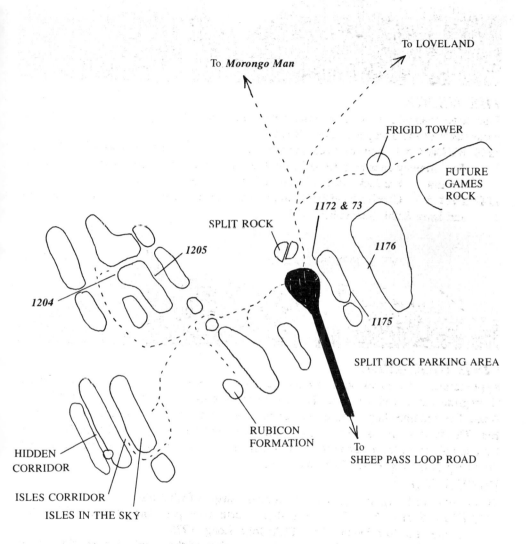

To LOVELAND

To *Morongo Man*

FRIGID TOWER

FUTURE
GAMES
ROCK

1172 & 73

SPLIT ROCK

1205

1176

1204

1175

SPLIT ROCK PARKING AREA

RUBICON
FORMATION

To
SHEEP PASS LOOP ROAD

HIDDEN
CORRIDOR

ISLES CORRIDOR

ISLES IN THE SKY

SPLIT ROCKS AREA

SPLIT ROCKS AREA

Take the marked road which heads north off the Sheep Pass Loop Road at a point 1.2 miles past Jumbo Rocks Campground. This road ends at the Split Rocks Parking Lot about ½ mile northwest of Sheep Pass Loop Road. Map, page 330.

SPLIT ROCKS – EAST PARKING AREA

The following routes lie generally east of the Split Rocks Parking Lot, but within the Split Rocks Area. Map, page 337.

1171 SPLIT ROCKS 5.8   The obvious split boulder north of the parking lot may be climbed via a layback on the east face.   FA: Bob Boyle, 1958.

1172 IN AND OUT 5.9   This route is northeast of the parking lot in an A-shaped alcove left of a large block. Climb the offwidth crack on the left side of an alcove.   FA: John Bald and Clark Jacobs, December 1976

1173 BIG BOY 5.9   This takes the hand crack on the right side of the alcove mentioned in route #1172.   FA: Bald and Jacobs, December 1976.

1174 WORTHY OF IT 5.8   to the right of routes #1172 and 1173, on the northwest corner of the formation, follow flakes up to an obvious roof.   FA: Mike Guardino and others, 1983.

SPLIT ROCK – EAST FACE

The east face of the formation containing routes #1172 to 1174 lies in a small valley.

1175 CLEARED FOR TAKEOFF 5.11a   This is a prominent overhanging crack on the east face and across from route #1176.   FA: Jon Lonne, Herb Laeger and Rick Smith, February 1979.

1176 BLOOD AND CUTS 5.9   The west facing wall of the valley mentioned above has many crack systems. Climb the hand crack 20' left of a left facing corner.   FA: Alan Nelson and Alan Patey, December 1981.

FRIGID TOWER

This large boulder/rock is split along its east-west axis by a chimney which lies directly on the trail from the Split Rock Parking Lot to Future Games Rock. Map, page 337.

1177 PUSS WUSS 5.10a On the north face of Frigid Tower climb a crack to a horizontal slot which accesses the steep face above. Two bolts protect face climbing to another crack that leads to the summit. FA: Hans Lippuner and Mike Beck, 1982.

FUTURE GAMES ROCK

This is the steep north facing face which lies about ¼ mile northeast of the parking lot. Map, page 337.

1178 THERAPEUTIC TYRANNY 5.11a ★★ This is the very thin crack near the left end of the face. A large flared section (the "Pod") is located about 20' up the route. FA: John Long and Mike Lechlinski (TR), December 1978. First lead: Jonny Woodward, 1982.

1179 CONTINUUM 5.8 + ★★★★ This is the fine dogleg crack which leans right at the top. FA: John Long, Mike Lechlinski and Mari Gingery, December 1978.

1180 INVISIBILITY LESSONS 5.9 ★★★★ This is the thin crack that starts behind an oak tree on the right side of the face. FA: Long, Lechlinski and Gingery, December 1978.

1181 SANDBLAST 5.7 This is the short crack to the right of *Invisibility Lessons*. It is sort of loose. FA: Rick Sylvester, January 1983.

1182 CASUAL AFFAIR 5.10d FA: Vaino Kodas and Herb Laeger, September 1985.

SPLIT ROCKS – WEST PARKING AREA

The following routes generally lie to the west of the Split Rocks Parking Lot. Map, page 337.

1183 GRAND CANYON DONKEY TRAIL 5.9+ ★ This face climb is located on the east face of a long wall located about 250 yards southwest of the parking lot. FA: Dave Houser and Jan McCollum, December 1978.

1184 RUBICON 5.10d ★★★★ (*direct start* 5.11+) This excellent thin crack lies on the east face of a very large boulder/rock to the west of the face with *Grand Canyon Donkey Trail*. Climb a hand crack on the right to reach a hand traverse left to the base of this right-arching finger crack. FA: John Bald and Hank Levine, 1976. FFA (TR):John Long and others. First lead: Jon Lonne, Herb Laeger, Rich Smith and Eve Uiga, December 1978.

ISLES IN THE SKY

This formation is about ½ mile southwest of the Split Rocks Parking Lot. Several obvious cracks are located high on the east face. Easy scrambling leads up low angled slabs to a ledge system. Map, page 337.

1185 BEE GEES 5.10d   FA: unknown

1186 NECTAR 5.4   FA: unknown

1187 DEAD BEES 5.10a ★   FA: unknown

1188 DOLPHIN 5.7 ★★   FA: John Long, March 1974.

1189 BIRD OF FIRE 5.10a ★★★   FA: John Long and Ray Ochoa, May 1874.

1190 RITES OF SPRING 5.9   FA: John Long and Mike Jaffe, May 1974.

ISLES CORRIDOR – LEFT (West) SIDE

This narrow corridor has several good cracks on both sides of the corridor. Approach from the left (south) end of the ledge system on Isles In The Sky. Map, page 337.

1191 DESCENT CRACK 5.2   This is the easy crack which can be used for a descent. It is the first crack on the left.   FA: unknown

1192 CRACK #2 5.6   The second crack on the left.   FA: unknown

1193 GROUNDER 5.9   The third crack on the left.   FA: Mike Jaffe, John Bald and Bill Heiman, January 1974.

1194 CRACK #4 5.10c   The fourth crack on the left.   FA: unknown

1195 CRACK #5 5.9+   The fifth crack on the left.   FA: unknown

1196 CRACK #6 5.10a   The sixth crack on the left.   FA: unknown

ISLES CORRIDOR – RIGHT (East) SIDE

1197 CRACK A 5.7+ The first crack on the right   FA: unknown

1198 CRACK B 5.9 The second crack on the right   FA: unknown

1199 MOUBIT 5,10a Third crack on the right.   FA: Mike Jaffe and John Bald, January 1974.

1200 HOUR OF POWER 5.10a Fourth crack on the right.   FA: Matt Cox and John Bald, 1974.

1201 CRACK C 5.10c Fifth crack on the right.   FA: unknown

HIDDEN CORRIDOR

This corridor lies directly west of Isles Corridor; it is spanned by a giant chockstone at the south end. Map, page

1202 WEDLOCK 5.11a On the right (east) side, near the south end, climb a thin crack up to a chockstone.   FA: Tony Yaniro and Vaino Kodas, 1982.

1203 ROUTE 1203 5.10a Climb a right leaning crack system on the left side of the corridor.   FA: unknown

The following routes lie on the formation lying north of the open plain between **Grand Canyon Donkey Trail** and Isles In The Sky. Map, page 337.

1204 ANGULAR MOMENTUM 5.9+ (TR) This obscure route lies on the north face of a corridor capped by a very large rock approximately 300 yards north of Isles In The Sky. Walk up the gully/canyon north of the Isles face, then look right into a narrow corridor with dark brown rock on both sides. Climb the face just right of a rotton crack.   FA: Randy Vogel and Alan Roberts (TR), 1984.

1205 BRITS IN DRAG 5.10b ★★ Fifty yards to the right (east) of the gully mentioned in route #1204 is a very narrow corridor/canyon. Walk into this until it narrows. A two-pitch route lies on the east (left) face. Two bolts protect face climbing to a two-bolt belay. Follow a crack to the top.   FA: Dave Evans and others, 1980.

LOVELAND

This loose conglomeration of large boulders and small formations lies north and northeast of the Split Rocks Parking Area. A ¾ to 1 mile walk northeast of the parking area will take you to Loveland. An alternate approach for some of the climbs is to drive about 1½ miles past the Split Rocks turnoff along the Sheep Pass Loop Road to where a dirt mining road heads north. Hike along the mining road until the main wash is reached, about a 1¼ mile hike. Map, pages 330, 337.

1206 MORONGO MAN 5.11b ★★ This route is technically not in the Loveland area, but is best treated at this point since it lies almost ¾ mile due north of the Split Rocks Parking Area. FA: Jon Lonne, December 1978.

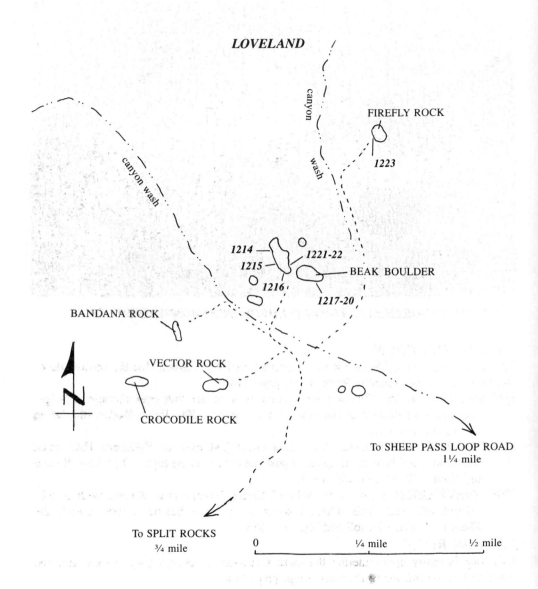

LOVELAND

canyon

wash

FIREFLY ROCK

1223

canyon wash

1214
1215
1221-22
1216
BEAK BOULDER
1217-20

BANDANA ROCK

VECTOR ROCK

N

CROCODILE ROCK

To SHEEP PASS LOOP ROAD
1 ¼ mile

To SPLIT ROCKS
¾ mile

0   ¼ mile   ½ mile

LOOKING NORTHEAST TOWARD LOVELAND FROM SPLIT ROCKS

CROCODILE ROCK

Up the hill and west of Vector Rock is a small enclosed canyon. On the south side of this little canyon is Crocodile Rock. Map, page 344.

1207 B-MOVIE 5.10b Follow a hand crack in a corner that goes through a bulge. There is a small pine at the base of the crack. FA: Vaino Kodas and Diana Leach, January 1983.

1208 CLAIM JUMPER 5.11a Start in a crack just right of *B-Movie*. This crack disappears, and face climbing leads past three bolts to the top. FA: Alan Nelson and Gaute "Tom" Einevoll, 1984.

1209 HEAVY GOLD 5.10a 100' right of *Claim Jumper* is a dihedral with a gold colored left wall. This dihedral starts on a ledge behind a tree. Climb the dihedral. FA: Einevoll and Nelson, 1984.

VECTOR ROCK

This rock is easily upon entering the main Loveland wash as a large corner near the south end of the hillside to the west. Map, page 344.

1210 VECTOR 5.11c ★★★★ This follows the thin, right-arching crack on the left wall of the Vector Rock dihedral. FA: Tony Yaniro and Randy Leavitt, December 1982.

1211 ALL LOIN 5.10c From the base of *Vector,* walk right around the corner and into a corridor. *All Loin* climbs the slightly overhanging finger crack on the left (south) wall. FA: Alan Nelson and Gaute "Tom" Einevoll, 1984.

BANDANA ROCK

This rock lies on the hillside about 200 yards north of the Vector Rock. Map, page 344.

1212 MORE FOOL ME 5.9   This route climbs a hand crack which leads to the top of a pedestal. Follow a clean offwidth up the corner above.   FA: Alan Nelson, Mike Beck and Suzanne Sanbar, January 1983.

1213 SUZANNA'S BANDANA 5.7   To the right of *More Fool Me,* climb up and left on a flake until it is possible to reach a crack that leads up and right to the top.   FA: Mike Beck and Suzanne Sanbar, January 1983.

THE BEAK BOULDER ROCKS

These rocks lie on the hillside to the east (right) of the main wash. The southern formation has a prominent beaked boulder near the southwest side. Map, page 344.

1214 SOMETHING HEINOUS 5.9   100 yards left (north) and down from the Beak Boulder is a west facing wall with some left-slanting cracks. This route climbs the leftmost cracks up to and over a roof before continuing to the top.   FA: Mike Beck and Suzanne Sanbar, January 1983.

1215 GOIN' DOWN THE ROAD FEELIN' BAD 5.10c   50 feet right of *Something Heinous* is a clean left facing thin crack. Face climb or follow a crack on the right up to the leaning thin crack. Follow it to the top.   FA: Nelson, Beck and Sanbar, 1983.

1216 HEAVY SLANDER 5.10a (TR)   50 feet right of route #1214, climb a right leaning, slightly overhanging finger crack/lieback.   FA: Alan Nelson, January 1983.

1217 DESERT QUEEN 5.8   Climb the prominent hand crack on the wall below and to the right of the Beak Boulder.   FA: Alan Nelson, December 1982.

1218 FOR SURE 5.3   100 yards right of the Beak Boulder is an interesting configuration of flakes and boulders. This route climbs the chimney behind the flakes to the left.   FA: Denise Brown and Alan Nelson, January 1983.

1219 TOTALLY TUBULAR 5.8   Behind the flakes and boulders comprising *For Sure* is a totally enclosed, triangular shaped slot/chimney; tunnel up this to the top.   FA: Nelson and Brown, 1983.

1220 SQUEEZE PLAY 5.10a   Climb the overhanging, converging and flared V-slot just outside and right of *Totally Tubular.*

On the backside (north and east) of the Beak Boulder Rocks are three prominent offwidth cracks.

1221 MODERN WARFARE 5.10a   Climb the middle of the three cracks, passing a bulge at the top.   FA: Ray Olsen and Alan Nelson, January 1984.

1222 KAMAKAZE 5.10c   50 feet right of *Modern Warfare,* climb the offwidth in the corner.   FA: Nelson and Olsen, 1983.

FIREFLY ROCK

This rock lies on the hillside across a canyon/wash east of the Beak Boulder Rocks. This rock lies about 150 yards north of an obvious rock with two dikes. Map, page 344.

1223 FIREFLY 5.11b (TR)   Stem and lieback up a left facing, bottom less corner up to a roof about half-way up. Jam the crack above to the top.   FA: unknown

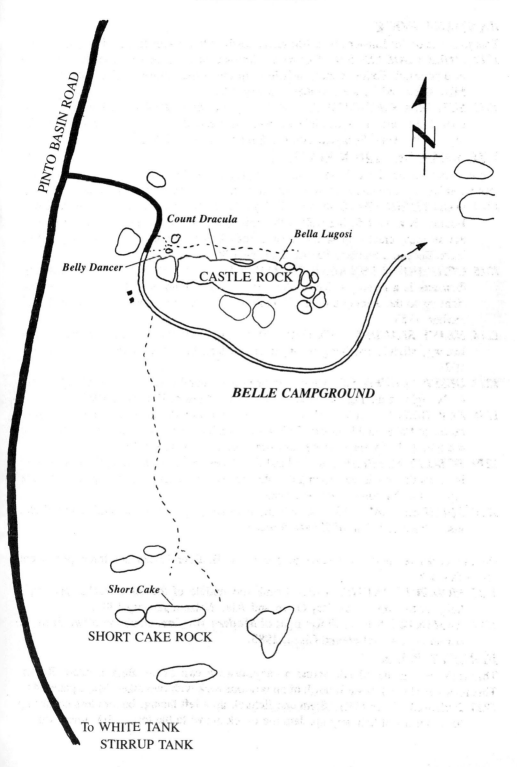

PINTO BASIN ROAD

Count Dracula

Bella Lugosi

Belly Dancer

CASTLE ROCK

BELLE CAMPGROUND

Short Cake

SHORT CAKE ROCK

To WHITE TANK
STIRRUP TANK

BELLE CAMPGROUND

Approximately 3½ miles northeast of the Jumbo Rocks Campground along the Sheep Pass Loop Road, the road takes a sharp turn left (north), becoming Gold Park Road and descending, in eight miles, to 29 Palms. A road also splits off to the south; this is the Pinto Basin Road. A long and beautiful drive along the Pinto Basin Road eventually leads to U.S.10. Although the vast Pinto Basin and surrounding mountains are all part of the Monument, little climbing potential exists.

Belle Campground is located about 1¼ miles south of the Pinto Basin Road from its juncture with the Sheep Pass Loop Road. Most of the recorded climbs lie on the large oblong formation in the middle of the campground, named Castle Rock.

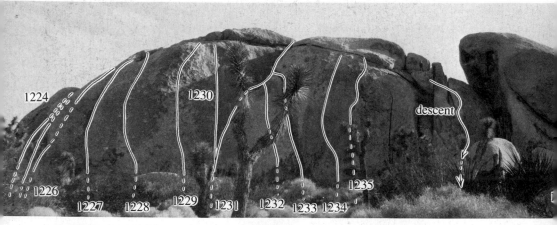

CASTLE ROCK – NORTH FACE

1224 HALF CRACK 5.3   FA: unknown

1225 ONE POINT CRACK 5.4   FA: unknown

1226 TWO POINT CRACK 5.1   FA: unknown

1227 MUSIC BOX 5.8   FA: unknown

1228 BELLA LUGOSI 5.11b ★   FA: Don O'Kelley and Dave Davis, October 1970. FFA (TR): Kevin Powell, 1977. First lead: Craig Fry and Randy Vogel, January 1978.

1229 THAT OLD SOFT SHOE 5.10c ★★   FA: Herb Laeger, Dave Houser, Eve Uiga and Jan McCollum, May 1977.

1230 TRANSYLVANIA TWIST 5.10b   FA: Herb Laeger and Ron Carson, November 1984.

1231 JUNCTION CHIMNEY 5.2   FA: unknown

1232 GROUND FINALE 5.10a   FA: Larry Reynolds and R. Kyle Horst, November 1979.

1233 CHIMNEY SWEEP 5.0   FA: unknown

1234 COUNT DRACULA 5.10d ★★★   FA: Kevin Powell and Darrell Hensel, December 1978.

1235 DIAGNOSTICS 5.6   FA: unknown

1236 BELLY DANCER 5.10d ★★★   FA: Mike Jaffe, Randy Vogel and Dennis Knuckles, April 1977.

CASTLE ROCK – EAST FACE
1237 BONNIE BRAE 5.7   FA: unknown
1238 BUBBA'S TOURIST TRAP 5.9   FA: David Rubine, Martin Wiensley, Sheri
  Levine and Jeff, 1983.

SHORT CAKE ROCK
This formation is about 200 yard south of Castle Rock. It has a prominent dike system
up the middle of the rock. Map, page 347.
1239 SHORT CAKE 5.10a ★   Climb the dike past two bolts.   FA: Jan McCollum
  and Dave Houser, October 1977.
1240 SHORT FLAKE 5.6   Climb the flake and crack 25' right of ***Short Cake***.   FA:
  R.Kyle Horst and Larry DeAngelo, December 1979.

WHITE TANK CAMPGROUND
White Tank Campground lies about 1¼ miles south of Belle Campground, on the east
side of the Pinto Basin Road. Lots of rocks here, but not too many routes.
1241 UPEVIL 5.6   This route lies on a rock west of the road just south of the
  campground. On the east side of the largest block, either lieback up a crack or
  climb the face next to the crack.   FA: Don O'Kelley, Jr. and Don O'Kelley,
  April 1969.
1242 DESIDERIOUS DELIGHT 5.4   This route lies on the southeast corner of a
  pinnacle about 100 yards east of the campground and just west of a cement tank/
  dam.   FA: Don O'Kelley and Dave Davis, April 1969.

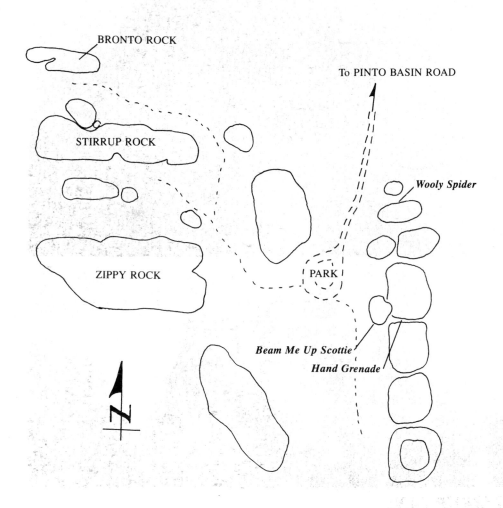

BRONTO ROCK

To PINTO BASIN ROAD

STIRRUP ROCK

Wooly Spider

ZIPPY ROCK

PARK

Beam Me Up Scottie

Hand Grenade

STIRRUP TANK

STIRRUP TANK

Stirrup Tank is reached by way of a dirt road which is found about ⅓ mile south of White Tank Campground along the Pinto Basin Road. A paved parking area on the west side of the road marks the start of the dirt road. Follow this for about 1½ miles to a parking area. The rocks near the parking lot have many established routes, and within a short walk remains much potential for new routes. Map, page 350.

1243 TARANTULA 5.2   FA: unknown

1244 WOOLY SPIDER 5.2   FA: unknown

1245 BEAM ME UP SCOTTIE 5.10a ★   FA: Todd Gordon and others, 1974.

1246 HAND GRENADE 5.10a   This climbs the slanting hand crack in the corridor to the east of route #1245.   FA: Don Reid and Alan Bartlett, December 1984.

ZIPPY ROCK

This rock lies directly west of the parking area, and the following routes are on the east face. Map, page 350.

1247 GARGOYLE 5.6   FA: unknown

1248 FREE AS CAN BE 5.7   FA: Mike Beck, December 1982.

1249 DIE YOUNG 5.9   FA: Alan Nelson, December 1982.

1250 JEDI MASTER 5.10c   FA: Nelson, 1982.

1251 HANS SOLO 5.9   FA: Nelson, 1982.

STIRRUP ROCK – SOUTH FACE

This formation lies about 150 yards northwest of the parking area, and is easily distinguished by the very dark brown rock on the south face. Map, page 350.

1252 DANCIN' DAZE 5.8   FA: Alan Nelson and others, December 1982.

1253 PETER EASTER PUMPKIN EATER 5.10b ★★   FA: Mike Waugh, Nick Badyrka, Dave Houser and Jan McCollum, December 1977.

1254 OVERPOWERED BY FUNK 5.11c· ★★   FA: Houser and McCollum, April 1981. FFA: Vaino Kodas, 1982.

STIRRUP ROCK – NORTH FACE
1255 NEW TOY 5.6   FA: Alan Nelson and Mike Beck, December 1982.
1256 JUGULAR VEIN 5.8   FA: Dave Houser, Bob Molloy and Jan McCollum,
    February 1978.
1257 FRECKLE FACE 5.11a (TR)   FA: Alan Nelson, January 1983.
1258 DO OR DIKE 5.9   FA: Alan Nelson and Denise Brown, January 1983.

BRONTO ROCK

This formation is just north of Stirrup Rock and is distinguished by the "X" on its south face, formed by a crack and a dike. Map, page 350.

1259 STEGASAURUS 5.10a (TR)   FA: Alan Nelson and Denise Brown, January 1983.

1260 CRACK' N' UP 5.4   FA: Nelson and Brown, 1983.

1261 TREMOR 5.10b (TR)   FA: Nelson, 1983.

1262 FLASHFLOOD 5.11a (TR)   FA: Nelson, 1983.

1263 STINGER 5.10a (TR)   FA: Brown and Nelson, January 1983.

1264 JUNKIE THRILL 5.6   FA: Nelson, 1983.

INDIAN HEAD

INDIAN HEAD

This large south facing formation lies high on the hillside west of Gold Park Road/Utah Trail (the main road from 29 Palms into the Monument), at a point about 3 miles south of the 29 Palms Highway. A fairly long (1 mile) and uphill (about 1,000 ft.) hike leads to the base. Plan on about an hour for the approach.

1265 RUDE AWAKENING 5.10c ★★★★   This two pitch face climb goes up the steep face left of *Goof Proof Roof*. Four bolts protect this route, together with a selection of nuts, Lost Arrows and Knifeblades. There are some runout sections.   FA: Charles Cole, Gib Lewis, Herb Laeger and Eve Laeger, February 1980.

1266 GOOF PROOF ROOF 5.8 A2+   Climb on aid past 8 bolts to a sling belay just left of an obvious large roof. Nail out right along the lip of the roof, then up to another sling belay. Aid and free climb straight up to the top. A good selection of thin pins is needed.   FA: Herb Laeger, Dave Houser and Jai Watts, April, 1978.

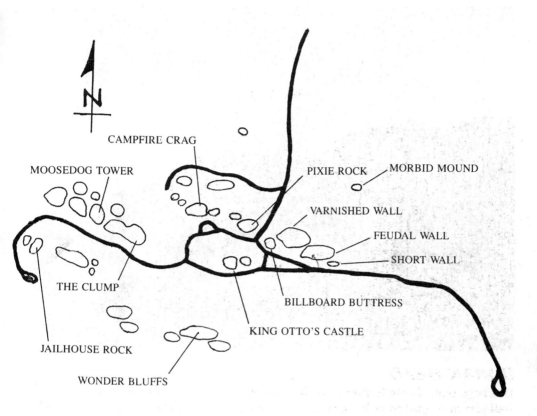

INDIAN COVE

This area is located along the northern edge of the Wonderland of Rocks. It is reached by driving east from the town of Joshua Tree about nine miles. There, a small sign and some buildings point the way to the remaining three miles to Indian Cove Campground. Besides being isolated from the other climbing areas of the Monument, Indian Cove tends to have somewhat warmer temperatures, due to a lower altitude.

PIXIE ROCK

This rock lies just to your right (west) as you enter the campground. The right hand edge of the south face is an extremely steep but bucketed face. To the left is a lower angled slab. Map, page 357.

1267 VAINO'S LOST IN POT 5.7   FA: Alan Nelson, December 1982.

1268 WHO'S FIRST 5.6   FA: Bill Squires and Craig Parsley, February 1975.

1269 RHYTHM OF THE HEART 5.8   FA: unknown

1270 SILENT SCREAM 5.10a ★★   FA: Alan Nelson and Mike Beck (TR), December 1982. First lead: Glenn Svenson and Mark Pfundt, November 1983.

1271 PIXIE STICK 5.10a (TR)   FA: Mike Beck and Alan Nelson, December 1982.

CAMPFIRE CRAG

This large formation is located west of Pixie Rock and overlooks the ranger campfire area where nature programs are conducted. The routes are located on the east face. Map, page 357.

1272 PICNIC 5.6   Behind campsite #2 are two shallow water chutes. Climb up the left chute until you can traverse right, past a horn, over to the right chute. Follow this to the top.   FA: Norm Saude and Bob Dominick, February 1970.

1273 FOOL'S RUBY 5.6   This route climbs a rib right of *Picnic* up to a cave; above this continue left and up to the summit.   FA: Jeff Morgan and Bruce Nyberg, 1977.

1274 OMEGA 5.7   FA: Bob Dominick and Norm Saude, April 1970.

1275 DATURA 5.12a (TR)   FA: Jim Boone and Stu Hughes, September 1978. FFA (TR): John Long and Lynn Hill, 1979.

1276 KLINGON PIZZA 5.6   FA: Jim Boone, September 1978

1277 FAT MAN'S MISERY 5.6   FA: Jim Boone, Lance Reynolds, Stu Hughes and Dave, September 1978.

CAMPFIRE CRAG
1278 NICKEL SLOTS 5.7   FA: Boone and Hughes, September 1978.
1279 OSTRICH SKIN 5.7   FA: Hughes and Boone, September 1978.
1280 AWFUL LOOSE 5.6   FA: Boone and Hughes, August 1978.
1281 PREJUDICIAL VIEWPOINT 5.11a   FA: Jeff Morgan and Bruce Nyberg, 1977. FFA: John Long, May 1978.
1282 CAMPFIRE GIRL 5.11d (TR)   FA: John Svenson and Jim Barker, 1968. FFA: John Long, May 1978.

CIRCLE CRAG
This low wall lies behind the campfire circle, about 100 yards north of Campfire Crag.
1283 SCOTCH 5.6   Climb a steep face, directly behind the campfire circle, up to a dark colored "bowl." Follow cracks left and up.   FA: unknown
1284 WHISKEY 5.6   Just right of *Scotch,* climb the face to an easy gully which is followed to the top.   FA: unknown

THE CLUMP

West along the campground road from the campfire circle are a series of "towers" of rock, which lie to the north of the road. The southeast spur of these towers is called The Clump. Map, page 357.

1285 FINALLY 5.4 At the far right end of an overhanging orangish-colored face, a large shallow hole in the rock will be seen about ten feet off the ground. Climb up to the hole, continue up and left until a "wait-a-minute" bush forces one up and right to the top.   FA: unknown

1286 AT LAST 5.9 Climb to the hole on *Finally,* but exit right and up to pass a deep hole on the way to the top.   FA: Chris Gonzalez, November 1978.

1287 MOMMA SPIDER 5.9 To the left of routes #1285 and 1286 about 100 feet is a wide chimney capped by a roof. Climb the chimney, then exit out left to the top.   FA: Jim Boone, August 1978.

DOS EQUIS WALL

This steep, brown, west facing wall lies behind campsite #80.

1288 SCARE WAY 5.10b   FA: unknown

1289 FLARE PLAY 5.10a   FA: unknown

1290 AIR PLAY 5.10d (TR)   FA: Alan Nelson, December 1982.

MOOSEDOG TOWER

This formation lies behind campsite #91. Rappel off the north side. Map, page 357.

1291 THIRD TIME'S A CHARM 5.10b ★★   FA: Bob Dominick and Dave Maher, February 1972. FFA: John Long and Keith Cunning, February 1978.

1292 WANDERING WINNEBAGO 5.8+ ★   FA: Norm Saude and Bob Dominick, February 1970.

1293 DIRECT SOUTH FACE 5.9 ★★   FA: Jim Barker, John Mokri, Bob Dominick and Norm Saude, January 1969. FFA: Chris Gonzalez, May 1975.

1294 TRANQUILITY 5.6   FA: unknown

1295 QUIEN SABE 5.7   Climbs the right-angling ramp located in the middle of the east face.   FA: unknown

JAILHOUSE ROCK

Jailhouse Rock is located at the extreme right (west) end of the campground. See map, page 357. Drive to the end of the road and walk around to the rear of the large formation near the parking area.

1296 CELLBOUND 5.5 ★★   Climb the arête at the extreme right (southwest) end of Jailhouse Rock. Start in a short gully, then ascend the arête using a dike and thin crack to a lieback corner that leads to the summit.   FA: Todd Swain, May 1984.

1297 JAILBREAK 5.3   This route ascends the right-facing corner 30 feet left (west) of *Cellbound.*   FD: Todd Swain, May 1984.

KING OTTO'S CASTLE

This formation lies in the middle of the campground. (See the map on page 357.) The only recorded routes lie on the south face.

1298 SWEAT BAND 5.10c ★★★   This fine route was unfortunately placed on rappel, despite the fact that it could have been put up on the lead.   FA: Keith Cunning, 1979.

1299 TARAWASSIE WIGGIE 5.10b   FA: Mike Beck, Dave Tapes and Alan Nelson, December 1982.

1300 PLAIN BUT GOOD HEARTED 5.6   FA: Todd McMasters, Bruce Linton and Bob Vinnacombe, March 1977.

CONDOR ROCK
This rock is obvious from King Otto's Castle as a large left facing, left leaning, orange corner.

1301 THE CONDOR 5.11d ★★★★   Climb the dihedral; small nuts, Friends, and a couple fixed pins protect the route.   FA: Perry Beckham, January 1984.

WONDER BLUFFS
This crag lies a couple hundred yards southwest of King Otto's Castle. Map, page 357.

1302 SLAM DUNK 5.8 ★★   Climb the corner at the left end of the cliff.   FA: John Long and Keith Cunning, December 1979.

1303 CONNIPTION 5.10b ★★★   This climbs up to the right side of the black triangular hole, then up a nice hand crack to the top.   FA: John Long and Keith Cunning, December 1979.

1304 BLUEWIND 5.10b   Climb the straight crack right of *Conniption*.   FA: Long and Cunning, December 1979.

1305 DRY RAIN 5.7   Climb a small left facing corner and continue up and right to the top.   FA: Long and Cunning, December 1979.

1306 GOMER PILE 5.9   Start up *Dry Rain,* but head up and left to the middle of three cracks.   FA: Long and Cunning, 1979.

1307 NEGRO VORTEX 5.10a   Start up *Dry Rain,* traverse sharply left, and follow an awkward crack to face climbing that leads to a thin crack and the summit.   FA: Long and Cunning, 1979.

1308 PENCIL NECK GEEK 5.10b ★★   This takes the straight thin crack on the right side of the cliff.   FA: Long and Cunning, 1979.

BILLBOARD BUTTRESS

This small face lies just east of the split in the road as you enter the campground. This is about 100 yards south of Pixie Rock, and it faces west. Map, page 357.

1309 SHEET BENDS 5.8   This is the left facing corner around to the left of the main face.   FA: unknown

1310 CERAMIC BUS 5.11   FA: unknown

1311 SQUAT ROCKETS 5.4   FA: unknown

1312 WE DIVE AT DAWN 5.7   FA: Howard King and Scott Stuemke, 1977.

1313 GAIT OF POWER 5.10a   FA: Scott Stuemke and Dick Armstrong.

1314 THE REVEREND 5.8   FA: unknown

1315 KNAUG AND HYDE 5.3   This route climbs a pillar before traversing up and left onto a knobby wall.   FA: unknown

WILLIT TOWER

1317

1318

1316

1319

VARNISHED WALL

This wall lies to the northeast of Billboard Buttress and southeast of Pixie Rock. This wall faces to the north and toward the entrance to the campground. Map, page 357.

1316 WITH MALICE AND FORETHOUGHT 5.7   This route follows a right-slanting crack on the left side of the Varnished Wall. Climb over several roofs.   FA: Scott Stuemke and Dick Armstrong, 1977.

1317 DOUBLE CRUX 5.7   FA: Jim Boone, Lance Reynolds and Stu Hughes, September 1978.

1318 MOSAIC 5.8   FA: Mike Anderson and Jim Boone, October 1978.

1319 CRANK QUEENIE 5.8   FA: Scott Stuemke and Howard King, 1977.

INDIAN PALISADES CORRIDOR

1320

1321

WILLIT PILLAR
This formation is near the road behind campsite #3 and about 75 yards right of Billboard Buttress.

1320 UNKNOWN HIGHWAY 5.10c   FA: unknown. FFA: Vaino Kodas, 1982.

1321 UNNAMED 5.10b   FA and FFA: unknown

INDIAN PALISADES CORRIDOR
This boulder filled canyon lies around to the right and behind Willit Pillar. Two routes have been recorded on the left wall of the Corridor.

1322 WHEAT CHEX 5.7   Twenty feet left of a large roof in the center of the face, climb an arching crack to a hole, then follow a crack just right of the arch until face climbing leads to the top.   FA: Scott Stuemke and Dick Armstrong, 1977.

1323 WATER MOCCASIN 5.4   On the right side of the face several bolts protect face climbing to a ledge.   FA: unknown

DARK SHADOWS ROCK
This formation lies about 40 yards east of Willit Pillar, directly behind a campsite. The dark colored, steep face has a very shallow crack which arches up and left.

1324 NAIL 'N GRAVEL 5.10d   Climb the arching crack to just below a ledge, climb straight up to the ledge and follow a vertical crack to the top.   FA: John Wolfe and Dick James, 1968. FFA: John Long and Lynn Hill, 1979.

1325 FORGOTTEN GALAXY 5.11a   This route lies just left of *Nail 'n Gravel.*   FA: Lynn Hill and John Long, 1979.

THE FEUDAL WALL

To the right (east) of Billboard Buttress and Willit Pillar a large formation can be seen lying above a small wash/canyon to the north of the road. This is the Feudal Wall. See the map, page 357. The low formation forming the south side of the wash/canyon is the Short Wall.

1326 ROUTE 1326 5.2 Climb a crack just left of *Scaramouch* and just right of a pillar. FA: unknown

1327 SCARAMOUCH 5.2 On the extreme left hand side of the Feudal Wall, start just left of a prominent bulge, at the base of a brownish pillar of rock. Climb up using small flakes and a crack. Follow a jam crack to the summit. FA: unknown

1328 SWISHBAH 5.7 Start to the right of *Scaramouch* and climb a right facing corner to the top. FA: unknown

1329 LA REINA 5.9 FA: John Long and John Wolfe, March 1974.

1330 DUCHESS LEFT 5.4 FA: unknown

1331 DUCHESS 5.6 FA: Chris Gonzalez and Rob Stahl, February 1974.

1332 DUCHESS RIGHT 5.7 FA: Chris Gonzalez and John Wolfe, March 1974.

1333 THE CASTRUM 5.10c FA: Jim Boone, August 1978. FFA: John Long and Keith Cunning, 1979.

1334 COURT JESTER 5.7 FA: Rob Stahl and John Wolfe, February 1974.

1335 MARCHESA 5.2 FA: unknown

1336 DUM ROODLE 5.6 FA: unknown

1337 PRINCESS 5.7 FA: Chris Gonzalez and Rey Creed, February 1974.

1338 THE MIKADO 5.6 FA: lots of people, April 1975.

1339 CALIFORNIA CRACK 5.11a FA: Don O'Kelley and Dave Davis, April 1969. FFA: unknown, 1979.

1340 EL REY 5.10a FA: Chris Gonzalez, September 1976.

1341 MINION 5.4 FA: Gonzalez and others, March 1974.

1342 CUBAN CONNECTION 5.8 FA: Chris Gonzalez and Jim Nagas, March 1974.

1329
1330
1331
1332
1333
1334
1335
1336

1335
1336
1337
1338
1339
1340
1341
1342

SHORT WALL
This wall lies just south of the Feudal Wall, and the routes lie on the south face. Map, page 357.

1343 *STEP 'N OUT* 5.10a   FA: John Wolfe and Dick James, 1968. FFA: Keith Cunning and John Long, 1979.

1344 *MAD RACE* 5.4   FA: unknown

1345 *BOMBAY* 5.8   FA: unknown

1346 *CALCUTTA* 5.6   FA: Chris Gonzalez and Rob Stahl, April 1975.

1347 *LEFT V CRACK* 5.11b   FA: unknown. FFA: John Long and Keith Cunning, 1979.

1348 *RIGHT V CRACK* 5.10a ★★   FA and FFA: unknown.

1349 *LINDA'S CRACK* 5.2   FA: unknown

1350 *LINDA'S FACE* 5.6   FA: unknown

1351 *CHOCKSTONE CHIMNEY* 4th Class   FA: unknown

1352 *TIGHT SHOES* 5.7   FA: unknown

1353 *DOUBLE CRACK* 5.3   FA: unknown

1354 *UP TO HEAVEN* 5.8   FA: unknown

1355 *TOE JAM EXPRESS* 5.3   FA: unknown

1356 *STEADY BREEZE* 5.7   FA: unknown

1357 *S.O.B.* 5.6   FA: unknown

1358 *MORNING WARM-UP* 5.9   FA: unknown

1359 *GOTCHA BUSH* 5.4   FA: unknown

1360 *RIGHT N UP* 5.8   FA: unknown

1361 *DONNA T'S ROUTE* 5.5   FA: unknown

1362 *BIG STEP* 5.8   FA: unknown

1363 *OUT OF STEP* 5.7   Follow up a flake on the extreme right end of the face until it crosses *Big Step* and leads to *Donna T's Route*.   FA: unknown

43

1344

1345 1346

1347

1348

48

1361

1362

1349 1350 1351 1352 1353 1354 1355 1356 1357 1358 1359 1360

MORBID MOUND

This small rock is about 400 yards northeast of the Varnished Wall and the entrance to the campground. Map, page 357.

1364 BE WARY 5.2   Climb a short, right facing corner in the center of the south face.   FA: Jim Boone, October 1979.

1365 DISAPPEARING BELAYER 5.7   Start at *Be Wary,* and after ten feet climb up and left to a large flake, then on to the top.   FA: Ted Chapin and Jim Boone, October 1979.

1366 HILLSIDE STRANGLER 5.4   Climb the chimney left of *Disappearing Belayer* past a bush.   FA: Jim Boone and Ted Chapin, November 1979.

1367 FLIES ON THE WOUND 5.7   Just left of *Hillside Strangler* climb a steep face and crack system.   FA: Ted Chapin, Bill Fournier and Jim Boone, October 1979.

1368 BRIMSTONE STAIRWAY 5.1   Climb the dike that is just left of *Flies on the Wound.*   FA: Jim Boone, October 1979.

1369 BOUNCER 5.8   Follow a discontinuous crack system on the steep wall of *Brimstone Chimney.*   FA: unknown. FFA: Jim Boone and Ted Chapin, October 1979.

1370 3RD CLASS IT 5.8   Around the corner and left of *Bouncer,* climb off a boulder to a bowl and follow two short cracks to the top.   FA: Boone and Chapin, October 1979.

1371 AMBULANCE DRIVER 5.1   This route lies just right of *Be Wary* and climbs a left leaning flake/crack.   FA: unknown

1372 MYRMECOCYSTUS EWARTI   Climb the second flake right of *Be Wary* up to a bowl, traverse left, and climb the face to the top.   FA: Boone and Chapin, November 1979.

1373 MORITURI TE SALUTAMUS 5.9   Start at the previous route, but climb up and right on face holds past a roof, and follow a prow to the top.   FA: Chapin and Boone, November 1979.

1374 A LAST CIGARETTE SEÑOR? 5.9   Around the corner and right of route #1373, climb a steep crack past a bush to a ledge. Above, climb past a roof, then up a wide crack to the top.   FA: Chapin and Boone, October 1979.

ROUTES BY RATING

5.6 Jessica's Crack Solo 1/8/88
5.6 Solo

☑ **5.7**

☐ *Andromeda Strain*
☐ *As the Crags Turn* ★★★
☐ *As the Wind Blows*
☐ *Aztec Twostep*
☐ *Ballbury*
☐ *Barely Crankin'*
☐ *Beck's Bear*
☐ *Bleed Proof*
☐ *Bonnie Brae*
☐ *Bonzo Dog Band* ★
☐ *Buissonier* ★★
☐ *Bushcrack* ★
☐ *Captain Kronos* ★
☐ *Clearasil*
☐ *Court Jester*
☐ *Cranny* ★
☐ *Deceptive Corner*
☐ *Die-hedral*
☐ *Dimorphism*
☐ *Disappearing Belayer*
☐ *Dolphin* ★★
☐ *Double Crux*
☐ *Double Dogleg* ★★★
☐ *Double Start*
☐ *Drawstring*
☐ *Dry Rain*
☐ *Duchess Right*
☐ *Dung Fu*
☐ *Easy as Pi*
☐ *Elusive Butterfly* ★★★
☐ *Flies on the Wound*
☐ *Frankenwood*
☐ *Free As Can Be*
☐ *Freeway*
☐ *Frosty Cone* ★★ os
☐ *Grand Theft Avocado*
☐ *Granny Goose*
☐ *Hemroidic Terror* ★
☐ *Hex*   Solo
☐ *Hex Marks the Poot* ★★★
☐ *Hoblett*
☐ *Howard's Horror*
☐ *I'm So Embarrassed For You*
☐ *Illusion*
☒ *Jumping Jehosaphat* ★ 1/10/88 os Solo
☐ *Jungle*

☐ *Knight Mare*
☐ *Last Ticket to Obscuritiville* ★
☒ *Lazy Day* ★★ 1/11/88 os Solo
☐ *Lickety Splits* ★★★
☐ *Little Rock Candy Crack*
☐ *Lizard's Landing* ★
☐ *Lost and Found*
☐ *Lumping Fat Jennie*
☐ *M.F. Dirty Rat*
☐ *Middle Finger*
☐ *Mr. Misty Kiss* 1/13/88 Solo
☒ *Nereltne* ★★
☐ *Nickel Slots*
☐ *One Way Up*
☐ *Ostrich Skin*
☐ *Other Voices*
☐ *Out of Step*
☒ *Overhang Bypass* ★★★ Solo 89
☐ *Palm-u-Granite*
☐ *Pile, The*
☐ *Pinnacle Stand*
☐ *Power Line*
☐ *Presto in C Sharp*
☐ *Princess*
☐ *Progressive Lizard*
☐ *Quien Sabe*
☐ *Resurrection*
☐ *Ripples*
☐ *Roast Leg of Chair*
☐ *Rock-a-Lot*
☐ *S Crack, Left*
☐ *Sandblast*
☐ *Scrumdillishus* ★★
☐ *Skinny Dip* ★★
☐ *Slippery When Wet*
☐ *Smooth as Silk*
☐ *Spud Patrol*
☐ *Steady Breeze*   Black Tide
☒ *Stichter Quits* ★★★ Black 12/21/88
☐ *Suzanna's Bandana*
☐ *Swift, The*
☐ *Swishbah*
☐ *Thrutcher*
☐ *Tight Shoes*
☐ *Tiptoe* ★★
☒ *Toe Jam* ★★ Solo 89

5.7

- [ ] Tom Bombadil
- [ ] Unwed Mudders
- [ ] Vaino's Lost in Pot
- [ ] We Dive at Dawn
- [ ] West Face Overhang ★
- [ ] Wheat Chex

- [ ] Where Janitors Dare
- [ ] White Lightning ★★★
- [ ] White Powder
- [ ] Willard ★
- [ ] Wisest Crack ★★★
- [ ] With Malice and Forethought
- [ ] Zigzag

5.7+

- [ ] Crack A
- [ ] Double Cross
- [ ] Mental Physics ★★★★
- [ ] Walk on the Wild Side ★★★★

5.8

- [ ] 3rd Class It
- [ ] All-Reet Arête
- [ ] Are We Ourselves
- [ ] Arturo's Special ★
- [ ] Baby Roof ★★★
- [ ] Baby-Point-Five
- [ ] Beck's Bet
- [x] Berkeley Dyke Solo #1/2/88
- [ ] Big Step
- [ ] Bimbo
- [ ] Bivo Sham
- [ ] Blue Nun
- [ ] Bombay
- [ ] Boulder Crack
- [ ] Bouncer
- [ ] Buckets to Burbank ★
- [ ] Bullocks Fashion Center
- [ ] C.F.M.F.
- [ ] Cashews Will be Eaten
- [ ] Catch a Falling Star ★★
- [ ] Cerro Torre, SW Face ★
- [ ] Chaffe n' Up
- [ ] City H ★
- [ ] Crank Queenie
- [ ] Cryptic ★★★
- [ ] Cuban Connection
- [ ] Dancin' Daze
- [ ] Dappled Mare ★★
- [ ] Deliver Us From Evil ★
- [ ] Desert Queen
- [ ] Dinkey Doinks ★★
- [ ] Dogleg ★★★
- [ ] Edge of the Knife ★
- [ ] Eff Eight
- [ ] False Tumbling Rainbow
- [ ] Fat Freddie's Escape
- [ ] Fat Man's Folly

- [ ] Fatal Flaw
- [ ] Feltoneon Physics
- [ ] Five-Four-Plus
- [ ] Flake and Bake
- [x] Flake, The ★★ Solo 89
- [ ] Flared Bear
- [ ] Flue, The ★★★
- [ ] Fun Stuff
- [ ] Funky Dung
- [ ] Funny Bone
- [ ] Gem ★★
- [ ] Generic Route
- [ ] Go 'Gane
- [ ] Go for Broke
- [ ] Gumby Goes to Washington
- [ ] H.R. Hardman ★
- [ ] Ham Sandwich
- [ ] Hands Off ★★★
- [ ] Hang Ten
- [ ] Hard Science ★
- [ ] I Am Not a Crook
- [ ] Isotope ★★
- [ ] Jack the Ripper
- [x] Jam Crack
- [ ] Jugular Vein
- [ ] Kickoff
- [ ] Laid Back ★
- [ ] Leader's Fright ★★★
- [ ] Lost in Space
- [ ] Lucky Lady ★★
- [ ] Luminous Breast
- [ ] Lurleen Quits
- [ ] Monkey Business ★★
- [ ] Monument Manor ★
- [ ] More Hustle Than Muscle
- [ ] Mosaic
- [ ] Mr. Bunny vrs Six Unknown Agents

- [ ] Music Box
- [ ] Nurn's Romp ★★
- [ ] Old Man and the Poodle, The
- [ ] On the Air
- [ ] Owatafooliam
- [ ] Parental Guidance Suggested ★
- [ ] Penalty Runout ★★
- [ ] Peyote Crack, Right ★★
- [ ] Poodle in Shining Armor
- [ ] Pumpkin Pie
- [ ] Quivering Lips
- [ ] R & R
- [ ] R.M.L. ★★
- [ ] Raindance
- [ ] Raker Mobile
- [ ] Ranger Danger
- [ ] Rat Ledge ★
- [ ] Red Eye ★★
- [ ] Reverend, The
- [ ] Rhythm of the Heart
- [ ] Right n Up
- [ ] Roan Way ★
- [ ] Robotics
- [ ] S Crack, Right
- [ ] Safe Muffins
- [x] Sail Away ★★★★ Solo on sight
- [ ] Savwafare ist Everywhere
- [ ] Sawdust Crack, Right ★★
- [ ] Season Opener ★★
- [ ] Sheet Bends

- [ ] Slam Dunk ★★
- [ ] Small but Short
- [ ] Snnfchtt
- [ ] Solar Wind ★★
- [ ] Solo
- [ ] Soma
- [ ] Southwest Passage
- [ ] Span-nish Fly
- [ ] Sparkle
- [ ] Spider
- [ ] Split Rocks
- [ ] Straight Flush
- [ ] Tabby Litter
- [x] Tennis Shoe Crack ★ Solo 89
- [ ] Ticket to Nowhere
- [ ] Totally Tubular
- [ ] Tri-step
- [ ] Troglodyte Crack
- [ ] Ulysses' Bivouac
- [ ] Unicorner ★★
- [ ] Up to Heaven
- [ ] Urine Trouble
- [ ] V Cracks
- [ ] W.A.C. ★
- [ ] Wallaby Crack
- [ ] We'll Get Them Little P's
- [ ] What
- [ ] White Collar Crime
- [ ] Worthy of It
- [x] Zardoz ★★

5.8+

- [ ] Bambi Meets Godzilla ★★★
- [ ] Breakfast of Champions ★
- [ ] Continuum ★★★★
- [ ] Nobody Walks in LA ★
- [ ] Orange Flake ★★
- [x] Pinched Rib ★★★ 1/6/88 os n.p.
- [ ] Punked Out Porpoise ★★
- [ ] Such a Poodle
- [ ] T.S. Special ★★★
- [ ] Wandering Winnebago ★
- [x] ZZZZZ ★★★★

5.9

- [ ] A Farewell to Poodles
- [ ] A Last Cigarette Señor?
- [ ] Ace of Spades
- [ ] Alice in Wonderjam ★★★
- [ ] American Express ★
- [ ] An Eye to the West ★
- [ ] Ancient Future

- [ ] Archimedes' Crack, Right
- [ ] Ass of Dog
- [ ] At Last
- [ ] Atomic Pile
- [ ] Baby Route
- [ ] Big Boy
- [ ] Big Brother

5.9

- [ ] *Birdman from Alcatraz*
- [ ] *Biskering*
- [ ] *Black Eye*
- [ ] *Blood and Cuts*
- [ ] *Bloodymir*
- [ ] *Bolivian Freeze Job*
- [ ] *Boom Boom Room* ★★
- [ ] *Boulder Dash*
- [ ] *Bubba's Tourist Trap*
- [ ] *Buster Brown* ★★
- [ ] *Buster Hymen*
- [ ] *Cake Walk* ★★★
- [ ] *Calgary Stampede* ★★
- [ ] *Casual* ★
- [ ] *Chalk Up Another One* ★★★
- [ ] *Charlie Brown*
- [ ] *Chocolate Chips*
- [ ] *Cling Peaches* ★★
- [ ] *Cole-Lewis*
- [ ] *Colorado Crack* ★★★★
- [ ] *Controversial*
- [ ] *Crack B*
- [ ] *Credibility Gap*
- [ ] *Crystal Keyhole*
- [ ] *DMB, The* ★★
- [ ] *Damper* ★
- [ ] *Dazed and Confused* ★★★
- [ ] *Deep Throat*
- [ ] *Defoliation* ★
- [ ] *Die Young*
- [ ] *Direct South Face* ★★
- [ ] *Dirty Surprise*
- [ ] *Do or Dike*
- [ ] *Dos Peros Negros* ★
- [ ] *Downpour*
- [ ] *Drop a Frog* ★
- [ ] *Dummy's Delight* ★★★
- [ ] *Enchanted Stairway* ★★
- [ ] *Enforcer, The* ★
- [ ] *Enter the Dragon*
- [ ] *Euthyphro*
- [ ] *Exit Stage Right* ★★
- [ ] *Fiendish Fists*
- [ ] *Fishing Trip*
- [ ] *For Whom the Poodle Tolls*
- [ ] *Frets Don't Fail Me Now* ★
- [ ] *General Hospital* ★★★
- [ ] *Glumpies*
- [ ] *Gomer Pile*
- [ ] *Good Book, The*
- [ ] *Grain and Bear It*
- [ ] *Grounder*
- [ ] *Hairline Fracture* ★★

- [ ] *Hand Wobler Delight*
- [ ] *Hands Away*
- [ ] *Hans Solo*
- [ ] *Herman*
- [ ] *High Strung* ★★
- [ ] *Hunkloads to Hermosa*
- [ ] *I Can't Believe It's a Girdle* ★★★★
- [ ] *I Got It*
- [ ] *In and Out*
- [ ] *Infectious Smile*
- [ ] *Innervisions*
- [ ] *Invisibility Lessons* ★★★★
- [ ] *It*
- [ ] *Jack of Hearts* ★★★
- [ ] *Joan Jetson* ★
- [ ] *Junkyard God*
- [ ] *Just Another Crack From L.A.* ★
- [ ] *Just Another New Wave Route*
- [ ] *Just Another Roadside Attraction* ★
- [ ] *Kiddie Corner*
- [ ] *Killer Bees*
- [ ] *Kippy Korner*
- [ ] *Krakatoa*
- [ ] *La Reina*
- [ ] *Lead Us Not Into Temptation* ★★★
- [ ] *Lean Two*
- [ ] *Lechlinski Crack, Left* ★
- [ ] *Lechlinski Crack, Right* ★
- [ ] *Legal Briefs*
- [ ] *Live From Tasmania* ★
- [ ] *Looney Tunes* ★★★
- [ ] *Lust We Forget*
- [ ] *Lust in the Wonderland* ★
- [ ] *M & M's Plain* ★★
- [ ] *Made in the Shade*
- [ ] *Mare's Tail*
- [ ] *Midnight Dreamer*
- [ ] *Momma Spider*
- [ ] *More Fool Me*
- [ ] *Morituri te Salutamus*
- [ ] *Morning Warm-up*
- [ ] *My Laundry* ★★★
- [ ] *Negasaurus*
- [ ] *Nobody Walks in L.A.* ★★★
- [ ] *Nobody's Right Mind*
- [ ] *North Overhang* ★★★
- [ ] *Norwegian Wood*
- [ ] *Nuke the Whales*
- [ ] *Nurses in Bondage*
- [ ] *Nuts are for Men Without Balls*
- [ ] *OK Korner*
- [ ] *Opus Dihedral*
- [ ] *Orphan* ★★★

- ☐ Over the Hill
- ☐ Overseer ★★
- ☐ Owl ★
- ☐ Pacyderms to Paradise
- ☐ Peabody's Peril ★★
- ☐ Perhaps
- ☐ Pete's Handful
- ☐ Peyote Crack, Middle ★★
- ☐ Pig in Heat
- ☐ Pinhead ★
- ☐ Poetry in Motion
- ☒ Pope's Crack ★★★ 12/29/87 RP
- ☐ Pope's Hat
- ☐ Popular Mechanics ★★★
- ☐ Prepackaged ★★
- ☐ Psoriasis ★
- ☐ Pterodactydl Crack
- ☐ Pygmy Village
- ☐ R.A.F. ★★
- ☐ Rad
- ☐ Rites of Spring
- ☐ Roberts Crack ★
- ☐ Rock & Roll Girl
- ☐ Rock Candy ★★★
- ☐ Room to Shroom ★★★★
- ☐ Route 182
- ☐ Rush Hour
- ☐ Same As It Ever Was
- ☐ Shakin' the Shirts
- ☐ Short but Sweet ★★
- ☐ Sine Wave
- ☐ Smithereens
- ☐ Smoke-a-Bowl
- ☐ Snow Falls
- ☐ Soft Core ★★
- ☐ Something Heinous
- ☐ South Face Center (Headstone) ★★
- ☐ Sphincter Quits ★★★
- ☐ Split Personality ★★★
- ☐ Stemulation
- ☐ Stick to What ★★★
- ☐ Strawberry Jam ★★

- ☐ Sugar Daddy
- ☐ Sugar Daddy (L.R. Candy Mtn.) ★
- ☐ Sullivan From Colorado
- ☐ Super Roof ★★★
- ☐ Tails of Poodles
- ☒ Take Two They're Small 1/9/88 SB
- ☐ Teenage Enema
- ☐ The Harder They Fall ★★★
- ☐ Thin Air
- ☐ Thin Flakes ★★
- ☐ Thin Man's Nightmare
- ☐ Thin is In
- ☐ Third World ★★
- ☐ Thrash or Crash
- ☐ Throat Warbler Mangrove
- ☐ Thumbs Down Left ★★
- ☐ Toad Crack
- ☐ Todd Squad
- ☐ Tofu the Dwarf
- ☐ Top 40 to Middle Toilet
- ☐ Totally Nuts
- ☐ Touch and Go ★★★★
- ☐ Touche Away ★
- ☐ Trashman Roof ★
- ☐ Trembling Toes ★
- ☐ True Democracy ★
- ☐ Tumbling Rainbow ★★
- ☐ Turkey Terror
- ☐ Two Our Surprise
- ☐ Unconscious Obscenity
- ☐ Voice Buddy
- ☐ Waterchute, The
- ☐ Weathering Frights
- ☐ Western Saga ★
- ☐ What's Left
- ☐ Which Witch
- ☐ Wild Gravity
- ☐ Wild Wind ★★
- ☐ Wind Sprint
- ☐ Wise Crack
- ☐ Working Overtime ★★
- ☐ X-Rated Tits ★
- ☐ Young Lust

5.9+

- ☐ Angular Momentum
- ☐ Aqua Tarkus ★
- ☐ Comic Book ★★★
- ☐ Crack #5
- ☐ Early Bird ★★
- ☒ Effigy Too ★★★
- ☐ Flaming Arrow ★
- ☐ Grand Canyon Donkey Trail ★

- ☐ Java
- ☐ No Holds Barred
- ☐ Primal Flake
- ☐ Route 1056
- ☒ Sidewinder ★★★★
- ☐ Uncertainly Principal
- ☐ Wanna Bong
- ☐ Workout at the Y ★

5.10a

- [ ] A-Jill-ity
- [ ] Aero Space
- [ ] Against the Grain
- [ ] Alligator Lizard
- [ ] Archimedes' Crack, Left
- [ ] Arraignment, The
- [ ] Ash Gordon
- [ ] Axe of Dog ★
- [ ] Bad Lizards ★★
- [ ] Ball Bearing ★★
- [ ] Ballbearings Under Foot
- [ ] Ballet ★
- [ ] Baskerville Crack, Right
- [ ] Beam Me Up Scottie ★
- [ ] Berserk
- [ ] Bird of Fire ★★★
- [ ] Bird on a Wire ★★★
- [ ] Blue Nubian ★
- [ ] Blues Brothers ★★★
- [ ] Boogers on a Lampshade ★
- [ ] Bottle in Front of Me ★★
- [ ] Broken Glass
- [ ] Buenos Aires ★
- [ ] C.S. Special ★★★
- [ ] Candelabra ★
- [ ] Caramel Crunch
- [ ] Championship Wrestling ★
- [ ] Closed on Mondays ★
- [ ] Cole-Evans ★
- [ ] Cole-Lewis, The ★★
- [ ] Cornerstone, The (Touch and Go)
- [ ] Cosmic Debris ★
- [ ] Crack #6
- [ ] Cranking Skills or Hospital Bill
- [ ] Crystal Calisthenics ★
- [ ] Dandelion ★★
- [ ] Dangling Woo Li Master ★★★★
- [ ] Dead Bees
- [ ] Death of a Decade
- [ ] Deception
- [ ] Defibrillation
- [x] Deja Vu ★
- [ ] Desert Delirium ★★★
- [ ] Deviate
- [ ] Diamond Dogs ★★★
- [ ] Dodo's Delight ★
- [ ] Don't Think Just Jump ★
- [ ] Drano ★★
- [ ] El Rey
- [ ] Enos Mills Glacier
- [ ] Exhibit A
- [ ] Exorcist ★★★★
- [ ] Face It ★★
- [ ] Face Race
- [ ] Face Route
- [ ] Feeling Groovy
- [ ] Female Mud Massacre
- [ ] Fire or Retire ★
- [ ] Fist Full of Crystals ★★
- [ ] Fists of Fury
- [ ] Flare Play
- [ ] 42N8
- [ ] Free Climbing
- [ ] Frontal Lobotomy ★★★
- [ ] Frostline
- [ ] Frotal Logranity
- [ ] Full Frontal Nudity ★★★
- [ ] Gait of Power
- [ ] Gemstoner
- [ ] Gnarly
- [ ] Gone in 60 Seconds ★
- [x] Good to the Last Drop ★★
- [ ] Gripped Up the Hole ★
- [ ] Gross Chimney
- [ ] Ground Finale
- [ ] Half Track ★
- [ ] Halfway to Paradise ★★★
- [ ] Hand Grenade
- [ ] Hawks Retreat
- [ ] Head Over Heals ★★★
- [x] Heart and Sole ★★★★ 12/21/88
- [ ] Heavy Gold
- [ ] Heavy Slander
- [ ] Heavy Water
- [ ] Holes in the Head ★★
- [ ] Holy Cross
- [ ] I Just Told You ★
- [ ] Ice Climbing
- [ ] Illusion Dweller ★★★★★
- [ ] Immuno Reaction ★
- [ ] In Elke's Absence ★
- [ ] In The Pit ★
- [ ] Jack Grit
- [ ] Jamburger
- [ ] Jerry Brown ★★
- [ ] Jughead
- [ ] Julius Seizure
- [ ] Kickin' Bach
- [ ] Knick
- [ ] Ledges to Laundale ★
- [ ] Left Route
- [ ] M & M's Peanut
- [ ] Mama Woolsey ★★
- [ ] Mel Crack, Right ★★
- [ ] Mind Over Splatter
- [ ] Modern Warfare

5.10a

- [ ] Monster Mash
- [ ] More Funky Than Junky
- [ ] Mother Lode ★★★
- [ ] Moubit
- [ ] Mr. Bunny Quits ★
- [ ] Mr. Bunny's Refund Check ★
- [ ] Negro Vortex
- [ ] New Day Yesterday
- [ ] Nip in the Air
- [ ] No Calculators Allowed ★★
- [ ] Not Forgotten
- [ ] Not a Hogan
- [ ] O.W.
- [ ] Orc, The ★★
- [ ] Out to Grunge
- [ ] Overseer, Direct Start ★
- [ ] Oversight
- [ ] Phineas P. Phart
- [ ] Picking up the Pieces
- [ ] Pictures at an Exhibition
- [ ] Pixie Stick
- [ ] Pretty Gritty
- [ ] Prime Time
- [ ] Profundity
- [ ] Puss Wuss
- [ ] Quarter Moon Crack ★
- [x] Quick Draw McGraw ★★ *Rich 12/29/57 RP*
- [ ] Raven's Reach
- [ ] Ray's Cafe
- [ ] Ride a Wild Bago ★★
- [x] Rollerball ★★★★ *05 RP 60*
- [ ] Roof, The
- [ ] Roofing Company ★★
- [ ] Route 1203
- [ ] Route 152
- [ ] Route 251
- [ ] Safety in Numbers
- [ ] Second Thoughts ★
- [ ] Short Cake ★
- [ ] Silent Scream ★★
- [ ] Snatch, The ★

- [ ] Sole Food ★★
- [ ] Solid Gold ★★★★
- [ ] Space Slot
- [ ] Spiderman ★★
- [ ] Spitwad
- [ ] Squeeze Play
- [ ] Squid of My Desire
- [ ] Start Trundling
- [ ] Stegasaurus
- [ ] Step'n Out
- [ ] Stinger
- [ ] Sublimation
- [ ] Sudden Death ★
- [ ] Tax Evasion ★★
- [ ] Tax Man ★★★★
- [ ] Ten Conversations at Once
- [ ] The Good, the Bad and the Ugly
- [ ] The Old Man Down the Road
- [ ] Thumbs Up
- [ ] Thunderclap
- [ ] Tipples in Rime
- [ ] Top Flight
- [ ] Tossed Green ★★★
- [ ] Tower of Godliness ★
- [ ] True Dice ★★
- [ ] Unknown
- [ ] Unknown Route, The ★★
- [ ] Use it or Loose it
- [ ] V Crack, Right ★★
- [ ] Vaino's Renegade Lead
- [ ] Visual Nightmare
- [ ] Vortex
- [ ] War Crimes
- [ ] War Games ★★
- [ ] Watanobe Wall ★★★
- [ ] Weak Force, The ★
- [ ] What's Hannen
- [ ] White Rabbit ★★
- [ ] Yardy-Hoo and Away ★★★
- [ ] Yogi the Overbear
- [ ] Zarmog the Dragon Man ★
- [ ] Zondo's Perks ★

5.10b

- [ ] Aftermath ★★★★
- [ ] Ali Shuffle ★★
- [ ] An Eye for an Eye and a Route for a Route ★★★
- [ ] B-Movie
- [ ] B.L.T.
- [ ] Banana Crack, Left ★
- [ ] Barnie Rubble ★★

- [ ] Baskerville Crack, Left
- [ ] Ben ★★
- [ ] Between a Rock and a Hard Place
- [x] Bitchin'
- [ ] Bloody Tax Break ★
- [ ] Bluewind
- [ ] Book of Changes ★★★★
- [ ] Brits in Drag ★★

5.10b

- [ ] Burn Out ★
- [ ] Caught on a Big Set ★★★★★
- [ ] Chemical Warefare ★★★
- [ ] Chicken Lizard
- [x] Clean and Jerk ★★★★ 0S.RP TR. 1/10/88
- [ ] Conniption ★★★
- [ ] Delightful Lady ★
- [ ] Direct Start, Pig in Heat
- [x] Dog Day Afternoon ★★★ 1/11/88 0S.RP.
- [ ] Dyno in the Dark ★
- [ ] Edge of Doom ★★★
- [ ] Energy Crisis
- [ ] Event Horizon ★★
- [ ] Eyes Without a Face ★
- [ ] Figures on a Landscape ★★★★★ ⸺
- [ ] Fisticuffs ★★★
- [ ] Flaring Rhoid ★
- [ ] Flue Right ★★
- [ ] Friendly Hands ★★★★
- [ ] Fusion Without Integrity 12/31/87 RP
- [x] Grain Surgery ★★★
- [ ] Great Unknown, The ★★★
- [ ] Ham & Swiss
- [ ] Handsaw
- [x] Hobbit Roof ★★ 12/31/87 RP
- [ ] Howard's Horror, Direct
- [ ] Insolvent ★★
- [ ] Jemiomagina ★★
- [ ] Jet Stream ★★
- [ ] Judas ★
- [ ] Jungle Cruise ★★★
- [ ] Ladder Back
- [ ] Let it all Hang Out
- [ ] Light Sabre ★★
- [ ] Loose Lady ★★★★
- [ ] Lower Band ★★
- [ ] Magnetic Woose
- [ ] Make or Break Flake
- [ ] Maltese Falcon, The ★
- [ ] Matt's Problem
- [ ] Mental Bankruptcy ★★
- [ ] Mesopotamia ★★★
- [ ] Ming Dallas, The
- [ ] My Favorite Things ★★★
- [ ] Napkin of Shame ★
- [ ] Narwhal, The ★★
- [ ] No Biggy ★
- [ ] None of Your Business ★★
- [ ] Not For Loan ★★★
- [ ] Nuclear Waste

- [ ] Offshoot
- [ ] On the Nob
- [ ] Ordinary Route ★★ 1/1/88 RP
- [x] Papa Woolsey ★★★ 1/1/88 RP
- [ ] Papillon
- [ ] Pencil Neck Geek ★★
- [ ] Peter Easter Pumkin Eater ★★
- [ ] Poodle Boy
- [ ] Poodle Woof ★
- [ ] Poodles Are People Too ★★★★
- [ ] Pop Rocks
- [ ] Power Drop ★
- [x] Pumping Ego ★★ 1/1/88 RP
- [ ] Rhythm & Blues ★★
- [ ] Rope Drag
- [ ] Run For Your Life ★★★★
- [ ] Scare Way
- [ ] Schrodinger Equation, The ★★★
- [ ] Scope & Hope
- [ ] Shooting Gallery ★★
- [ ] Shovling-Cole
- [ ] Sinner's Swing ★
- [ ] Ski Track, Lower Right ★★★
- [ ] Slim Pickings
- [ ] Solosby
- [ ] Sound Asleep
- [ ] Space Odyssey ★
- [ ] Strike it Rich ★★
- [ ] Surrealistic Pillar ★
- [ ] Sympathy to the Devil
- [ ] Tales of Powder
- [ ] Tarawassie Wiggie
- [ ] That
- [ ] Third Time's a Charm ★★
- [ ] Tinker Toys ★★
- [ ] Toad Warrior ★
- [ ] Too Loose to Trek ★
- [ ] Tower of Cleanliness ★★★
- [ ] Transylvania Twist
- [ ] Treinte Anos
- [ ] Tremor
- [ ] Tube, The
- [ ] Tubular Balls ★
- [ ] U.B. Kool
- [ ] Unnamed
- [ ] Vice President ★★★
- [ ] Waugh Crack ★★
- [ ] Whatchasay Dude
- [ ] Wired ★★★
- [ ] Worth Bagly Dihedral ★★
- [ ] Y Knot ★

5.10

- [ ] *Bolt Heaven*
- [ ] *Cyclotron*
- [ ] *Forsaken Mein-key, The*
- [ ] *Get the Balance Right* ★★★
- [ ] *Peyote Crack, Left* ★★
- [ ] *Unknown*

5.10c

- [ ] *A Woman's Work is Never Done* ★★★
- [ ] *Absolute Zero* ★
- [ ] *All Loin*
- [ ] *Anacram* ★★★
- [ ] *Atari* ★★
- [ ] *Baby Fae* ★★
- [x] *Band Saw* ★★ 12/27/87 RP
- [ ] *Bearded Cabbage* ★★★
- [ ] *Beginner's Twenty-Six*
- [ ] *Beverly Drive*
- [ ] *Billabong* ★★
- [ ] *Bongledesh*
- [ ] *Brief Case*
- [ ] *British Airways* ★★★
- [ ] *Brownian Motion*
- [ ] *Bruiser, The* ★★★
- [ ] *Carnage*
- [ ] *Castrum, The*
- [ ] *Cat on a Hot Tin Roof*
- [ ] *Church Bazaar*
- [ ] *Cole Sore* ★★
- [ ] *Common Law Marriage*
- [ ] *Compassion of the Elephants, The* ★★★
- [ ] *Corner of Foreigner*
- [ ] *Crack #4*
- [ ] *Crack C*
- [ ] *Crescent Wrench* ★
- [ ] *Crime of the Century* ★★★
- [ ] *Cruising for Burgers* ★
- [ ] *Daddy Long Legs* ★
- [ ] *Dike Da Doodad*
- [ ] *Dike, The* ★★
- [ ] *Dirty Cat*
- [ ] *Disco Sucks*
- [ ] *Don't Dik With Walt*
- [ ] *Double Jeopardy* ★★
- [x] *EBGB's* ★★★★ 12/28/87 RP
- [ ] *El Blowhole* ★
- [ ] *Episcopalian Toothpick*
- [ ] *First Eleven*
- [ ] *Flakes of Grasp*
- [ ] *Fumblers Below the Roof*
- [ ] *Goin' Down the Road Feelin' Bad*
- [ ] *Good Grief*

- [ ] *Greenhorn Dihedral* ★★★
- [ ] *Grit Roof* ★★
- [ ] *Gumshoe* ★★★
- [ ] *Hallow Friction*
- [x] *Harlequin* ★★★★ 1/13/88 OS. RP.
- [ ] *Hawk Wind* ★★★
- [ ] *Heaven Can Wait* ★★★
- [ ] *Hermanutic* ★★
- [ ] *Hintertoiser Traverse, The*
- [ ] *Hour of Power*
- [ ] *Inauguron, The* ★★
- [ ] *Indian Giver* ★★★
- [ ] *Iron Mantle*
- [ ] *Jah Loo* ★★★
- [ ] *Jedi Master*
- [ ] *Kamakaze*
- [ ] *Knack* ★★
- [ ] *Kook Book*
- [ ] *Laid Back and Doing It*
- [ ] *Legolas*
- [ ] *Life in the Fast Lane* ★★
- [ ] *Make That Move or Six Foot Groove* ★
- [ ] *Martin Quits* ★
- [ ] *Memorial Meowzer*
- [ ] *Mental Siege Tactics* ★
- [ ] *Modern Jazz*
- [ ] *Nestle Crunch* ★
- [ ] *No Self Confidence* ★★
- [ ] *O'Kelley's Crack* ★★★★★
- [x] *Official Route of the 1984 Olympics* ★★★ 12/31/87 OS RP
- [ ] *One Move Leads to Another* ★★
- [ ] *Orc Sighs*
- [ ] *Out for a Bite* ★★
- [ ] *Piggle Pugg* ★★★
- [ ] *Pile in the Sky*
- [ ] *Point of No Return* ★
- [ ] *Polytechnics* ★★
- [ ] *Primal Scream*
- [x] *Pullups to Pasadena* 1/6/88 OS.RP
- [ ] *Quantum Jump* ★★★★
- [ ] *Regular Route (Plymouth Rock)*
- [ ] *Rice Cake Roof* ★
- [ ] *Right Route*
- [ ] *Roark*

5.10c

- [ ] Route 499 ★★
- [ ] Rude Awakening ★★★★
- [ ] Ruff Stuff
- [ ] S Cracker, The ★★★
- [ ] Sandbag
- [ ] Sawdust Crack, Left
- [x] Serious Fashion ★   11b?
- [ ] Sexy Sadye ★★★ 1/10/88 OS RP.
- [ ] Sinbad the Sailor
- [ ] Slip Skrig ★★★
- [ ] Smear Tactics
- [ ] Solstice ★
- [ ] Studebaker Hawk ★★
- [x] Surface Tension ★★★ 1/1/68 RP
- [ ] Sweat Band ★★★

- [ ] T.K.O.
- [ ] Take it for Granite ★★★
- [ ] Telegram for Mongo ★★
- [ ] That Old Soft Shoe ★★
- [ ] The Importance of Being Ernest ★★★★
- [ ] The Three Best Friends Your Car Ever Had ★★
- [ ] Trespassers Will Be Violated ★★★
- [ ] Try Again ★★
- [ ] Two Scoops Please ★★
- [ ] Unknown Highway
- [ ] Welcome to Joshua Tree ★★
- [ ] When Sheep Ran Scared ★★
- [ ] Winter Wine ★★★
- [ ] Yabo Phone Home

5.10d

- [ ] A Cheap Way to Die ★★★
- [ ] Air Play
- [ ] Banana Splits ★★
- [ ] Bee Gees
- [ ] Belly Dancer ★★★
- [ ] Big Brown Eye ★★★
- [x] Black President ★★★★★ 1/9/88 1 Fall
- [ ] Blind Me With Science
- [ ] Casual Affair
- [ ] Cedric's Deep Sea Fish Market ★
- [ ] Centurion
- [ ] Child's Play ★★
- [ ] Cinnamon Girl ★★
- [ ] Count Dracula ★★★
- [ ] Crazy Climber
- [x] Decompensator of Lhasa, The ★★★★ OS RP. 1/6/88
- [ ] Doing That Scrapyard Thing ★★
- [ ] El Brujo ★★
- [ ] Fatty Winds His Neck Out
- [ ] Foreign Legion ★★★★
- [ ] Fractured Fissure
- [ ] Freeway Jam ★★
- [ ] Grain of Truth ★
- [ ] Grungy
- [ ] Hang and Swing ★★
- [ ] Henny Penny
- [ ] Hot Knife
- [ ] Hyperventilation
- [ ] I Eat Cannibals ★
- [ ] Imaginary Voyage ★★★★
- [ ] Janus
- [ ] Jolly Rancher Firestix
- [ ] Kidney Stone
- [ ] Kool Aid ★

- [ ] Last Unicorn, The ★★★★★
- [ ] Mel Crack, Left ★★
- [ ] Middle Band
- [ ] Minute Man
- [ ] Morning Thunder ★★★
- [ ] Nail 'n Gravel
- [ ] No Falls
- [ ] No Self Respect ★★★
- [ ] No Shirt Needed ★★
- [ ] Perpetual Motion ★★★★
- [ ] Pinky Lee ★
- [ ] Presbyterian Dental Floss
- [ ] Pussy Galore ★
- [ ] Rain Dance ★
- [ ] Raked Over the Coles ★★★
- [ ] Raker's Blaring Hat Rack ★★
- [ ] Rat Race ★★
- [ ] Rock Star ★★★
- [x] Rockwell 41C ★★ 5/6/68 RP. 4 Tries
- [ ] Rocky Road ★
- [ ] Rubicon ★★★★
- [ ] Scared Bare
- [ ] Semi Tough ★★
- [ ] Squatter's Right
- [ ] Surrealistic Colgate
- [ ] Tax Free
- [ ] Thunderclap Direct
- [ ] Too Secret To Find ★★★★
- [ ] Uncle Fester
- [ ] Wage and Price Ceiling ★
- [ ] Wet Rock Day ★
- [ ] What's it to You ★★★
- [ ] Zion Train ★★
- [ ] Zulu Dawn

5.11a

- [x] Abstract Roller Disco ★★★
- [ ] Acid Rock ★
- [ ] Adult Books ★★
- [ ] Amazing Grace ★
- [ ] Android Lust
- [ ] Are You Experienced? ★
- [ ] Ayatollah, The ★★
- [ ] Bad Fun
- [ ] Bebop Tango
- [x] Big Moe ★★★ .89
- [ ] Breaking Away
- [ ] Brown 25 ★★★
- [x] Butterfly Crack ★★★
- [ ] California Crack
- [ ] Claim Jumper
- [ ] Cleared for Takeoff
- [x] Coarse and Buggy ★★★★
- [ ] Colossus of Rhoids, The
- [ ] Comic Relief ★
- [ ] Congratulations ★★
- [ ] Cretin Bull Dancer ★
- [ ] Dick Enberg ★★
- [ ] Dimp for A Chimp ★
- [ ] Direct Wrench
- [ ] Discoy Decoy ★★
- [ ] Dwindling Greenbacks ★★
- [ ] Flashflood
- [ ] Forgotten Galaxy
- [ ] Freckle Face
- [ ] Gold Hunk, The
- [ ] Goldenbush Corner
- [ ] Gravity Waves ★★★★★
- [ ] High and Dry
- [ ] Hook and Ladder ★★
- [ ] Hot Lava ★
- [ ] Hyperion ★★★★
- [ ] Ignorant Photons From Pluto ★
- [ ] Jugline
- [ ] Jumping Jack Crack ★★★

- [ ] Killer Pussy
- [ ] Lay Back and Do It
- [ ] Layaway Plan ★
- [ ] Lithophiliac ★★★
- [ ] Loose Lips ★★★
- [ ] Mere Illusion ★★
- [ ] Naked Reagan ★★★
- [ ] Natural Selection ★★★★
- [ ] No Mistake or Big Pancake ★★
- [ ] No San Francisco
- [ ] Out to Lunge
- [ ] Outsiders, The
- [ ] Poodle Smasher, The ★★★
- [ ] Popeye ★★
- [ ] Prejudicial Viewpoint
- [x] Preparation H 12/22/88 +
- [ ] Psychokenesis
- [ ] Quest for Fire
- [ ] Red Headed Stranger ★★
- [ ] Red Snapper ★★★
- [x] Ripper 12/26/87 Sdo
- [ ] Rubberfat Syndrome, The
- [ ] S Crack ★
- [ ] S Crack, Middle
- [ ] Scar Wars
- [ ] Ski Track, Left ★★★
- [ ] Static Cling
- [ ] Such a Savage ★★★★★
- [x] Swept Away ★★★★ OS RP 89
- [ ] Swift ★
- [ ] Taming of the Shoe, The ★★
- [ ] Therapeutic Tyranny ★★
- [ ] Traverse of no Return
- [ ] Venucian Fece
- [ ] Wedlock
- [ ] Weekend Warrior ★
- [ ] Winds of Whoopee ★★★
- [ ] Wren's Nest ★★★
- [ ] Young Frankenstein ★

Unknown 11 - 1/8/88 (new)

5.11b

- [ ] Animalitos ★★
- [ ] Atom Ant ★★
- [ ] Banana Crack, Right ★★
- [ ] Bella Lugosi ★
- [ ] Catapult ★★★★
- [ ] Chick Flakey ★ 12/22/88
- [x] Compound W - 12/22/88
- [ ] Desert Song ★★★★
- [ ] Fang, The
- [ ] Fingers of Frenzy
- [ ] Fingers on a Landscape

- [ ] Firefly
- [ ] Ho Man!
- [ ] Hot Rocks ★★★★★ 11 10/88
- [ ] Knight In Shining Armor, The ★★★★
- [ ] Latin Swing
- [ ] Middle Age Crazy ★★★
- [ ] Mission Impossible ★★★
- [ ] More Monkey Than Funky ★★★
- [ ] Morongo Man ★★
- [ ] Overnight Sensation ★★
- [ ] Pat Adams Dihedral ★★★

5.11b

- [ ] Poaching Bighorn ★★★★
- [ ] Porky Pig ★
- [x] Private Idaho
- [ ] Quantum Mechanics ★★
- [ ] Rainy Day, Dream Away ★★★
- [ ] Route 1060

- [ ] Scary Poodles ★★★
- [ ] Up 40 ★★
- [ ] V Crack, Left
- [ ] Walking Pneumonia ★★★
- [ ] White Bread Fever ★★★

5.11

- [ ] Ceramic bus
- [ ] Comfortably Numb ★★
- [ ] Gunsmoke ★★★★
- [ ] High Cost of Living, The ★★★★
- [ ] If it's Brown, Flush it ★
- [ ] Mr. DNA

5.11c

- [ ] Animalargos ★★★
- [ ] Anti-Gravity Boots
- [ ] Buried Treasure
- [ ] Carribean Cruise
- [ ] Castaway
- [ ] Chicago Nipple Slump ★
- [ ] Conceptual Continuity
- [ ] Cool But Concerned ★★★
- [ ] Dial Africa ★★
- [ ] Digital Watch ★★
- [ ] Famous Potatoes
- [ ] Frigid Dare
- [ ] Gravity Works ★★★
- [ ] Hands Down
- [ ] Hands to Yourself
- [ ] Hercules ★★★
- [ ] Human Sacrifice
- [ ] It's Easy to be Distant When Your're Brave ★★
- [ ] Let's Get Horizontal ★
- [ ] Magma
- [ ] Mighty High

- [ ] Nihilistic Pillar ★★
- [ ] On the Back
- [x] Overpowered by Funk ★★ T.R.
- [ ] Riddles in the Dark ★★
- [ ] Rockwork Orange ★★★
- [ ] Secret Agent Man ★★
- [ ] Shamrock Shooter
- [ ] Shin Bashers ★
- [ ] Simple Simon ★★★
- [ ] Soviet Union ★★
- [ ] Spider Line ★★★★
- [ ] The Bronto's or Us ★★
- [ ] The Sound of One Hand Slapping ★★★★
- [ ] Thin Line ★★
- [ ] Tombstone, The ★★
- [ ] Top of the Rope ★
- [ ] Vector ★★★★
- [ ] Wangerbanger ★★★★
- [ ] Wet T-Shirt Night ★★★★
- [ ] When You're a Jet ★★★
- [ ] Whistling Sphincter

5.11d

- [ ] Baby Huey Smokes An Ant-Pipeload
- [ ] Campfire Girl
- [ ] Condor, The ★★★★
- [ ] Dawn Yawn ★★★
- [ ] Dirty Tricks
- [ ] Dynamic Panic
- [ ] Functional Analysis
- [ ] Hidden Arch ★★★
- [ ] It Don't Mean a Thing if it Ain't Got That Swing ★★★

- [ ] Leave it to Beaver ★★★★★
- [ ] Living Conjunction, The ★★
- [ ] Power Fingers
- [ ] Rubicon Direct
- [ ] Scary Monsters ★★★
- [ ] Super Spy ★★
- [ ] 29 Palms ★★★★
- [ ] Watusi, The ★★
- [ ] Where Eagles Dare ★★

5.12a

- [ ] *Arms Control* ★★★
- [ ] *Bikini Whale* ★★★
- [ ] *Brain Death* ★★★
- [ ] *Chief Crazy Horse* ★★★
- [ ] *Datura*
- [ ] *Emotional Rescue* ★★
- [ ] *Fingers of Frenzy*
- [ ] *Great Escape, The* ★★★★

- [ ] *Ionic Strength* ★★★
- [ ] *It's Easy to be Brave From a Safe Distance* ★★
- [ ] *Nuclear Arms* ★★★
- [ ] *Slightly Ahead of Our Time* ★
- [ ] *Sole Fusion* ★★★★
- [ ] *Transfusion* ★★
- [ ] *Waltzing Worn* ★★

5.12b

- [ ] *5 Crying Cowboys* ★★★★
- [ ] *Apollo*
- [ ] *Baby Apes* ★★★
- [ ] *Chameleon, The* ★★★
- [ ] *Mohawk, The* ★★★★
- [ ] *Warrior Eagle* ★★★
- [ ] *Zombie Woof* ★★

5.12

- [ ] *Marathon Crack*
- [ ] *Obsidian*
- [ ] *Thin Red Line*

5.12c

- [ ] *No Self Control* ★★★★

5.12d

- [ ] *Acid Crack, The* ★★★★
- [ ] *Equinox* ★★★★★
- [ ] *Moonbeam Crack, The* ★★

5.12 +

- [ ] *Asteroid Crack*
- [ ] *Ship Wrecked*
- [ ] *Book of Brilliant Things* ★★★★★

? New Routes

° 10b R of Heart & Sole 12/31/88

11a

INDEX